BUILDING COMMUNITIES FROM THE INSIDE OUT:

A PATH TOWARD FINDING AND MOBILIZING A COMMUNITY'S ASSETS

JOHN P. KRETZMANN · JOHN L. McKNIGHT

The Asset-Based Community Development Institute
Institute for Policy Research
Northwestern University
2040 Sheridan Road
Evanston, IL 60208-4100
Phone: 847-491-3518
Fax: 847-491-9916

Distributed exclusively by:
ACTA Publications
4848 North Clark Street
Chicago, IL 60640
Phone: 800-397-2282
Fax: 800-397-0079

ACKNOWLEDGEMENTS

This guide reflects the hard work of lots of good people. Estella Walsh, Xandria Birk and Alice Murray provided stellar administrative support for the Neighborhood Innovations Network. Valuable research was contributed by Xandria Birk, Rebecca Deaton, Mark Ellis, Christine George, Yvonne Newsome, Darrell Moore, Deborah Puntenney, Jon Schmidt, Tamara Serwer, and Juliet Wilson. Valued colleagues Stan Hallett, Charles Payne and Tom Dewar helped shape the frameworks which undergird this work. And final writing, editing and production depended heavily on the considerable talents of Audrey Chambers, Valerie Lorimer and Gene Walsh.

We are particularly grateful to the Searle family and the Chicago Community Trust for funding much of this work, and to the Center for Urban Affairs and Policy Research at Northwestern University for providing a stimulating and hospitable site for exploring the challenges facing communities.

Obviously, the real authors of this guide are the hundreds of creative and committed neighborhood leaders in Chicago and across the country who have graciously consented to be our teachers. To them and to their rich visions of community goes the credit for anything valuable this guide might contribute.

—John Kretzmann, John McKnight
November 1993

HOW TO USE THIS BOOK

The Table of Contents that follows is long and quite detailed. To help the reader use this guide more productively, here is a brief introduction to each of the chapters. Readers are encouraged to consult those sections that apply most directly to their own community-building context and challenges.

Introduction. This brief section introduces the basic framework for the guide. It suggests that communities cannot be rebuilt by focusing on their needs, problems, and deficiencies. Rather, community building starts with the process of locating the assets, skills and capacities of residents, citizens associations, and local institutions.

Chapter One. Releasing Individual Capacities introduces ways to find and use the gifts and talents of local people. Helpful tools such as a "capacity inventory" are introduced. People who are sometimes thought not to have many talents and gifts receive particular attention. Brief sections suggest ways to find and mobilize the capacities of young people, people with disabilities, older people, people experiencing welfare, and local artists.

Chapter Two. Releasing the Power of Local Associations and Organizations describes how hundreds of groups of local people across the country come together to solve problems on a voluntary basis. Methods for locating and activating these groups, which we call "associations," are introduced. Churches and cultural organizations, two important types of community-building associations, receive special attention.

Chapter Three. Capturing Local Institutions for Community Building describes how local institutions enter into strong community partnerships with each other, as well as with local residents and citizens associations. The institutional "assets" that receive particular emphasis, and whose community-building stories are summarized, include parks, libraries, schools, community colleges, police, and hospitals.

Chapter Four. Rebuilding the Community Economy highlights three ways in which communities can capture and build upon the economic assets that are already in place. First, the chapter outlines stories and strategies in which the budgets and resources of local institutions such as schools, libraries, and hospitals can help to build the local economy. Second, two community-based structures designed to capture savings and provide local credit are described. Finally, the chapter outlines successful efforts to reclaim the often hidden physical assets of the community such as abandoned space and waste materials.

Chapter Five. Asset-Based Community Development: Mobilizing an Entire Community summarizes the community-building process and describes briefly the five key steps:
Step 1—Mapping Assets
Step 2—Building Relationships
Step 3—Mobilizing for Economic Development and Information Sharing
Step 4—Convening the Community to Develop a Vision and a Plan
Step 5—Leveraging Outside Resources to Support Locally Driven Development

Chapter Six. Providing Support for Asset-Based Development: Policies and Guidelines suggests ways in which people and institutions from outside the community can support asset-based community- building activity. Examples of guidelines for foundations as well as some modest advice for governments are included.

TABLE OF CONTENTS

INTRODUCTION

CHAPTER ONE
RELEASING INDIVIDUAL CAPACITIES

TABLE OF CONTENTS

CHAPTER TWO
RELEASING THE POWER OF LOCAL ASSOCIATIONS AND ORGANIZATIONS

TABLE OF CONTENTS

CHAPTER THREE
CAPTURING LOCAL INSTITUTIONS FOR COMMUNITY BUILDING

TABLE OF CONTENTS

CHAPTER FOUR
REBUILDING THE COMMUNITY ECONOMY

TABLE OF CONTENTS

CHAPTER FIVE
ASSET-BASED COMMUNITY DEVELOPMENT: MOBILIZING AN ENTIRE COMMUNITY

CHAPTER SIX
PROVIDING SUPPORT FOR ASSET-BASED DEVELOPMENT: POLICIES AND GUIDELINES

This is a guide about rebuilding troubled communities. It is meant to be simple, basic and usable. Whatever wisdom it contains flows directly out of the experience of courageous and creative neighborhood leaders from across the country.

Most of this guide is devoted to spreading community-building success stories. These stories are organized into a step-by-step introduction to a coherent strategy that we have learned about from neighborhood leaders. We call this strategy "asset-based community development." Before beginning to outline the basic elements of this approach, it will be helpful to remember how so many of our communities came to be so devastated, and why traditional strategies for improvement have so often failed.

The Problem: Devastated Communities

No one can doubt that most American cities these days are deeply troubled places. At the root of the problems are the massive economic shifts that have marked the last two decades. Hundreds of thousands of industrial jobs have either disappeared or moved away from the central city and its neighborhoods. And while many downtown areas have experienced a "renaissance," the jobs created there are different from those that once sustained neighborhoods. Either these new jobs are highly professionalized, and require elaborate education and credentials for entry, or they are routine, low-paying service jobs without much of a future. In effect, these shifts in the economy, and particularly the disappearance of decent employment possibilities from low-income neighborhoods, have removed the bottom rung from the fabled American "ladder of opportunity." For many people in older city neighborhoods, new approaches to rebuilding their lives and communities, new openings toward opportunity, are a vital necessity.

Two Solutions, Two Paths

In response to this desperate situation, well-intended people are seeking solutions by taking one of two divergent paths. The first, which begins by focusing on a community's needs, deficiencies and problems, is still by far the most traveled, and commands the vast majority of our financial and human resources. By comparison with the second path, which insists on beginning with a clear commitment to discovering a community's capacities and assets, and which is the direction this guide recommends, the first and more traditional path is more like an eight-lane superhighway.

INTRODUCTION

The Traditional Path—A Needs-Driven Dead End

For most Americans, the names "South Bronx," or "South Central Los Angeles," or even "Public Housing" call forth a rush of images. It is not surprising that these images are overwhelmingly negative. They are images of crime and violence, of joblessness and welfare dependency, of gangs and drugs and homelessness, of vacant and abandoned land and buildings. They are images of needy and problematic and deficient neighborhoods populated by needy and problematic and deficient people.

These negative images, which can be conceived as a kind of mental "map" of the neighborhood (see page 3) often convey part of the truth about the actual conditions of a troubled community. But they are not regarded as part of the truth; they are regarded as the whole truth.

Once accepted as the whole truth about troubled neighborhoods, this "needs" map determines how problems are to be addressed, through deficiency-oriented policies and programs. Public, private and non-profit human service systems, often supported by university research and foundation funding, translate the programs into local activities that teach people the nature and extent of their problems, and the value of services as the answer to their problems. As a result, many lower income urban neighborhoods are now environments of service where behaviors are affected because residents come to believe that their well-being depends upon being a client. They begin to see themselves as people with special needs that can only be met by outsiders. They become consumers of services, with no incentive to be producers. Consumers of services focus vast amounts of creativity and intelligence on the survival-motivated challenge of outwitting the "system," or on finding ways—in the informal or even illegal economy—to bypass the system entirely.

There is nothing natural or inevitable about the process that leads to the creation of client neighborhoods. In fact, it is important to note how little power local neighborhood residents have to affect the pervasive nature of the deficiency model, mainly because a number of society's most influential institutions have themselves developed a stake in maintaining that focus. For example, much of the social science research produced by universities is designed to collect and analyze data about problems. Much of the funding directed to lower income communities by foundations and the United Way is based on the problem-oriented data collected in "needs surveys," a practice emulated by government human service agencies. Finally, the needs map often appears to be the only neighborhood guide ever used by members of the mass media, whose appetite for the violent and the spectacularly problematic story seems insatiable. All of these major institutions combine to create a wall between lower income communities and the rest of society—a wall of needs which, ironically enough, is built not on hatred but (at least partly) on the desire to "help."

Neighborhood Needs Map

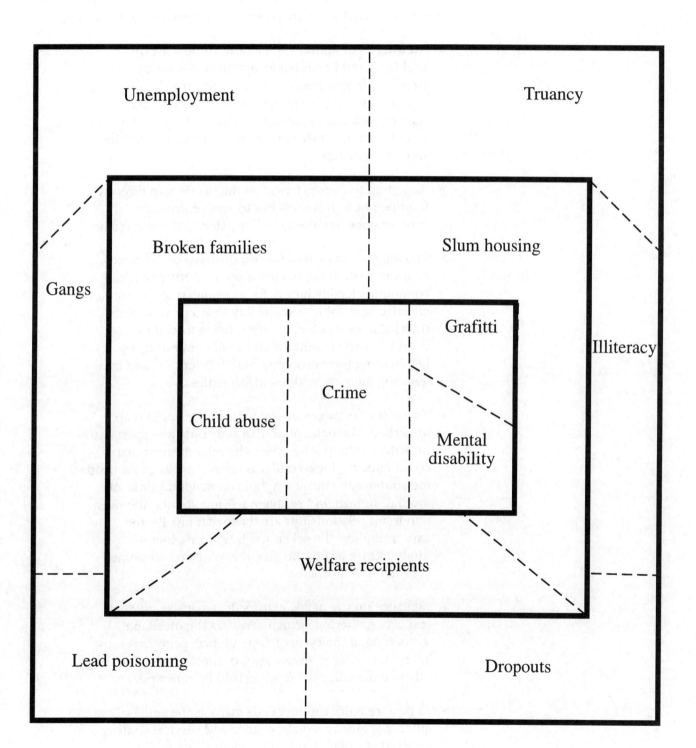

The fact that the deficiency orientation represented by the needs map constitutes our only guide to lower income neighborhoods has devastating consequences for residents. We have already noted one of the most tragic—that is, residents themselves begin to accept that map as the only guide to the reality of their lives. They think of themselves and their neighbors as fundamentally deficient, victims incapable of taking charge of their lives and of their community's future. But other consequences flow as well from the power of the needs map. For example:

- Viewing a community as a nearly endless list of problems and needs leads directly to the much lamented fragmentation of efforts to provide solutions. It also denies the basic community wisdom which regards problems as tightly intertwined, as symptoms in fact of the breakdown of a community's own problem-solving capacities.

- Targeting resources based on the needs map directs funding not to residents but to service providers, a consequence not always either planned for or effective.

- Making resources available on the basis of the needs map can have negative effects on the nature of local community leadership. If, for example, one measure of effective leadership is the ability to attract resources, then local leaders are, in effect, being forced to denigrate their neighbors and their community by highlighting their problems and deficiencies, and by ignoring their capacities and strengths.

- Providing resources on the basis of the needs map underlines the perception that only outside experts can provide real help. Therefore, the relationships that count most for local residents are no longer those inside the community, those neighbor-to-neighbor links of mutual support and problem solving. Rather, the most important relationships are those that involve the expert, the social worker, the health provider, the funder. Once again, the glue that binds communities together is weakened.

- Reliance on the needs map as the exclusive guide to resource gathering virtually ensures the inevitable deepening of the cycle of dependence: problems must always be worse than last year, or more intractable than other communities, if funding is to be renewed.

- At best, reliance on the needs maps as the sole policy guide will ensure a maintenance and survival strategy targeted at isolated individual clients, not a development plan that can involve the energies of an entire community.

❧ Because the needs-based strategy can guarantee only
survival, and can never lead to serious change or
community development, this orientation must be
regarded as one of the major causes of the sense of
hopelessness that pervades discussions about the future
of low income neighborhoods. From the street corner to
the White House, if maintenance and survival are the
best we can provide, what sense can it make to invest in
the future?

The Alternative Path: Capacity-Focused Development

If even some of these negative consequences follow from our total
reliance upon the needs map, an alternative approach becomes imperative. That alternative path, very simply, leads toward the development of policies and activities based on the capacities, skills and assets
of lower income people and their neighborhoods.

In addition to the problems associated with the dominant deficiency
model, at least two more factors argue for shifting to a capacity-oriented emphasis. First, all the historic evidence indicates that significant
community development takes place only when local community
people are committed to investing themselves and their resources in
the effort. This observation explains why communities are never built
from the top down, or from the outside in. (Clearly, however, valuable
outside assistance can be provided to communities that are actively
developing their own assets, a topic explored further in Chapter Six.)

The second reason for emphasizing the development of the internal
assets of local urban neighborhoods is that the prospect for outside
help is bleak indeed. Even in areas designated as Enterprise Zones, the
odds are long that large-scale, job-providing industrial or service
corporations will be locating in these neighborhoods. Nor is it likely,
in the light of continuing budget constraints, that significant new
inputs of federal money will be forthcoming soon. It is increasingly
futile to wait for significant help to arrive from outside the community.
The hard truth is that development must start from within the community and, in most of our urban neighborhoods, there is no other
choice.

Creative neighborhood leaders across the country have begun to
recognize this hard truth, and have shifted their practices accordingly.
They are discovering that wherever there are effective community
development efforts, those efforts are based upon an understanding,
or map, of the community's assets, capacities and abilities. For it is
clear that even the poorest neighborhood is a place where individuals
and organizations represent resources upon which to rebuild. The key
to neighborhood regeneration, then, is to locate all of the available
local assets, to begin connecting them with one another in ways that
multiply their power and effectiveness, and to begin harnessing those

local institutions that are not yet available for local development purposes.

This entire process begins with the construction of a new "map" (see page 7). Once this guide to capacities has replaced the old one containing only needs and deficiencies, the regenerating community can begin to assemble its strengths into new combinations, new structures of opportunity, new sources of income and control, and new possibilities for production.

The Assets of a Community: Individuals, Associations, Institutions

Each community boasts a unique combination of assets upon which to build its future. A thorough map of those assets would begin with an inventory of the gifts, skills and capacities of the community's residents. Household by household, building by building, block by block, the capacity mapmakers will discover a vast and often surprising array of individual talents and productive skills, few of which are being mobilized for community-building purposes. This basic truth about the "giftedness" of every individual is particularly important to apply to persons who often find themselves marginalized by communities. It is essential to recognize the capacities, for example, of those who have been labeled mentally handicapped or disabled, or of those who are marginalized because they are too old, or too young, or too poor. In a community whose assets are being fully recognized and mobilized, these people too will be part of the action, not as clients or recipients of aid, but as full contributors to the community-building process.

In addition to mapping the gifts and skills of individuals, and of households and families, the committed community builder will compile an inventory of citizens' associations. These associations, less formal and much less dependent upon paid staff than are formal institutions, are the vehicles through which citizens in the U.S. assemble to solve problems, or to share common interests and activities. It is usually the case that the depth and extent of associational life in any community is vastly underestimated. This is particularly true of lower income communities. In fact, however, though some parts of associational life may have dwindled in very low income neighborhoods, most communities continue to harbor significant numbers of associations with religious, cultural, athletic, recreational and other purposes. Community builders soon recognize that these groups are indispensable tools for development, and that many of them can in fact be stretched beyond their original purposes and intentions to become full contributors to the development process.

Beyond the individuals and local associations that make up the asset base of communities are all of the more formal institutions which are located in the community. Private businesses; public institutions such

Community Assets Map

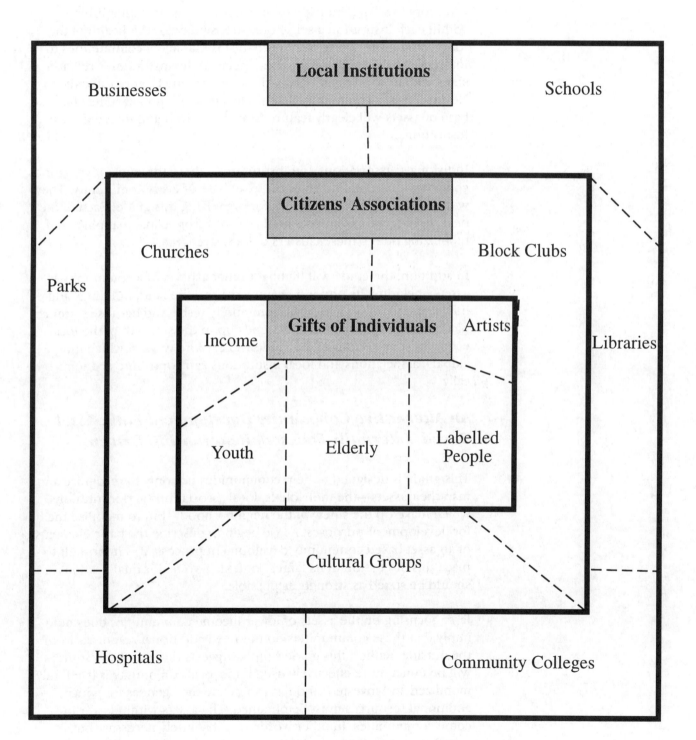

as schools, libraries, parks, police and fire stations; nonprofit institutions such as hospitals and social service agencies—these organizations make up the most visible and formal part of a community's fabric. Accounting for them in full, and enlisting them in the process of community development, is essential to the success of the process. For community builders, the process of mapping the institutional assets of the community will often be much simpler than that of making an inventory involving individuals and associations. But establishing within each institution a sense of responsibility for the health of the local community, along with mechanisms that allow communities to influence and even control some aspects of the institution's relationships with its local neighborhood, can prove much more difficult. Nevertheless, a community that has located and mobilized its entire base of assets will clearly feature heavily involved and invested local institutions.

Individuals, associations and institutions—these three major categories contain within them much of the asset base of every community. They will also provide the framework for organizing this guide. Each of the next three sections explores methods for recognizing, mapping, and mobilizing one of these clusters of local strengths.

In addition, the guide will highlight other aspects of a community's assets, including its physical characteristics—the land, buildings and infrastructure upon which the community rests. And because so much of a community's well-being depends upon the strength of the local economy, one section of the guide will explore ways in which individuals, associations and local institutions can contribute economically.

An Alternative Community Development Path: Asset-Based, Internally Focused, Relationship Driven

This guide is designed to help communities not only to recognize and map their assets—the individuals, local associations and institutions which make up the sinew of the neighborhood—but to mobilize them for development purposes. As we begin to describe the basic elements of an asset-based community development process, it is important to place this discussion in its larger context. Two major qualifications should be stated as strongly as possible.

First, focusing on the assets of lower income communities does not imply that these communities do not need additional resources from the outside. Rather, this guide simply suggests that outside resources will be much more effectively used if the local community is itself fully mobilized and invested, and if it can define the agendas for which additional resources must be obtained. The assets within lower income communities, in other words, are absolutely necessary but usually not sufficient to meet the huge development challenges ahead.

Second, the discussion of asset-based community development is intended to affirm, and to build upon the remarkable work already going on in neighborhoods across the country. Asset-based community development acknowledges and embraces particularly the strong neighborhood-rooted traditions of community organizing, community economic development and neighborhood planning. In fact, experienced leaders in these three areas have been among our most valuable sources of inspiration and guidance. The approach outlined in this guide is intended to complement, and sometimes to precede, their efforts—not to substitute for them.

These caveats understood, then, "asset-based community development" deserves a little more introduction and definition. As will become apparent in more detail in the chapters that follow, this process can be defined by three simple, interrelated characteristics:

   ❧ Obviously enough, the first principle that defines this process is that it is "asset-based." That is, this community development strategy starts with what is present in the community, the capacities of its residents and workers, the associational and institutional base of the area—not with what is absent, or with what is problematic, or with what the community needs.

   ❧ Because this community development process is asset-based, it is by necessity "internally focused." That is, the development strategy concentrates first of all upon the agenda building and problem-solving capacities of local residents, local associations and local institutions. Again, this intense and self-conscious internal focus is not intended to minimize either the role external forces have played in helping to create the desperate conditions of lower income neighborhoods, nor the need to attract additional resources to these communities. Rather this strong internal focus is intended simply to stress the primacy of local definition, investment, creativity, hope and control.

   ❧ If a community development process is to be asset-based and internally focused, then it will be in very important ways "relationship driven." Thus, one of the central challenges for asset-based community developers is to constantly build and rebuild the relationships between and among local residents, local associations and local institutions.

Skilled community organizers and effective community developers already recognize the importance of relationship building. For it is clear that the strong ties which form the basis for community-based problem solving have been under attack. The forces driving people apart are many and frequently cited—increasing mobility rates, the separation of work and residence, mass media, segregation by race and age and not least from the point of view of lower income communities, increasing dependence upon outside, professionalized helpers.

Because of these factors, the sense of efficacy based on interdependence, the idea that people can count on their neighbors and neighborhood resources for support and strength has weakened. For community builders who are focused on assets, rebuilding these local relationships offers the most promising route toward successful community development. This guide will stress the importance of relationship building for every person and group in the community, and will underline the necessity of basing those relationships always upon the strengths and capacities of the parties involved, never on their weaknesses and needs.

That, then is the skeleton of the simple development process sketched in this guide—it is a community-building path which is asset-based, internally focused and relationship driven.

How to Use This Guide

This introduction to asset-based development is not a novel. It is not meant to be read straight through from beginning to end. Rather its various sections are meant to be consulted as they are needed, and as they apply to the actual conditions and challenges of particular communities.

After this initial overview, the guide is divided into six more chapters. Chapters one, two and three address the major categories of community-based assets—individuals, citizens' associations, and local institutions. Each of these chapters, in turn, is divided into sections that outline successful approaches to mapping and developing particular assets. Within the chapter devoted to individual capacities, for example, sections introduce community development activities which successfully incorporate the gifts of young people, of older people, and of those who are developmentally disabled. Similarly, the chapter on institutions introduces simple ideas about mobilizing schools, parks, libraries, community colleges and even local police stations for community-building purposes.

These three chapters should be sampled for their relevance to the reader's particular community. Not every chapter will be useful in every context. Each community's collection of assets will be unique, as will the particular sequence of development strategies, the major players, the local priorities, etc.

This guide, in other words, must not be regarded as a cookie cutter set of solutions. It is rather a starting point, a prod, an open invitation to start down a somewhat different path. All of the really creative work remains for community leadership to perform.

The fourth chapter turns a specifically economic spotlight on the approaches suggested in this guide. What does it mean to take seriously a devastated community's already existing economic assets? How might the full economic potential of every community be harnessed for development purposes?

The fifth chapter offers commentary on some central issues related to the asset-based community development process. It outlines a simple neighborhood planning process which intends to involve and activate all of the representatives of a community's asset base in constructing a common vision and a powerful strategy for realizing that vision.

The sixth chapter offers some modest advice to those in philanthropy and in the public sector who may wish to help this internally focused process without overdirecting it or snuffing out its energies. And it grapples with at least a few of the objections occasionally raised to the asset-based approach.

Finally, we should acknowledge the numerous stories of creative community-building that are included in this guide, and recommend their creators as potential advisors and helpers. Key words which follow most examples in parentheses will in most cases guide the reader to a specific project name and location. But use these references with some caution. We cannot vouch for the currency of the stories; nor have we included them as guides to the details of particular community-building strategies. Rather they are cited to excite, to spark the imagination, to underline the idea that these approaches need not be daunting or overcomplicated. We hope that at least a few of them can connect with the realities encountered in every reader's own community.

Persons at the Center of Community—Persons at the Margins of Community

Every single person has capacities, abilities and gifts. Living a good life depends on whether those capacities can be used, abilities expressed and gifts given. If they are, the person will be valued, feel powerful and well-connected to the people around them. And the community around the person will be more powerful because of the contribution the person is making.

Each time a person uses his or her capacity, the community is stronger and the person more powerful. That is why strong communities are basically places where the capacities of local residents are identified, valued and used. Weak communities are places that fail, for whatever reason, to mobilize the skills, capacities and talents of their residents or members.

While the raw material for community-building is the capacity of its individual members, some communities have failed to understand this. One of the reasons this basic resource is undeveloped in weak communities is because the community has come to focus largely on the deficiencies rather than the capacities of its members. This deficiency focus is usually described as a concern about the needs of local members. And these needs are understood to be the problems, shortcomings, maladies and dilemmas of people.

It is clear that every individual has needs or deficiencies. It is also clear that every individual has gifts and capacities. This fact reminds us of the glass of water filled to the middle. The glass is half full and it is half empty. Local residents, likewise, have capacities and they also have deficiencies. However, the part of people that builds powerful commu-

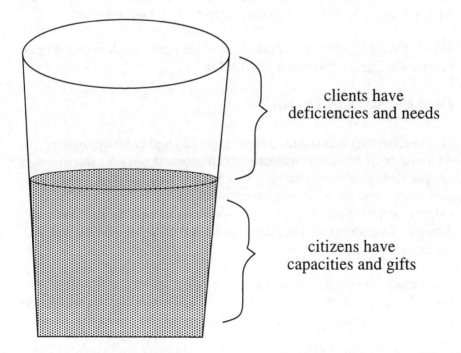

clients have
deficiencies and needs

citizens have
capacities and gifts

nities is the capacity part of its members. Therefore, the basic information needed to develop strong communities is an inventory of the capacities of its residents.

Unfortunately, in some communities local residents have come to mistakenly believe they can build their community by an inventory of deficiencies. The common name for this deficiency inventory is a "needs survey." It is basically an effort to count up the emptiness in an individual or a neighborhood. The problem is that this information is not useful for community-building because it deals with people as potential clients and consumers. To be powerful, a community must have people who are citizens and producers.

Think of a carpenter who has lost one leg in an accident years ago. Clearly, he has a deficiency. However, he also has a skill. If we know he has a missing leg, we cannot build our community with that information. If we know he has a capacity as a wood worker, that information can literally build our community.

Mapping Individual Capacities: An Inventory

In order to focus on the capacities of community members, it may be necessary to use a new tool that does not focus on needs. This tool is called a *Capacity Inventory*. An example follows beginning on page 19.

This particular *Capacity Inventory* was designed to identify the abilities of people in two older Chicago neighborhoods. Therefore, it is merely an example of one approach to identifying what local citizens can contribute to community-building. However, it has demonstrated its usefulness in communities across North America where it has been adapted for various groups, associations and neighborhoods.

The *Capacity Inventory* is divided into four parts. Look over each part before reading the following description.

Part I—Skills Information

This section lists many skills people have learned at home, in the community or at their workplace. It is important to point out to people taking the inventory that it is more than a list of skills learned on paying jobs. Many people have valuable skills learned outside the workplace and these skills are often valuable to neighbors, community groups and employers. They can also be the basis for starting a new business.

The list was developed based upon the particular skills reported by lower income people in two inner-city neighborhoods. Therefore, the list should be understood as simply an example. It can be shortened or added to depending on the particular people being inventoried. For example, a very different list might be developed if school parents are being interviewed to determine what additional classes they could teach in the evening, what they could contribute to the operation of their children's school or what skills they could help young people develop.

Similarly, a different list might be developed based upon capacities of seniors in the neighborhood. What particular gifts can they offer, no matter how physically limited?

At the conclusion of the list of skills is a section called Priority Skills. Here, the person being interviewed is asked to identify their best skills as listed in questions A and B. **This is usually the most important information in this section,** because the person with the skills is usually best able to assess their own abilities. And, they are most likely to feel confident about these skills. Therefore, they are more likely to be willing to contribute them to the community or sell them in the marketplace.

These Priority Skills are the foundation of community building. Therefore, identifying and mobilizing these skills is the basic work of leaders, associations and local institutions that are building on the assets of the neighborhood.

Part II—Community Skills

This section identifies the kinds of community work the person has participated in and then asks what kind of work they would be willing to do in the future. The work the person is willing to do in the future is the "raw material" for community building. Connecting these potential gifts with local community groups is vital work for local leaders and asset building organizations.

The particular list of activities in this section is only one example. It should be amended or added to as appropriate in the neighborhood where it is used.

Part III—Enterprising Interests and Experience

This part seeks two kinds of information. First, it determines whether the person has considered starting a business. Second, it asks if they presently are engaged in a business of any kind.

In asking questions about business, it is important to emphasize that your group is interested in any kind of business activity. It could be babysitting, selling perfume to neighbors, sewing, repairing broken windows, lawn care, etc. Often, people will not call this activity a business. Therefore, the interviewer should make clear that any money-making activity is of interest. This is because most small businesses grow step-by-step and often, the most important step is the first one—the sale of any goods or services.

This leads to the most important information in Part III for asset developing leaders and groups. This information is the answers to questions A4 and B5.

Question A4 identifies the barriers the person feels prevent them from starting some kind of enterprise. Helping remove these barriers is the work of asset developing leaders and groups.

Question B5 identifies the factors that could build the person's current business. Helping deal with these factors is the role of local leaders and groups committed to developing local capacities and assets.

Part IV—Personal Information

The items listed are the minimum information usually necessary for follow-up. However, other information may be added if it is useful in developing the capacities of the person.

Additional Advice for Groups Using the Capacity Inventory

The wording of the *Capacity Inventory* is for use when one person is interviewing another person to gather the information. However, some groups have revised the wording so that the Inventory can be given to a person who will fill out the answers themselves. Also, the Inventory has been given to groups of people, each of whom fills it out at the same time. This allows one person to explain what to do and to answer questions while many people are filling in the information.

At first glance, the Inventory may seem to be very long. It may be necessary therefore, to cut it back and revise it for the individuals using it. However, it may be best to try to gather all the information possible and see whether people interviewed actually object. Often, people will provide a great deal of information if they feel the interviewer is genuinely interested and the answers will be used to help them or their community.

One problem that may be encountered in using the *Capacity Inventory* is that some people may feel it asks some questions that are too personal or private. This may be especially the case in regard to the questions about business interests and activities. Therefore, those who use the inventory must be sensitive to these concerns and tell people that they should not answer any questions they do not care to answer.

A few of the groups who have used the Capacity Inventory have told the person interviewed that the information will be kept confidential. However, they found that they couldn't use the information for capacity development because of this promise. They could only use the information for a general study summarizing numbers of skills or capacities. Unfortunately, this information is of little practical use to the people being interviewed and may contribute to their frustration or anger because they were "studied" rather than helped or given an opportunity to contribute.

This leads to **the most important advice about using the *Capacity Inventory.*** We have found there are two basic questions that determine whether the *Capacity Inventory* is a useful development tool.

First, is its basic purpose to gather information about a specific person in order to help that person contribute to the community, develop employment or businesses? Will the information help this person—Mary Jones—give her gifts, contribute her talents or increase her income? The purpose of the *Inventory* is to help a particular person contribute. If the information is not primarily used for this purpose, Mary Jones may feel "used" and her time wasted. This result will weaken the community by alienating people who often feel they are being uselessly "studied" by outsiders.

Therefore, it should be emphasized that the *Capacity Inventory* is not designed to do a study of neighborhood residents that will primarily result in tables and charts showing numbers of skills, activities and enterprises. If this kind of study is the primary outcome, the inventory will not lead to its basic purpose as a tool for developing the capacities of local residents.

The second basic question is to ask what will be done with the information collected from Mary Jones in order to help her to contribute her gifts, skills and capacities and develop her income or enterprise? This question should be answered in detail before beginning the inventory.

Therefore, the groups involved in asking the questions should first have a plan that outlines how they will:

- Connect Mary Jones' skills to other residents, associations, institutions or enterprises.

- Connect Mary Jones' community skills to local community groups or activities.

- Connect Mary Jones to individuals, groups, programs or financing that will assist her in creating or developing an enterprise.

In summary, the information in each of these four sections is not useful until local individuals, leaders, associations or organizations act to enable the capacities to be used. Community development is the process by which local capacities are identified and mobilized. This mobilization mainly involves *connecting* people with capacities to:

- ☙ other people
- ☙ local associations
- ☙ local businesses
- ☙ local institutions
- ☙ capital and credit.

Therefore, growing community power requires local groups focused upon connecting people's capacities so they can be useful.

Capacity Inventory

Hello. I'm with (local organization's name). We're talking to local people about their skills. With this information, we hope to help people contribute to improving the neighborhood, find jobs or start businesses. May I ask you some questions about your skills and abilities?

Part I—Skills Information

Now I'm going to read to you a list of skills. It's an extensive list, so I hope you'll bear with me. I'll read the skills and you just say "yes" whenever we get to one you have.

We are interested in all your skills and abilities. They may have been learned through experience in the home or with your family. They may be skills you've learned at church or in the community. They may also be skills you have learned on the job.

Health

Caring for the Elderly _____
Caring for the Mentally Ill _____
Caring for the Sick _____
Caring for the Physically Disabled or Developmentally Disabled _____

(If yes answered to items 1, 2, 3 or 4, ask the following:)

Now, I would like to know about the kind of care you provided.

Bathing _____
Feeding _____
Preparing Special Diets _____
Exercising and Escorting _____
Grooming _____
Dressing _____
Making the Person Feel at Ease _____

Office

Typing (words per minute _____) _____
Operating Adding Machine/Calculator _____
Filing Alphabetically/Numerically _____
Taking Phone Messages _____
Writing Business Letters (not typing) _____
Receiving Phone Orders _____
Operating Switchboard _____
Keeping Track of Supplies _____
Shorthand or Speedwriting _____
Bookkeeping _____
Entering Information into Computer _____
Word Processing _____

Construction and Repair

Painting	_____
Porch Construction or Repair	_____
Tearing Down Buildings	_____
Knocking Out Walls	_____
Wall Papering	_____
Furniture Repairs	_____
Repairing Locks	_____
Building Garages	_____
Bathroom Modernization	_____
Building Room Additions	_____
Tile Work	_____
Installing Drywall & Taping	_____
Plumbing Repairs	_____
Electrical Repairs	_____
Bricklaying & Masonry	_____

(Stop here if no affirmative response by this point.)

Cabinetmaking	_____
Kitchen Modernization	_____
Furniture Making	_____
Installing Insulation	_____
Plastering	_____
Soldering & Welding	_____
Concrete Work (sidewalks)	_____
Installing Floor Coverings	_____
Repairing Chimneys	_____
Heating/Cooling System Installation	_____
Putting on Siding	_____
Tuckpointing	_____
Cleaning Chimneys (chimney sweep)	_____
Installing Windows	_____
Building Swimming Pools	_____
Carpentry Skills	_____
Roofing Repair or Installation	_____

Maintenance

Window Washing	_____
Floor Waxing or Mopping	_____
Washing and Cleaning Carpets/Rugs	_____
Routing Clogged Drains	_____
Using a Handtruck in a Business	_____
Caulking	_____
General Household Cleaning	_____
Fixing Leaky Faucets	_____

Mowing Lawns _____

Planting & Caring for Gardens _____

Pruning Trees & Shrubbery _____

Cleaning/Maintaining Swimming Pools _____

Floor Sanding or Stripping _____

Wood Stripping/Refinishing _____

Food

Catering _____

Serving Food to Large Numbers
  of People (over 10) _____

Preparing Meals for Large Numbers
  of People (over 10) _____

Clearing/Setting Tables for Large Numbers
  of People (over 10) _____

Washing Dishes for Large Numbers
  of People (over 10) _____

Operating Commercial Food
  Preparation Equipment _____

Bartending _____

Meatcutting _____

Baking _____

Child Care

Caring for Babies (under 1 year) _____

Caring for Children (1 to 6) _____

Caring for Children (7 to 13) _____

Taking Children on Field Trips _____

Transportation

Driving a Car _____

Driving a Van _____

Driving a Bus _____

Driving a Taxi _____

Driving a Tractor Trailer _____

Driving a Commercial Truck _____

Driving a Vehicle/Delivering Goods _____

Hauling _____

Operating Farm Equipment _____

Driving an Ambulance _____

Operating Equipment & Repairing Machinery

Repairing Radios, TVs, VCRs, Tape Recorders _____

Repairing Other Small Appliances _____

Repairing Automobiles _____

Repairing Trucks/Buses   _____
Repairing Auto/Truck/Bus Bodies   _____
Using a Forklift   _____
Repairing Large Household Equipment   _____
  (e.g., refrigerator)
Repairing Heating & Air Conditioning System   _____
Operating a Dump Truck   _____
Fixing Washers/Dryers   _____
Repairing Elevators   _____
Operating a Crane   _____
Assembling Items   _____

Supervision

Writing Reports   _____
Filling out Forms   _____
Planning Work for Other People   _____
Directing the Work of Other People   _____
Making a Budget   _____
Keeping Records of All Your Activities   _____
Interviewing People   _____

Sales

Operating a Cash Register   _____
Selling Products Wholesale or for Manufacturer   _____
  (If yes, which products?)
Selling Products Retail   _____
  (If yes, which products?)
Selling Services   _____
  (If yes, which services?)
How have you sold these products or services?
  (Check mark, if yes)
  Door to Door   _____
  Phone   _____
  Mail   _____
  Store   _____
  Home   _____

Music

Singing   _____
Play an Instrument   _____
  (Which instrument?)

Security

Guarding Residential Property   _____
Guarding Commercial Property   _____

Guarding Industrial Property   ____
Armed Guard   ____
Crowd Control   ____
Ushering at Major Events   ____
Installing Alarms or Security Systems ____
Repairing Alarms or Security Systems ____
Firefighting   ____

Other

Upholstering   ____
Sewing   ____
Dressmaking   ____
Crocheting   ____
Knitting   ____
Tailoring   ____
Moving Furniture or Equipment to
   Different Locations   ____
Managing Property   ____
Assisting in the Classroom   ____
Hair Dressing   ____
Hair Cutting   ____
Phone Surveys   ____
Jewelry or Watch Repair   ____

Are there any other skills that you have which we haven't mentioned?

Priority Skills

1. When you think about your skills, what three things do you think you do best?

a)
b)
c)

2. Which of all your skills are good enough that other people would hire you to do them?

a)
b)
c)

3. Are there any skills you would like to teach?

a)
b)
c)

4. What skills would you most like to learn?

a)

b)

c)

Part II—Community Skills

Have you ever organized or participated in any of the following community activities? (Place check mark if yes)

Boy Scouts/Girl Scouts   _____
Church Fundraisers   _____
Bingo   _____
School-Parent Associations   _____
Sports Teams .   _____
Camp Trips for Kids   _____
Field Trips   _____
Political Campaigns   _____
Block Clubs   _____
Community Groups   _____
Rummage Sales   _____
Yard Sales   _____
Church Suppers   _____
Community Gardens   _____
Neighborhood Organization   _____
Other Groups or Community Work?

Let me read the list again. Tell me in which of these you would be willing to participate in the future. (Place check mark if yes)

Part III—Enterprising Interests and Experience

A. Business Interest

1. Have you ever considered starting a business?   Yes_____   No_____
    If yes, what kind of business did you have in mind?

2. Did you plan to start it alone or with other people?   Alone_____   Others_____

3. Did you plan to operate it out of your home?   Yes_____   No_____

4. What obstacle kept you from starting the business?

B. Business Activity

1. Are you currently earning money on your own through the sale of services or products?
   Yes_____   No_____

2. If yes, what are the services or products you sell?

3. Whom do you sell to?

4. How do you get customers?

5. What would help you improve your business?

Part IV—Personal Information

Name_____

Address_____

Phone_____

Age_____ (If a precise age is not given, ask whether the person is in the teens, 20s, 30s, etc.)

Sex: F_____   M_____

Thank you very much for your time.

Source_____

Place of Interview_____

Interviewer_____

25

Connecting Capacity Information

In many communities, the natural ways of the local people and their associations and institutions constantly connect local capacities. For example:

❧ Neighbors have a tradition of helping each other by trading their skills. Mary repairs a dress while Sue watches her children.

❧ A local association of religious men combines their construction skills and builds a community center.

❧ A neighborhood school involves the local students in using the environmental knowledge they've gained to do a study for city council of whether a local pond is polluted.

In addition to these natural developments, other communities have intentionally used tools like the *Capacity Inventory* to identify local citizen talents. Then these groups have become active in making the necessary connections to mobilize the capacities. Some examples:

❧ A neighborhood organization interviewed over 100 local residents and found many women who had worked in hospitals, hotels or cared for sick and elderly people. Many of these women had families and were unemployed. They wanted to work part-time. The association brought them together and they formed a "company" to sell their services as home health care providers. There was great demand for their services and over 80 women were connected to neighbors needing community care. This connection met a community need and increased the income of the women.

❧ A group of residents of a public housing project organized and became powerful enough to gain control of their buildings. Their association took over the management and finances of the project. As a result they were able to employ residents to carry out the maintenance functions such as painting rooms, fixing broken windows, running a laundromat, etc. In order to exercise their new-found power, they needed to know which residents had the necessary skills to do the work of maintenance and management. They used a *Capacity Inventory* to gather this information and their association connected residents to the new job opportunities that improved the quality of the local buildings.

❧ A local association in a neighborhood collected information from local residents regarding skills that could be used at a job. Then they did an inventory of the kinds of jobs available at all local employers. They then created a brokerage effort connecting people with skills to employers needing skills.

It is significant to note two common characteristics of each of these efforts. First, a local group acted as a **connecter.** Second, the local group took people as they were and mobilized their existing capacities. They did not start with the idea that the local people needed to be trained, educated or treated. Instead, they started with the idea that capacities were there and that the community-building task was to:

❧ identify capacities

❧ connect them to people, groups and places that can use the capacities.

Does Everyone Have Capacities?

There are some people who seem to be without any gifts or capacities. They may appear to be like an empty glass. And so they get called names—names like mentally retarded, ex-convict, frail elderly, mentally ill, illiterate, and gang member. These are names for the emptiness some people see in other people. They are labels that focus attention on needs.

One effect of these labels is that they keep many community people from seeing the gifts of people who have been labeled. The label often blinds us to the capacity of the people who are named. They appear to be useless. Therefore, these labeled people often get pushed to the edge of the community, or they are sometimes sent outside the community to an institution to be rehabilitated or receive services.

Nonetheless, every living person has some gift or capacity of value to others. A strong community is a place that recognizes those gifts and ensures that they are given. A weak community is a place where lots of people can't give their gifts and express their capacities.

In weak communities there are lots of people who have been pushed to the edge or exiled to institutions. Often, we say these people **need** help. They are **needy.** They have nothing to contribute. The label tells us so.

For example, "She is a pregnant teenager. She needs counseling, therapy, residential services, special education." But also, "She is Mary Smith. She has a miraculously beautiful voice. We need her in the choir. She needs a record producer."

Her label, pregnant teenager, tells of emptiness and calls forth rejection, isolation and treatment. Her name, Mary Smith, tells of her gifts and evokes community and contributions.

Communities growing in power naturally or intentionally identify the capacities of all their members and ensure that they are contributed. However, the most powerful communities are those that can identify the gifts of those people at the margins and pull them into community life.

The following sections of this chapter describe how the gifts of various kinds of people have been identified and connected to the community's life. Included are descriptions of how neighborhoods grew more powerful because they identified and connected the special gifts and capacities of:

- people who are developmentally disabled

- people surviving on welfare

- young people and elderly people

- people with artistic gifts.

There are many other kinds of people with community contributions to make. Therefore, the following sections are merely examples of the thousands of possibilities for local individuals to contribute and develop their gifts, skills and capacities. The task of community builders is to expand the list of potential giftgivers and create methods to connect those gifts to other individuals, local associations and institutions.

Introduction—Youth and Community Renewal

At the present time many of the most innovative community leaders are rediscovering that youth can be essential contributors to the well-being and vitality of the community. Projects that connect young people productively with other youth and adults are now seen to be the foundations upon which healthy communities can be built. But for this task to be accomplished, youth must no longer be relegated to the margins of community life.

The unique energy and creativity of youth is often denied to the community because the young people of the neighborhood are all too often viewed only in terms of their lack of maturity and practical life experience. Categorized as the product of "immature" minds, the legitimate dreams and desires of youth are frequently ignored by the older, more "responsible" members of the community. As a result of this negative stereotyping, in many instances the youth of the community tend to be thought of as "incompetent individuals" who will wreck havoc on the established society if they are not tightly supervised and controlled.

With this attitude in mind, we can see how certain well-intentioned labels such as "at risk" can serve to immobilize youth within the community by defining the young in terms of their perceived deficiencies, rather than their potential capacities. Furthermore, labels of this sort tend to justify (and even to increase) the flood of social services that can further isolate youth from their friends, families and communities. In other words, service organizations by defining youth exclusively in terms of their problems and needs help to create barriers that make it difficult for young people to become productive members of the community. Thus youth can easily become trapped in a cycle of ongoing dependency, and the community itself will lose some of its greatest potential assets.

Given the proper opportunities, however, youth can always make a significant contribution to the development of the communities in which they live. What is needed for this to happen are specific projects that will connect youth with the community in ways that will increase their own self-esteem and level of competency while at the same time improving the quality of life of the community as a whole.

But how can these sorts of opportunities for youth be created and maintained? Just exactly how can community leaders go about tapping into the true capabilities of the young? The rest of this section will explore not only what the young have to offer but also will suggest specific means by which youth can be reintegrated into the life of the community through a series of productive, mutually-beneficial relationships.

Rediscovering Local Youth as Assets Within the Community

Clearly the category of youth represents a multitude of different individuals, each of whom is unique in terms of potential capabilities. Nevertheless, when "youth" are characterized as a group, most often their attributes are defined in negative terms and their positive qualities are totally ignored.

Rejecting this negative labeling, let us now examine the positive assets through which the young can make a unique contribution to the development of the community.

Time

❧ Usually youth have a certain amount of free time during the week which is not available to older members of the community who must work for a living. Often young people complain about not having anything to do on weekends and on long summer vacations when school is not in session. This unutilized time is an asset that could be filled with participation in constructive community projects.

Ideas and Creativity

❧ Infusion of new ideas and the kind of creativity so characteristic of the young can be great assets to community leaders who may be struggling to find novel solutions to recurring problems.

Connection to Place

❧ In most instances young people live at home and are confined throughout the week to the neighborhoods in which they live. This means that they have more of a stake in the well-being of the community than any other group and on a daily basis know more about what actually goes on there.

Dreams and Desires

❧ Many young people yearn to contribute meaningfully to their community and can be seen to flourish when they are given the opportunity to do so. There is no inherent reason for the most positive dreams of these young people to be deferred indefinitely. If their dreams are viewed as assets, they can at any given moment become partners in creating a better future for everyone.

Peer Group Relationships

❦ Even when youth have become marginalized from the more positive aspects of community life, they still generally remain well-connected with one another on a day-to-day basis. Gangs (and gang activities) are clear examples of the immense amount of peer group potential that is wasted because it is misdirected. When youth become connected in a positive manner with the community in which they live, they can become effective mobilizers of one another, and en masse can be powerful agents of community revitalization.

Family Relationships

❦ Most young people remain connected to their families. In families in which the parents have become isolated from community life—for example, in those situations in which the children speak English but the parents do not—young people can become very effective as a means to mobilize their parents into more effective participation in the life of the community.

Credibility as Teachers

❦ Although most young people are still students, they can also be teachers and role models. In many kinds of positive learning experiences, youth are often the most effective teachers and role models for other youth.

Enthusiasm and Energy

❦ Since they have not as yet experienced as many failures and disappointments as adults, young people usually possess a unique willingness to try to solve old problems and to create new opportunities. This fresh perspective and ability to remain undaunted by past failures are qualities that can make a young person an ideal entrepreneur.

Needless to say, this list should not be considered exhaustive. These eight characteristics are only a sample of the many assets that any young person or group of young people might be able to offer to the community.

Mapping Community Assets to Discover Potential Partners for Local Youth

Now that we have identified at least some of the assets that youth can bring to the process of community building, we must go on to examine the means by which neighborhood leaders can most effectively mobilize these assets and turn them into valuable resources for community building. This effort to connect local youth with the process of community building involves the utilization of a specific four-step process.

- First, make a thorough "capacity inventory" outlining all the various skills and assets for each of the youth with whom you are currently working.

- Next, compile an inventory of the key assets and resources of the community as these are represented by local individuals, associations, organizations and institutions. When this has been done, it will be discovered that these community assets fall into the following categories: (a) citizens associations and not-for-profit organizations of all types; (b) publicly funded institutions such as hospitals, parks, libraries, and schools; (c) the private sector including small businesses, banks and local branches of larger corporations; (d) local residents and special interest groups of labelled people such as "seniors," "disabled," and "artists."

- Then use the information that has been obtained from these inventories to build strong, concrete, mutually beneficial partnerships between local youth and the other individuals, organizations and associations that exist within the community.

- Finally, on the basis of these partnerships and the active participation of local youth in the community building process, go on to build new relationships with resources that exist outside the immediate community.

Let us look for a moment at two examples of how certain young people have "mapped" the capacities of their neighborhoods and have used this knowledge to make a significant contribution to the communities in which they live.

- Fifth and sixth graders who took part in an innovative curriculum at their school walked around their neighborhoods to learn about the buildings and the process of community planning. When officials of their town proposed razing an old barn to build a parking lot,

these students went to City Hall armed with information
that they had gathered as to why this should not be
done.

❧ A group of enterprising youth explored the vacant lots
in their neighborhood in search of discarded wood. As a
result of "mapping" their local resources, this group now
has a very successful firewood venture and has built
ongoing relationships with several businesses.

In both of these instances, groups of young people became productive
contributors because they knew how to use "mapping" techniques to
discover that even old unused buildings and illegally-dumped
scrapwood are valuable community resources that should not be
wasted. In other words, exact knowledge about existing community
assets is the necessary first step for young people who want to connect
with the positive aspects of community life.

As we have seen, relationship building depends on direct knowledge
of specific community resources. This means that young people who
have learned to "map" the assets of their neighborhoods are able to
place themselves in a much better position to connect and contribute
than would otherwise be possible.

Chart One on the next page illustrates the kinds of relationships that
can exist between local youth and their potential community partners.

Building Productive Relationships Between Local Youth and the Community

Most of the young are in school and, as a result, from an early age
continue to be involved constantly in social relationships that exist
outside the family. But their involvement in activities initiated in
school is only one of the many avenues along which youth can be
connected to other participants in the community-building process. In
each and every community there are many unique opportunities for
youth to become positively linked with potential partners. The following section examines various ways in which youth can effectively
connect with their potential partners in the community.

Local Youth and Community Associations

Citizens Associations

The direct participation of young people in the community can be
facilitated by associations and community organizations that are on the
alert for specific ways to utilize the unique capabilities of the young.
Opportunities should be looked for that will create this sort of connection not only with particular individuals but also with various groups
of young people. Examples include:

Chart One: Potential Partners

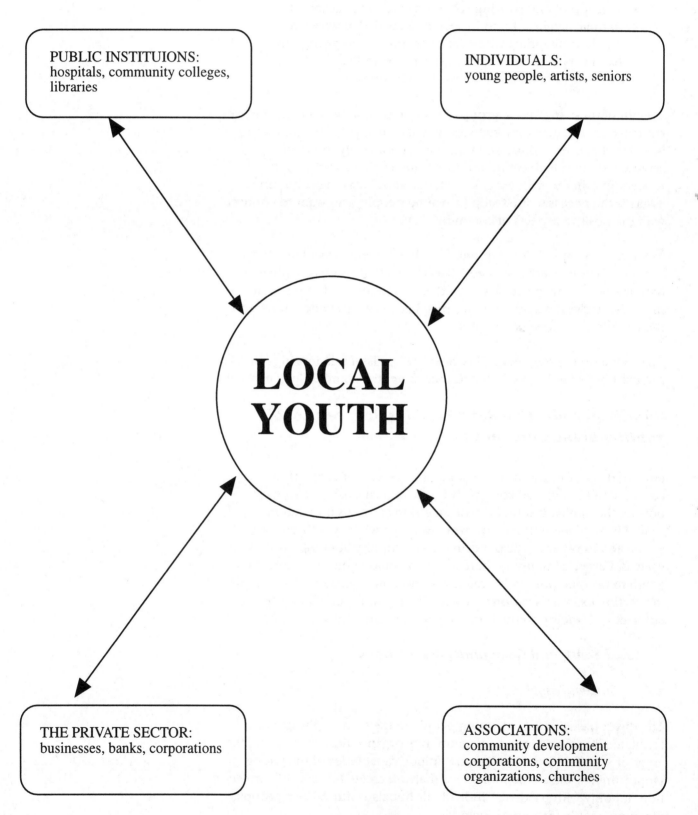

PUBLIC INSTITUIONS:
hospitals, community colleges,
libraries

INDIVIDUALS:
young people, artists, seniors

**LOCAL
YOUTH**

THE PRIVATE SECTOR:
businesses, banks, corporations

ASSOCIATIONS:
community development
corporations, community
organizations, churches

❧ A national organization with offices in several cities funds and supports youth-directed community-based projects. The board in each city is at least 50% youth. (Resources)

❧ A community center employs youth to do research on community organizations and institutions. Youth interview leaders or administrators at churches, schools, hospitals, businesses, health care centers and other organizations. At the end of the summer, the youth host a community forum to inform people about the resources in their community.

❧ Fifty-five community organizations form a coalition to employ 600 youth to rebuild their city. Youth are engaged in projects close to their homes: building a cement basketball court for a church, rehabilitating housing, painting murals, designing puppets for a parade, developing a "toxic tour" of the city's hazardous neighborhood, and educating residents about health issues. (Detroit)

❧ At a crisis intervention center youth and adults have the same duties. Youth are on the board of directors, are AIDS educators, and staff a 24 hour crisis hotline. (Emergency)

❧ Youth own and run a credit union, are the tellers and board members, plan meetings, set loan policies and age requirements, recruit youth, and send regular statements out to members. There are 110 members, each paying a minimum fee of $12. (Alternatives)

❧ Youth connected with a community center organize an anti-drug rally. They contact all the community people and make presentations to their peers about drugs. (Latino)

❧ Youth form a Leaders Club at their local YMCA. Members write their own constitution and plan activities such as the collection of recyclables from the neighborhood. (Logan)

❧ Youth are selected by YMCA staff and Resident Managers in their housing developments to participate in a six month fitness and leadership program. At the end of the training, the youth will be certified Y fitness leaders. They will structure and operate after-school and Saturday night programs for other youth in the neighborhood. (YMCA)

Religious Institutions

❦ A church invites a children's nursery school to become a tenant in its building. This newly expanded children's program helps the church to meet its bills and provides an opportunity for leadership by placing church members on the school's board. (UCRP)

❦ A youth service organization helps a church to establish a youth program at the church. (UCRP)

Cultural Organizations

❦ In most communities various cultural organizations exist that celebrate the specific ethnic heritage of their neighborhood. These organizations are always eager to include young people in their activities because it is these young people that will have the responsibility of keeping the ethnic heritage alive for future generations.

Local Youth and Public Institutions

Public institutions can effectively mobilize youth to become productive members of the community. Most young people are already connected with at least one public institution in their immediate neighborhoods: their schools. But youth can also form productive relationships with a wide variety of other public institutions as well.

Parks

❦ A group of youth organize 150 other youth to renovate a small park. A police officer helps the youth find funding and assist with the writing of the proposal. The youth are planning to organize businesses in the area for more funding. The major piece of their work will be the renovation of an abandoned community center at the park in order to make it available for public use. (Resources)

❦ Youth gain ownership of an empty lot and transform it into a children's park. They paint a huge mural on the wall of the church facing the park and renovate the basement of the church to create a youth center. (Action)

❦ Youth work at a community center doing community-related activities: one is the community historian, another works with the park district organizing teams and tournaments. (Hegewisch)

Libraries

❧ Through a program coordianted by the city, three teenagers who needed jobs worked for the summer at a severely understaffed local library. (Marshall Square)

❧ A children's librarian uses money leftover from a grant to buy books for preschoolers in order to hire local teenagers to design the learning program for these preschoolers. (Logan Square)

❧ Students enrolled in the literacy program at their local library are encouraged to become teachers for other students just coming into the program. (Stateway Gardens)

❧ A librarian compiles a mailing list of young people who come to the library so that they can receive a newsletter about library activities and be invited to help form an advisory council. (North Pulaski)

Community Colleges

❧ A coalition of parents, teachers, students, a community college and a community development corporation sponsors a curriculum at three vocational schools to combine traditional studies with practical economic ventures. Students run a credit union, a scholastic supply store and a "desk-top" catering business. (Bethel)

❧ About 60 youth leaders are trained to teach a youth empowerment curriculum to 700 younger kids. The curriculum, which develops self-esteem through a variety of non-traditional classes, offers youth alternatives to crime, gangs and drugs. The project is sponsored jointly by a community college and the neighborhood police precinct. (Wright)

Schools

❧ Fifth and sixth graders participate in an innovative educational program that takes them on tours around their neighborhoods to learn about the buildings and the process of community planning. Then the students create their own walking tour and slide presentation about the community. When officials of their town proposed razing an old barn to build a parking lot, 90 students went to City Hall with information about the barn's historical significance to the community. (CUBE)

Police

❦ A police department organizes a youth advisory panel to hear the youth perspective on policing issues, to change adult perceptions of youth, and to provide a vehicle for youth to be community leaders. The police department also sponsors a peer mediation project and overnight camping trips led by youth. (Minneapolis)

❦ A group of youth starts a "Safe Streets Initiative" to decrease the involvement of their peers in gangs. In partnership with the police the group holds forums for the community, arranges for their Y to be open from 9 to 1 every Friday night, sponsors youth forums, develops relationships with schools and renovates apartments for low-income families. The group was recently asked by one school to conduct a survey of students to find out about the weapons they own. (Tacoma)

❦ 800 youth attend an annual conference organized by the County Sheriff's Office. Youth present workshops to one another on community service work they are doing in their own communities. (Cook County)

In each of these stories, public institutions can be seen as extending beyond their traditionally passive service-providing function in order to create a positive and mutually beneficial relationship with the youth of their communities. These sorts of creative initiatives allow institutions to bring about positive change rather than simply reacting passively on demand to the constant flood of community needs and problems. Moreover, as the result of innovative programs such as these, the young people of the community have learned to see themselves in relation to public institutions not as recipients of social services but instead as essential contributors to the well-being of the community as a whole. This means that in the future they will be better prepared to take full responsibility for their own education, safety and health.

Local Youth and the Private Sector

Businesses and neighborhoods are mutually dependent: businesses can only thrive in neighborhoods that are viable, and no neighborhood can be viable without successful businesses. Therefore, it should be seen that it is in the best interest of the private sector to invest in developing local young people as essential neighborhood resources.

❦ Youth build their own coffeehouse. The space for the building is donated by the local Boy Scouts, and the youth organize all the resources they need to do the building: they get insurance, local businesses donate the lumber and other materials, and youth solicit the advice of local labor unions and contractors. (Tacoma)

❦ Youth contribute to the economic development of their communities by rehabilitating housing. They are paid and earn school credit. An industrial council made up of local businesses provides raw materials and offers talks, tours, and job training for the youth. Many of the youth eventually start their own businesses or are employed by one of the local businesses. (Resources)

❦ A bank collects and displays artwork from local youth. Many of the youth enroll in a summer program to produce arts and crafts which they sell at an enterprise they have established at the bank. (South Shore)

❦ Youth gather wood that is being illegally dumped in a vacant lot in their neighborhood and start a firewood business. They print fliers, make contacts with other landscaping companies, and deliver their wood to businesses where it is sold. The youth work on commission and many earn between $100-$300 per week. The youth have also developed other enterprises: silk-screened t-shirts with neighborhood scenes, hand-made postcards, Christmas tree deliveries, frozen coconut ice, and manure and wood chips. (Hunts Point)

❦ A settlement house finds internships for youth at community institutions and facilitates a mentoring relationship with the employer. Youth are paid to work 10 hours a week. (Nuevos Futuras)

❦ Students in a youth enterprise program manufacture t-shirts, caps and socks which they sell throughout the community. They do all the printing themselves and earn about $60 at the end of the summer. (McDowell)

❦ Youth connected with a community center in a summer program are trained in various skills which enable them to start their own enterprises. Youth produce and market a calendar, produce a video for fundraising purposes and start a carpet-laying business. (Latino)

❦ A statewide foundation decides to make youth "partners in philanthropy" in order to give them an opportunity to make decisions about projects in their communities that need financial support. The foundation identifies ten groups of young people and gives them $1,000 each to donate to nonprofit organizations of their choice. (Maine)

❦ Young people organize a coalition of youth and adults to lobby the City to create a funding stream for youth employment programs. (Action)

Partnerships such as these enable youth to learn valuable skills but also help to ensure that businesses have deeper and more productive relationships with the local community. Once these sorts of relationships are firmly established, they often develop in unforeseen and exciting ways that will bring further improvement to the entire community.

Local Youth and Individuals Within the Community

Local Residents

❦ Youth form a crime patrol in their housing complex. They monitor the playground and discourage fighting, involve adults to intervene when needed, and keep a watch on elderly residents. Youth also make presentations to other youth groups to encourage them to do similar projects. (Resources)

People with Disabilities

❦ Because of their energy and enthusiasm, young people can often be of special help in mainstreaming the most marginalized members of the community. Community leaders should always be alert and try to include local youth in their efforts to involve disabled individuals in the activities of the neighborhood.

Seniors

❦ Latch key kids who are feeling lonely, experiencing a crisis, or just want to chat, can call on the telephone from their homes to the homes of senior citizens through the "Grandma Please" program. (Uptown)

❦ Several men and women from a senior building are paired with foster children at a neighboring day care center. This partnership is facilitated by the Department of Aging. (Lincoln Park)

❧ On Saturdays during the spring, seniors meet with youth for games, activities and poetry writing. A booklet called *Flowers and Cold Concrete* is published containing works of many of the participants. (5th City)

Welfare Recipients

❧ An 18-year-old youth director organizes younger kids into committees to improve life in their public housing building. The youth maintain a garden, do shopping for elderly residents and paint over graffiti walls. (Ogden)

❧ Youth clean up and beautify the housing development in which they live. They plant shrubs and flowers and plan to look after them in the long term. (Resources)

Other Youth

Youth naturally form strong relationships with other youth. While many older members of the community may continue to make the assumption that youth brought together into peer groups will only serve as destructive forces in the community, in point of fact, groups of youth can work together to become creative forces for positive change.

❧ High school students are mentors and tutors to younger kids who participate in an after-school program run by a Settlement House. (Neuvos Futuras)

❧ Youth provide 45 children from local community centers and homeless shelters with a tutoring program two times a week, craft projects, and a recreation program. (Resources)

❧ A YMCA trains high school students as volunteer mentors for students in grades 6-8. In addition, these young people form a leadership club to discuss issues of relevance to their communities—and then form resolutions they present at the state Youth Assembly. (Kentucky)

❧ At a neighborhood youth conference, high school kids lead a workshop for other youth who want to design projects to ease junior high school kids into high school. (Northwest)

❧ Several cities have youth councils that promote youth programs and advise the city council. For example, one Commission has 11 members between the ages of 13 and 17. The youth report directly to the city council and the Mayor. They have an annual budget of $7,500 they spent last year on a youth conference. (Bellevue)

41

    ❧ Low-income youth are trained on the job to do housing rehabilitation for homeless youth. Sometimes they live in the houses they reconstruct and 65% of the workers go on to hold construction jobs. Some of the youth workers are on the advisory council to the training program. Along with several adults they decide who gets accepted and set the general direction of the program. (Action)

Artists

    ❧ Local companies donate paint for young artists and youth to collaborate on the designing and painting of murals in the community. (Tacoma)

    ❧ Youth become involved with a local youth shelter by doing some cooking. They then decide to make a promotional video for the shelter. They write the script, film the video, and make connections with a local cable company to edit and market it. (Snohomish)

    ❧ At a community-based youth center, youth hang out and eventually come together as groups to design their own artistic projects. A youth is on the board of directors and youth visit schools to lead workshops on the issues addressed by their performances. (Aunt Martha's)

What characterizes each of these partnerships is that in each instance both sides win. By working together and creatively combining their resources, both partners in the relationship become stronger, and their increased and revitalized energy builds a stronger and better community for all its residents.

Chart Two, "Strengthening Partnerships" (see next page), shows how local youth can actually become connected with the process of community building by creating partnerships within their own immediate community. Each story illustrates the creative, practical projects which can result when young people begin to form relationships with local businesses, associations and institutions.

Chart Three on page 44 represents a more complete network of actual partnerships that might exist for local youth whose abilities have become fully utilized as dynamic community assets. In this illustration, young people are at the very center of a web of practical, mutually beneficial local relationships. Each of these relationships matches the gifts and capabilities of young people with those of another neighborhood group or institution. This "wheel" of relationships, then, illustrates how young people might be much more fully mobilized as important community builders.

Chart Two: Strengthening Partnerships

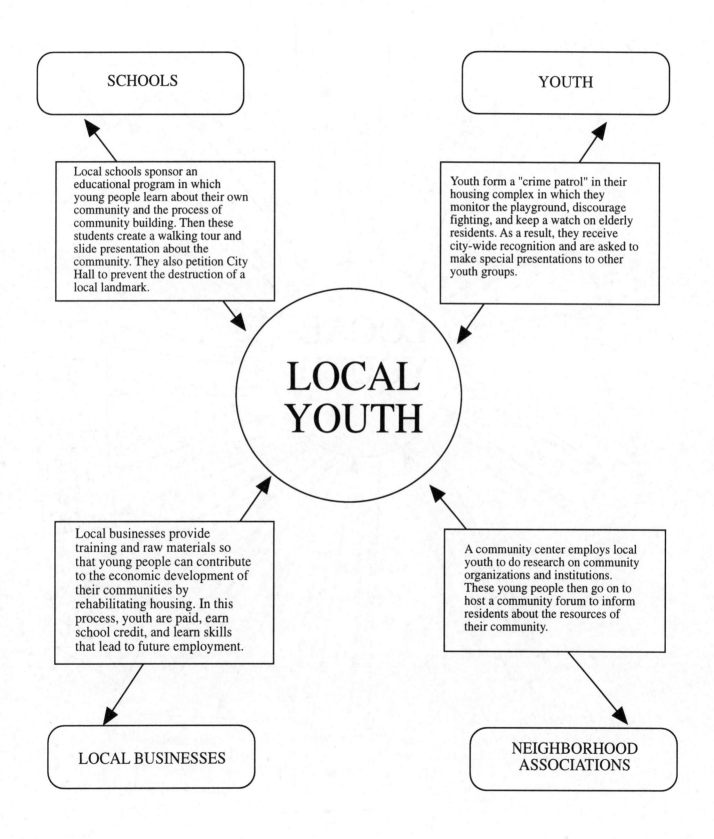

SCHOOLS

YOUTH

Local schools sponsor an educational program in which young people learn about their own community and the process of community building. Then these students create a walking tour and slide presentation about the community. They also petition City Hall to prevent the destruction of a local landmark.

Youth form a "crime patrol" in their housing complex in which they monitor the playground, discourage fighting, and keep a watch on elderly residents. As a result, they receive city-wide recognition and are asked to make special presentations to other youth groups.

LOCAL YOUTH

Local businesses provide training and raw materials so that young people can contribute to the economic development of their communities by rehabilitating housing. In this process, youth are paid, earn school credit, and learn skills that lead to future employment.

A community center employs local youth to do research on community organizations and institutions. These young people then go on to host a community forum to inform residents about the resources of their community.

LOCAL BUSINESSES

NEIGHBORHOOD ASSOCIATIONS

Chart Three: One-on-One Relationships

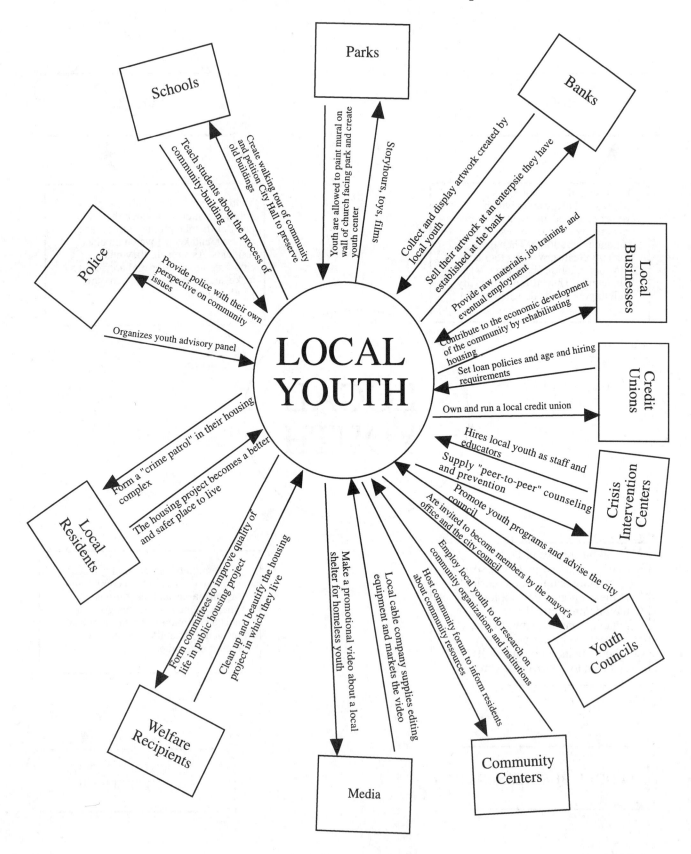

Building Bridges Between Local Youth and Resources Outside the Community

The specific needs and concerns of the young people of the community are expressions of problems and possibilities that exist for youth throughout our nation, whether their immediate community is urban, suburban or rural. Therefore, it is a natural process for young people in one community to feel great affinity for their peers in another, and thus it is possible in many instances to address mutual concerns in programs of combined action. Such programs can often become magnets for attracting "outside" resources and funding— on regional, statewide, and even national levels—into the local community. This can only occur, however, when the young people of the community are firmly connected in the process of community building with local organizations, institutions and concerned individuals.

Sources and Contacts for the "Stories" in This Section

Action

Youth in Action
1280 Fifth Avenue
New York, NY 10029
(212) 860-8170

Alternatives

Alternatives Credit Union
301 W. State Street
Ithaca, NY 14850

Aunt Martha's

Aunt Martha's
4343 Lincoln Highway, Suite 340
Matteson, IL 60443
(708) 747-2701 (Jennifer Kneeland)

Bellevue

Bellevue Youth Link
P.O. Box 90012
Bellevue, WA 98102
(206) 637-5254 (Penny Murphy)

Bethel

Bethel New Life, Inc.
367 N. Karlov
Chicago, IL 60623
(312) 261-3533 (Mildred Wiley)

Cook County

Cook County Youth Services
1401 S. Maybrook Drive
Maywood, IL 60153
(708) 865-2900 (Stan Dembouski, Assistant
Director)

CUBE

CUBE
5328 W. 67th Street
Prairie Village, KS 6228
(913) 262-0691 (Ginny Graves)

Detroit

Detroit Summer '92
2990 W. Grand Blvd., Room 307
Detroit, MI 48202
(313) 873-3216

Emergency

Youth Emergency Services (YES) of St. Louis
6816 Washington
University City, MO 63130
(314) 862-1334 (Deborah Phillips)

Fifth City	Fifth City Human Development Project 3350 W. Jackson Blvd. Chicago, IL 60624 (312) 265-1900 (Lela Moseley)
Hegewisch	Hegewisch Community Committee 13303 S. Baltimore Chicago, IL 60633 (312) 646-4488 (Ruth Zbinden)
Hunts Point	Hunts Point Farms Entrepreneurship Program Seneca Center, Inc. New York, NY (212) 731-8666 (R. Edward Lee, Executive Director)
Kentucky	Kentucky Youth Association State YMCA P.O. Box 577 Frankfort, KY 40602 (502) 227-7028 (Mike Haynes, S.T.A.Y. Project Director)
Latino	Latino Youth 2905 W. Cermak Chicago, IL 60623 (312) 277-0400 (Lori Rios & Hector Gamboa)
Lincoln Park	Lincoln Park Senior Center 2111 Halsted Street Chicago, IL (312) 542-6776 (Lorraine Myers)
Logan	Logan Square YMCA Aspira 3600 W. Fullerton Chicago, IL 60647 (312) 235-5150
Logan Square	Logan Square Library 3255 W. Altgeld Chicago, IL 60647 (312) 744-5295 (Pamela Martin-Diaz, Children's Librarian)
Maine	Maine Community Foundation 210 Main Street P.O. Box 148 Ellsworth, ME 04605

Marshall Square   Marshall Square Library
2724 W. Cermak
Chicago, IL 60608
(312) 747-0061 (Julie Lockwood, Branch Head)

McDowell   Mary McDowell Settlement House
1335 W. 51st Street
Chicago, IL 60609
(312) 376-5242 (Richard Ware)

Minneapolis   Minneapolis Police Department
CCP/SAFE Youth Programs
2717 S. Third Street
Minneapolis, MN 55401
(612) 673-3015 (Byron Lewis)

North Pulaski   North Pulaski Library
1330 N. Pulaski Road
Chicago, IL 60651
(312) 744-9573 (Nanette Freeman,
Children's Librarian)

Northwest   Northwest Youth Outreach
6417 W. Irving Park
Chicago, IL 60634
(312) 777-7112 (Lenny Lamkin)

Nuevos Futuras   Nuevos Futuras
Emerson House
645 N. Wood
Chicago, IL 60622
(312) 421-3551 (Lucy Gomez)

Ogden   Ogden Courts Youth Committee
2650 W. Ogden Avenue, Apt. 401
Chicago, IL 60608
(312) 762-8993 (Gervase Bolden)

Resources   Youth as Resources Project
Northwest Side Community Development
Corporation
5174 N. Hopkins Street
Milwaukee, WI 53209
(414) 532-3310 (Paula Allen)

Snohomish   Snohomish Youth Initiative
917 134th Street SW #A6
Everett, WA 98204
(206) 742-5911 (Laura Putnam)

South Shore   South Shore Bank
                       Junior Entrepreneurs Program
                       7054 S. Jeffrey Blvd.
                       Chicago, IL 60649
                       (312) 288-1000

Stateway Gardens   Stateway Gardens Library
                       3618 S. State Street
                       Chicago, IL 60609
                       (312) 747-6872 (Leanna Newson, Branch Head)

Tacoma   Washington Leadership Institute
                       Tacoma-Pierce County Office
                       PO Box 377
                       Tacoma, WA 98401
                       (206) 596-2501 (Jennifer Kurkoski)

Uptown   Uptown Center Hull House
                       4520 N. Beacon
                       Chicago, IL 60640
                       (312) 561-3500 (Monica Glaser)

UCRP   United Church of Rogers Park
                       Ashland and Morse Avenues
                       Chicago, IL 60626
                       (312) 761-2500 (Rev. Kerm Krueger)

Wright   Wright College
                       Adult Continuing Education
                       3400 N. Austin
                       Chicago, IL 60634
                       (312) 794-3200 (Sally Schwyn, Dean)

YMCA   YMCA Urban Services
                       1000 Church Street
                       Nashville, TN 37203
                       (615) 254-0631 (J. Lawrence-Reginald Tiller, Y-
                       Wolf Program Director)

Introduction—Seniors and Community Renewal

Up until the present time in most communities throughout the world, the elders of the community have been viewed as the primary sources of wisdom and experience. The elders of each group are thought to be responsible for the proper maintenance of cultural traditions. From this perspective the oldest members of the community are seen as primary contributors to the constantly continuing process of building community stability and development.

In highly competitive modern industrialized societies such as our own, however, senior members of the community often tend to be narrowly defined as *the elderly* and, as a result of this labelling, seniors become effectively marginalized from the activities of the mainstream, and their potential contributions to society become lost for both present and future generations. Moreover, once we allow the possibilities of senior citizens to be defined entirely by their perceived lack of economic mobility and their increasing need for social and medical services, the older members of the community tend to be seen only as a continuing drain on an already strained economy. In other words, the elderly are now often seen solely as recipients of services and social security checks. As a result of this myopic vision, we continue to rob ourselves of their true power to contribute to a more vibrant community.

This need not be so. For example, consider the experience of the members of one senior center:

❦ As retired persons entered the retirement community, center administrators and staff sensed a pervasive depression that comes when anyone is removed from his or her community. How did the center respond? Although the primary community of the residents had been lost, the center adopted a next best solution by organizing a variety of partnerships with businesses, the park system, local associations, etc., which connected seniors to their new communities. Residents were linked to the local park where two of the men watered plants and trees and did landscaping. Some other residents worked with the local neighborhood association as it built a new playground. Several residents were linked to the neighborhood day care center. Other members of the group put together an entertainment troupe and traveled to local churches and schools putting on presentations about African-American history. With their sense of community thus restored, the residents of the retirement community were able to recognize their continuing value to the community at large. (Lincoln Park)

Of course, not all institutions respond in such a creative and responsible manner. In fact, at the present time most of the institutions in
our society are structured to respond one-dimensionally to the perceived needs of the elderly "clients" which these institutions were
created to serve. As a result, institutions respond mainly to the medical
problems of retired persons and entirely neglect (and even serve to
deaden) the potential contributions which senior citizens might still be
able to make to the larger community in which they live.

Responsible community organizations can help to free these
marginalized elderly residents from this community isolation by
initiating projects that properly employ the unique talents and skills of
senior citizens. Just imagine what would happen if we all started to
think creatively of the elders in our community, not in terms of their
needs and deficiencies, but in terms of what specific contributions they
are able to make to the community as a whole.

Rediscovering Seniors as Assets Within the Community

Senior citizens possess a wide range of skills, talents and resources
which can be instrumental in the community development process. By
identifying the specific talents, resources and abilities that are present
in the older generation, we can begin to discover the appropriate roles
for them to play in the ongoing process of active community revitalization.

Economic Resources. The assumption that all retired persons are
economic liabilities simply is not true in our society at the present
time. As a matter of fact, the majority of retired people do not live in
senior care facilities or receive welfare services. Even more important
is the fact that retired persons represent more than 40% of the individual wealth in the United States and, as a result, represent a potentially powerful economic force in the communities where they live.

Culture, Tradition and History. Any senior who has lived in a
neighborhood for an extended period of time embodies a unique
perspective on the history of that community. As a Native American
educator once said: "You cannot do any good research without having
talked with the elderly." A community must know and understand its
roots in order to chart a meaningful path for the future, and there is
no more logical group of persons to be involved in this process than
the elderly. As one senior citizen recently said: "There is one thing that
always gets every senior excited and that's history!" As a matter of fact,
the sense of excitement that seniors generate can be contagious to
other members of the community as well.

In addition to a strong sense of history, seniors can also actively pass
down rich cultural traditions to younger members of the community.
Cultural institutions can be a natural setting for seniors to teach some

of their special skills to interested students of all ages. For example, an 85-year-old Mexican-American woman is currently teaching a traditional art and pottery course at the Mexican Fine Arts Museum in Chicago. At the Native American Educational Services College in the same city, two seniors are in the process of teaching their tribal languages to a younger generation. (NAES)

Experience and Skills. Most seniors have worked for several decades and in that process have accumulated pertinent personal and professional life experiences. This knowledge can and should be translated into resources which will serve to invigorate the daily life of the community. While it is true some seniors prefer and indeed deserve time to invest in themselves, it is also true most seniors would like to remain active in the community and would like to be connected in a meaningful way to organizations or groups that can use their services.

Time. In making the transition from full employment to retirement, seniors often find that they have a lot of extra time on their hands, and this is time that can be a useful resource for the revitalization of communities. In many instances once they have become involved in this ongoing process, seniors have discovered that even after retirement they can learn new skills and develop new talents which will be of use in a wide variety of venues.

Peer Groups. Whether living alone or in senior centers, retired persons often tend to congregate in peer groups which can in turn become active in a wide variety of projects which interface with the community at large. In Chicago, for example, the park district sponsors seniors clubs which were originally socially-oriented but which have also come to be rich centers of active participation and even leadership in the activities of the entire community.

The specific assets of retired persons will always be different from community to community and from individual to individual. In every instance, however, each community has the responsibility to locate and utilize its own hidden assets.

Mapping Community Assets to Discover Potential Partners for Local Seniors

Now that we have identified at least some of the assets local seniors can bring to the process of community building, we must examine the means by which neighborhood leaders can most effectively mobilize these assets and turn them into valuable resources for community building. This effort to "connect" local seniors with the process of community building involves the utilization of a specific four-step process.

❧ First, make a thorough "capacity inventory" outlining all the various skills and assets for each of the local seniors with whom you are currently working.

❧ Next, compile an inventory of the key assets and resources of the community as these are represented by local individuals, associations, organizations, and institutions. When this has been done, it will be discovered that these community assets fall into the following categories: (a) citizens associations and not-for-profit organizations of all types; (b) publicly funded institutions such as hospitals, parks, libraries, and schools; (c) the private sector including small businesses, banks and local branches of larger corporations; (d) local residents and special interest groups of "labelled people" such as "welfare recipients," "youth," "disabled," and "artists."

❧ Then use the information that has been obtained from these inventories to build strong, concrete, mutually beneficial "partnerships" between local "seniors" and the other individuals, organizations and associations that exist within the community.

❧ Finally, on the basis of these "partnerships" and the active participation of local seniors in the community building process, go on to build new relationships with resources that exist outside the immediate community.

Chart One on the next page illustrates the kinds of relationships that can exist between local seniors and their potential community partners.

Every community has a wide variety of potential partners for recon-necting senior citizens to the community building process. Seniors can either connect to local institutions and organizations on an individual basis or they can choose to connect as members of specific groups or organizations.

Chart One: Potential Partners

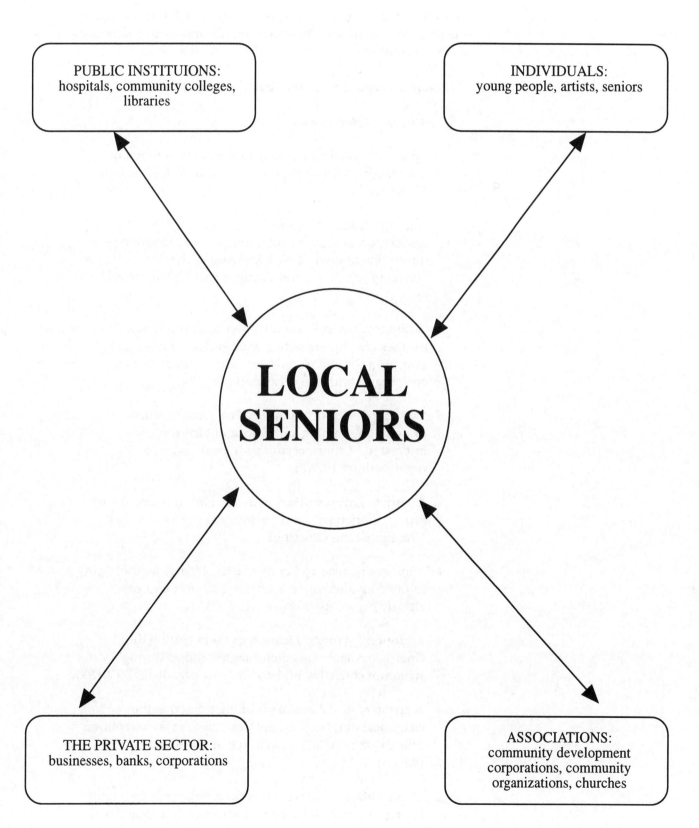

Building Productive Relationships Between Local Seniors and the Community

Let us now take a look at the specific ways in which constructive relationships can be built between seniors and their potential partners in the community.

Local Seniors and Community Associations

Citizens Associations.

❧ Seniors worked with a neighborhood development association in the design of a new building for seniors. (Claretian)

❧ A group of seniors worked with a neighborhood association to secure a loan from a local community development credit union in order to open a consignment shop administrated and staffed entirely by seniors.

❧ A nonprofit organization connects retired senior business executives with a wide variety of nonprofit groups in the city. Seniors volunteer primarily as consultants with the organizations. (ESC)

❧ The retired Senior Volunteer Program provides orientation, training and placement for seniors interested in volunteering with local nonprofit organizations. (RSVP)

❧ A seniors group worked with a community organizing group to open an intergenerational center at a park. (Greater Grand Crossing)

❧ Seniors organize and convince the Department of Aging to open an alternative nutrition site after two have already been closed down. (CLASP)

❧ A group of seniors is instrumental in getting the Guardian Angels into their neighborhood through signature collecting and community organizing. (CLASP)

❧ A group of 10-12 seniors is being trained at the Neighborhood Community Council to make telephone calls to get people involved in community activities. (Pilsen)

❧ Three elderly Chinese individuals volunteer on a daily basis to assist with classroom activities at a local day care center. (Chinese)

❧ A senior center works with tenant representatives from senior buildings to disseminate information regarding primarily crime and tenant issues. (Korean)

❧ Approximately 80% of a local food pantry is staffed by seniors at the Polish Welfare Association. (Polish)

❧ Many citizens groups and nonprofit associations (e.g., the American Association of Retired Persons) work specifically on social and economic issues related exclusively to the needs of seniors, but there are many other groups (e.g., the Grey Panthers) which stress a cross-generational approach to community problems in which the active participation of seniors is constantly encouraged. Other groups of seniors have been engaged in public advocacy work and have participated in coalitions which have been able to win concessions on factors such as transportation costs, accessibility issues, specific community health concerns, etc.

Religious Institutions

❧ High school students who are members of a local congregation establish an adoption program with seniors who are living in the affordable housing which was created by the church's development corporation. (Trinity)

❧ A congregation invites the city's Department on Aging to establish a senior nutrition site at the church. (North Shore)

Cultural Organizations

❧ A group of seniors that forms the East Side Historical Society works with a local high school in space provided by the park system in developing a museum which documents the history of four Chicago neighborhoods. (East Side)

❧ Seniors from the community help on the Day of La Posadas during which children go from house to house asking for shelter (as did Mary and Joseph in the Bible). (Pilsen)

❧ A group of seniors present skits, songs, historical presentations and cook southern-style food at local churches, synagogues and senior centers during Black History month. (Lincoln Park)

❧ A group of seniors active in the Vietnam Association organize an annual celebration in honor of the founding father of Vietnam. (Vietnam)

❧ Elderly from the Vietnamese community in a Chicago neighborhood contribute poetry to the Vietnamese Association's monthly publication. (Vietnam)

Local Seniors and Public Institutions

Parks

❧ Seniors worked with a neighborhood association on a renovation project at the local park performing some of the lighter tasks. (Lincoln Park)

❧ Seniors living in a Chicago Housing Authority building water and care for shrubbery and trees at a park which lies adjacent. (Lincoln Park)

❧ Seniors serve as docents at many museums and libraries.

Libraries

❧ Senior citizens who are ill at a local housing development call a neighborhood librarian for help. This librarian arranges to have library assistants deliver groceries to where the shut-ins live. (Stateway Gardens)

❧ A librarian works together with the president of the local historical society to collect oral histories from senior citizens with the purpose of compiling a book that will chronicle the history of the neighborhood. (Kelly)

❧ Senior citizens from a local quilting guild make a quilt depicting the library and the community, and this quilt is now on permanent display in the library's auditorium. (Beverly)

❧ A neighborhood librarian holds birthday and holiday dinners at the library for members of a seniors' self-help program, and once a week this librarian distributes clothing that these seniors have collected from the community. (Stateway Gardens)

❧ A librarian arranges for health providers from a local eye clinic to come to the library to screen seniors for cataracts. (Stateway Gardens)

❧ A library sponsors an intergenerational program that pairs seniors with first grade students in which they meet once a week to read and discuss books suggested by the library staff. (Connecticut)

❧ A retired schoolteacher uses local volunteers as assistants in the art classes for neighborhood children which he teaches at the local library. (Scottsdale)

Community Colleges

❧ Two seniors are on the faculty at a college where one teaches the Lakota language and the other is an instructor in Ojibwe. (NAES)

Schools

❧ Children from two day schools go to a senior center once a month, and seniors design special games for the children to play. (Lincoln Park)

❧ Seniors from a Chicago Housing Authority senior building meet with fourth graders from a local school once a week to conduct interviews with each other and, as a result, develop oral histories and act out skits based on the seniors' lives. (Illinois)

❧ Fifth and sixth graders from a local school meet with seniors after school over a 12-week period, participating together in a poetry reading program two days every week. As a result, the group creates a booklet including a biographical sketch, pictures and poetry from each participant. (Conrad)

Police

❧ A senior leader from the American Association of Retired Persons works together with the Chief of Police and a Police Sheriff to enhance delivery of law enforcement to the elderly. (TRIAD)

❧ Seniors work with the local police station to get foot patrol officers back into their neighborhood. (Metro Area)

❧ Seniors are recruited and trained to acquaint them with the local police station and other citywide departments. As a result, seniors visit other seniors in a door-to-door campaign in order to provide security evaluations and advice. (Cottage Grove/NNFCP)

Hospitals

❧ A wellness center, which came into being because of the advocacy work of seniors, provides preventative health care while facilities at a senior home provide medical care.

❧ A Shriner's Hospital is participating with seniors from a local retirement center who visit the hospital for one hour each day to read and play with the children.

❧ A group of seniors makes clothing for children at a hospital. (Eileen Ruff)

Local Seniors and the Private Sector

❧ A local restaurant which uses the parking lot of a senior center pays a group of seniors to help with a Christmas mailing. The restaurant also invites the seniors for a meal on Santa Lucia Day. (Lincoln Park)

❧ A local drug store chain offers discounted prescriptions to seniors and works with medical school doctors and a seniors group in the community in order to provide educational programs at local churches on medications and their proper usage. (Metro Area)

Local Seniors and Other Individuals Within the Community

Local Residents

❧ Seniors run a 55 Alive program for driver training which was originally intended for seniors but now has been opened to the entire community. (Abbott)

People with Disabilities

❧ Seniors are involved in the Visiting Important Persons program in which they visit less mobile elderly and try to assist with any practical problems. Seniors are trained to be able to provide CPR, to recognize drug abuse, to give bed baths and first aid, and to help with practical daily matters like budgeting and food selection and preparation. The oldest participant is an 82-year-old woman. (Little Brother's)

Welfare Recipients

❧ A seniors' club in the park system collects canned goods from among its members and provides food baskets for low income elderly. (Parks)

❧ Seniors provide tax preparation assistance for low
income elderly at local libraries. (Garfield Ridge)

Youth

Integenerational linkages between seniors and youth are natural
alliances. For example, when a local human service agency wanted to
find out how it could best provide services to a group of elderly in the
community, this agency decided to conduct a "needs assessment"
survey in order to quantify the problems experienced by this particular
group of seniors. Instead of revealing the true needs of the elderly,
however, this survey revealed that the elderly wanted to become active
players in the community and were eager to become re-connected
once again. In interpreting the results of this survey, therefore, the
human services agency listed "companionship" as the primary "deficiency" among seniors and set up a program which linked the elderly
to neighborhood kids via the telephone. Thus, even though still
thought of as having deficiencies, the seniors were unintentionally
utilized as resources in the community which could be used to fill a
gap in the lives of latch key children. (Uptown)

❧ Latch key kids who are feeling lonely, experiencing a
crisis, or just want to chat, can call on the telephone
from their homes to the homes of senior citizens
through the "Grandma Please" program. (Uptown)

❧ Several men and women from a senior building are
paired with foster children at a neighboring day care
center. This partnership is facilitated by the Department
of Aging. (Lincoln Park)

It seems that a major thrust today among those utilizing the special
talents and skills of the elderly is in developing intergenerational
programs. This connecting of the elderly to the young is not only a
pragmatic move in which seniors are seen as being able to fill some of
the gaps left by working parents but also enables the young to see
their own community and the wider world from a different and richer
perspective. For example, fourth graders from an elementary school in
one community developed a program in which they meet weekly with
seniors from a local public housing building. These school children
have learned to conduct interviews, to transcribe oral histories, and
even to create short plays in which they can act out tales from the lives
of their elders. This is not history just for its own sake. This is a means
of discovering and relating directly to the real roots of the community.
Thus the youth of the community become better able to understand
that a genuine community is not simply an amalgamation of people
and buildings and open spaces but is a woven tapestry of interconnected stories and possibilities. (Illinois)

☙ On Saturdays during the spring, seniors meet with youth for games, activities and poetry writing. A booklet called *Flowers and Cold Concrete* is published containing works of many of the participants. (5th City)

Other Seniors

Seniors also often share their capacities with the other seniors who live in their community. Those seniors who have been able to maintain a high degree of mobility can be connected to other less mobile seniors in order to enable them to remain in their own homes in the communities where they live. In other instances, seniors can be active as representatives or leaders for other seniors in service organizations and special advocacy programs.

☙ A group of 20 seniors throw birthday parties for other seniors at a senior center. (Little Brother's)

☙ Seniors teach other seniors crafts, sewing, music and arts at a senior center. (Little Brother's)

☙ Seniors lead and/or facilitate an Alzheimers support group, a low vision group and a weekly exercise group at a retirement house. (Little Brothers)

Artists

☙ Seniors learn traditional Greek fabric art and cross-stitching and then display their works at a senior center operated by the Department of Aging. (Greek)

☙ An 85-year-old Mexican-American woman teaches a six-week traditional art and pottery course to other senior citizens at the Mexican Fine Arts Museum. (Mexican)

What characterizes each of these partnerships which we have been discussing is that in each instance both sides win. In the intergenerational program, the stories told by seniors became living parts of the experience of the youngest members of the community. A community-based organization by connecting with seniors was able to obtain expert consultation which benefited the community as a whole. Seniors better than any other group of persons in each neighborhood embody the experience, the diversity, the changes, the development that make that particular community unique in its past, its present, and also its future possibilities.

Chart Two, "Strengthening Partnerships" (see next page), shows how local seniors can become connected with actual partners existing within the community in which these particular seniors currently reside. Each story exemplifies the creative practical projects which can

Chart Two: Strengthening Partnerships

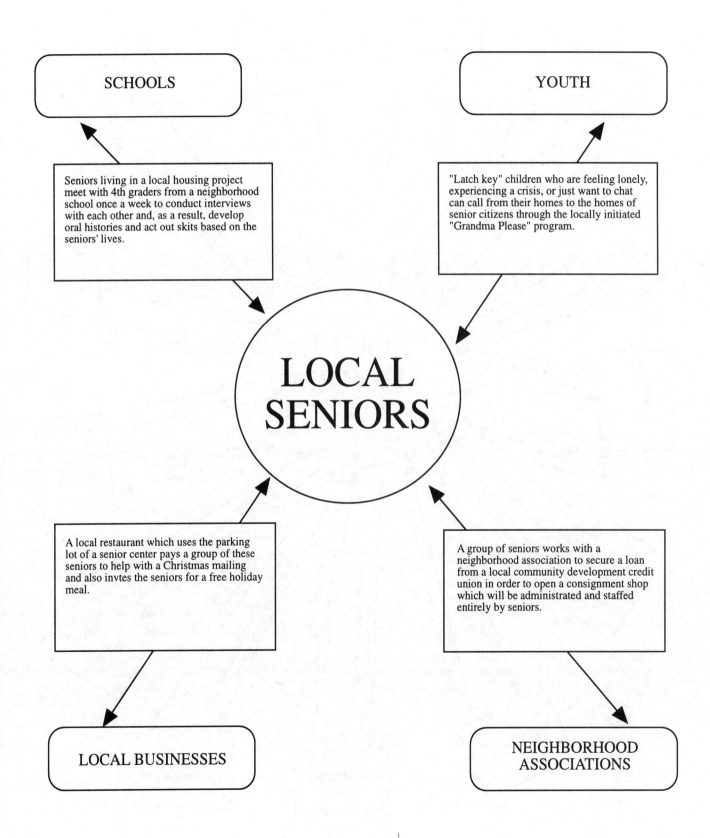

SCHOOLS

YOUTH

Seniors living in a local housing project meet with 4th graders from a neighborhood school once a week to conduct interviews with each other and, as a result, develop oral histories and act out skits based on the seniors' lives.

"Latch key" children who are feeling lonely, experiencing a crisis, or just want to chat can call from their homes to the homes of senior citizens through the locally initiated "Grandma Please" program.

LOCAL SENIORS

A local restaurant which uses the parking lot of a senior center pays a group of these seniors to help with a Christmas mailing and also invtes the seniors for a free holiday meal.

A group of seniors works with a neighborhood association to secure a loan from a local community development credit union in order to open a consignment shop which will be administrated and staffed entirely by seniors.

LOCAL BUSINESSES

NEIGHBORHOOD ASSOCIATIONS

Chart Three: One on One Relationships

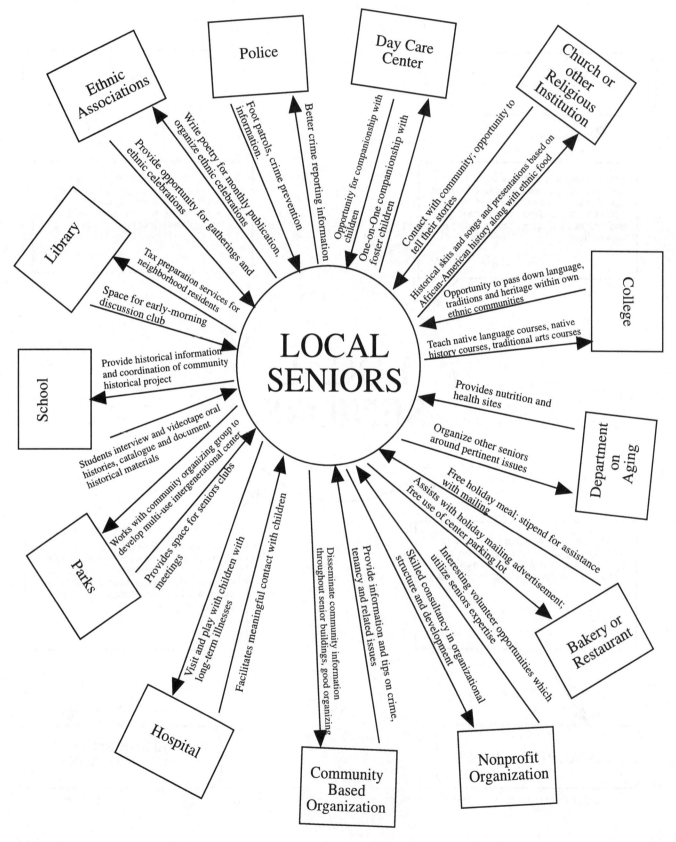

result when older citizens begin to form relationships with local businesses, associations and other groups and institutions.

Chart Three on page 64 represents the complex network of actual partnerships that might exist for local seniors whose abilities have been fully utilized as dynamic community assets. In this illustration, older people are at the very center of a web of practical, mutually beneficial local relationships. Each of these relationships matches the gifts and capabilities of older citizens with those of another neighborhood group or institution. This "wheel" of relationships, then, illustrates how older people might be much more fully mobilized as important community builders.

Sources and Contacts for the "Stories" in This Section

Abbott   Abbott Park
49 E. 95th Street
Chicago, IL 60628
(312) 264-1050 (Cecilia Wilkins)

Beverly   Beverly Library
2121 W. 95th Street
Chicago, IL 60643
(312) 747-9673 (Debbie Shillow,
Children's Librarian)

Chinese   Chinese-American Service League
310 W. 24th Place
Chicago, IL 60616
(312) 791-0418 (Larry So)

Claretian   Claretian Associates Neighborhood
    Development Office
205 W. Monroe
Chicago, IL 60606
(312) 236-7782 (Donna Drinian)

CLASP   CLASP
1545 W. Morse Avenue
Chicago, IL 60626
(312) 973-7888 (Karen Nielson)

Conrad   Conrad Center
2717 N. Leavitt
Chicago, IL
(312) 248-1093 (Miriam Jones, Intergenerational
Project)

East Side   East Side Historical Society
10833 Avenue D
Chicago, IL 60617
(312) 221-7349 (Frank Stanley)

ESC   Executive Service Corps
25 E. Washington, Suite 801
Chicago, IL 60602
(312) 580-1840 (John Eagen)

5th City

5th City Human Development Project
3350 W. Jackson Blvd.
Chicago, IL 60624
(312) 265-1900 (Lela Moseley)

Garfield Ridge

Garfield Ridge Library
6348 S. Archer
Chicago, IL 60638
(312) 747-6094 (Bruce Ziemer)

Greater Grand Crossing Greater Grand Crossing Organizing Committee
213 E. 79th Street
Chicago, IL 60619

Greek

Greek-American Community Service Center
3940 N. Pulaski
Chicago, IL 60641

Illinois

Illinois Intergenerational Project
Stateway Gardens Library
3618 S. State #106
Chicago, IL 60690
(312) 747-6872 (LeAnna Newsome)

Jane Addams

Jane Addams Senior Caucus
3212 N. Broadway
Chicago, IL 60657

Kelly

Kelly Library
6151 S. Normal Blvd.
Chicago, IL 60621
(312) 747-8418 (Linda Greene, Branch Head)

Korean

Korean Senior Citizen Center
4750 N. Sheridan
Chicago, IL 60640
(312) 878-7272 (Susan Kang)

Lincoln Park

Lincoln Park Senior Center
2111 Halsted Street
Chicago, IL
(312) 543-6776 (Lorraine Myers)

Little Brother's

Little Brother's Friends of the Elderly
1658 W. Belmont
Chicago, IL
(312) 477-7702 (Jamie Hirsch)

NAES   Native American Educational Services College
                        2838 W. Peterson Avenue
                        Chicago, IL 60659

North Shore   North Shore Baptist Church
                        5244 N. Lakewood
                        Chicago, IL
                        (312) 728-4200 (Pastor Marcus Pomeroy)

Polish   Polish Welfare Association
                        4101 S. Archer
                        Chicago, IL 60632

RSVP   RSVP
                        118 N. Clinton
                        Chicago, IL 60661
                        (312) 726-1526 (Janice Miles)

Scottsdale   Scottsdale Library
                        4101 W. 79th Street
                        Chicago, IL 60652
                        (312) 747-0193 (Bernadette Nowakowski,
                        Children's Librarian)

Stateway Gardens   Stateway Gardens Library
                        3618 S. State Street
                        Chicago, IL 60609
                        (312) 747-6872 (Leanna Newson, Branch Head)

TRIAD   TRIAD
                        American Association of Retired Persons Area V
                        2720 Des Plaines Ave., Suite 113
                        Des Plaines, IL 60018
                        (708) 298-2852 (Sonja Terry)

Trinity   Trinity United Church of Christ
                        532 W. 95th
                        Chicago, IL 60628
                        (312) 962-5650 (Rev. Jeremiah Wright)

Uptown   Uptown Center Hull House
                        4520 N. Beacon
                        Chicago, IL 60640
                        (312) 561-3500 (Monica Glaser)

Vietnamese   Vietnamese Association of Illinois
                        4842 N. Broadway
                        Chicago, IL 60640
                        (312) 728-3700 (Qua Dran)

Introduction—People with Disablities and Community Renewal

Once we have learned to understand that a community is composed of a series of partnerships which unlock the potential of each of the participants, we can begin to look creatively at ways to incorporate even the most excluded and "marginalized" individuals into the process of active community building. Therefore, let us now take a close look at those people who have been labelled as "disabled," "mentally retarded," "developmentally disabled," or severely "handicapped" in various ways. Each of these labels by focusing exclusively on what is different about these individuals serves to obscure their other qualities which are quite similar to all the rest of the members of the community. In other words, being misled by labels, we tend to forget that "disabled" individuals just like everyone else have deeply felt, personal needs for dignity, for pleasures, for friendship, for hope for the future, and for a useful place within the community. When these needs to give are denied, their lives become sad and empty. That is exactly what happens when these disabled people are taken out of their communities and placed instead in social service institutions where they are even further isolated. Institutionalization of this kind, though benign in its intention, creates problems that stand directly in the way of the process of dynamic community building.

First, there is the major financial expense that is imposed upon the rest of the community by the continued institutionalization of a growing number of its members. Second, and just as important, there is the even greater cost in human terms to those who are institutionalized and also to those that remain in the community who would be able to benefit from direct contact with those who have become marginalized.

But what exactly are the benefits that members of the community can derive from open and direct contact with people who are also disabled? In order to answer this question, we must examine some of the qualities that are required for the continuing development of a healthy, dynamic community.

Rediscovering the Gifts and Capacities of Disabled Individuals as Assets Within the Community

In order to understand the gifts that disabled people can bring to the community, we must learn to think inclusively in the language of genuine community and not exclusively in the language of social service systems that label certain individuals and isolate them from the process of community building. A true community is only able to grow and strengthen itself by including all of its members and finding room for them to develop their capacities within its own pattern of growth. Disabled people have been marginalized and forced to the edges of their society because they have been looked at exclusively in terms of their deficiencies. Let us reverse that tendency and now examine the positive gifts and capacities that disabled individuals can bring to the process of community building.

Skills. Every person has abilities including people labelled disabled. Identifying and mobilizing these abilities creates new benefits for all community members and builds the pride and self respect of the labelled person.

Hospitality. Every community has the latent capacity to be hospitable, but this hospitality is a quality that needs to be activated in order for it to become a genuine asset. It is the gift of the people who are disabled to be able to activate the hospitality of the community in which they reside. In relation to its most marginalized members, a community is enabled to demonstrate and develop its own inner strength and resiliency. By including the excluded, a community grows and creates new possibilities for its own further development.

Compassion. A strong community is always a compassionate community, and compassion is a quality that can only be released by establishing direct relationships with individuals who have become marginalized and isolated through no fault or desire of their own.

Friendship. Friendship goes beyond compassion and implies a certain degree of mutuality within a relationship. Once the pattern of isolating disabled individuals has been replaced by a process of active inclusion, then (and only then) can new possibilities for friendship be developed between disabled individuals and members of the rest of the community.

Happiness. Within the context of community relationships happiness is always a double gift: by giving happiness to others, in return we receive an equal amount of happiness of our own. In no situation is the mutuality of this process more clearly demonstrated than when a new partnership is established with a disabled individual. By bringing a source of meaningful connection and hope to an isolated, marginalized individual, we not only increase their personal happiness but also at the same time add greatly to our own.

Inspiration. Anyone who has ever established a genuine partnership with a disabled person knows exactly how inspiring such a relationship can often be. So many things that most of us have learned to take completely for granted come to be seen in a completely different light. To be able to participate in a process in which a marginalized individual is able to overcome great odds and is able for the first time to become productive in even a small way is a great privilege and a source of inspiration that is necessary for own productivity and that of the society of which we are a part.

This process of accepting and utilizing the gifts and capacities of disabled people means that when these marginalized individuals are placed in direct contact with appropriate and hospitable people and places, then the community as a whole is able to grow and become stronger—and this increased strength and capacity is precisely what we mean by community-building.

Mapping Community Assets to Discover Potential Partners for Disabled Individuals

Now that we have identified at least some of the gifts and capacities that disabled individuals can bring to the process of community building, we must go on to examine the means by which neighborhood leaders can most effectively mobilize these gifts and capacities and turn them into valuable assets for community building. This effort to connect local disabled individuals with the process of community-building involves the utilization of a specific four-step process:

- First, make a thorough capacity inventory outlining all the various gifts and capacities for each of the disabled individuals with whom you are currently working.

- Next, compile an inventory of the key assets and resources of the community as these are represented by other local individuals, associations, organizations, and institutions. When this has been done, it will be discovered that these community assets fall into the following categories: (a) citizens associations and not-for-profit organizations of all types; (b) publicly funded institutions such as hospitals, parks, libraries, and schools; (c) the private sector including small businesses, banks and local branches of larger corporations; (d) local residents and special interest groups of "labelled people" such as "seniors," "youth," and "artists."

- Then use the information that has been obtained from these inventories to build strong, concrete, mutually beneficial partnerships between local disabled individuals and the other individuals, organizations and associations that exist within the community.

- Finally, on the basis of these partnerships and the active participation of local disabled individuals in the community building process, go on to build new relationships with resources that exist outside the immediate community. Chart One on page 72 depicts these possibilities.

Chart One: Potential Partners

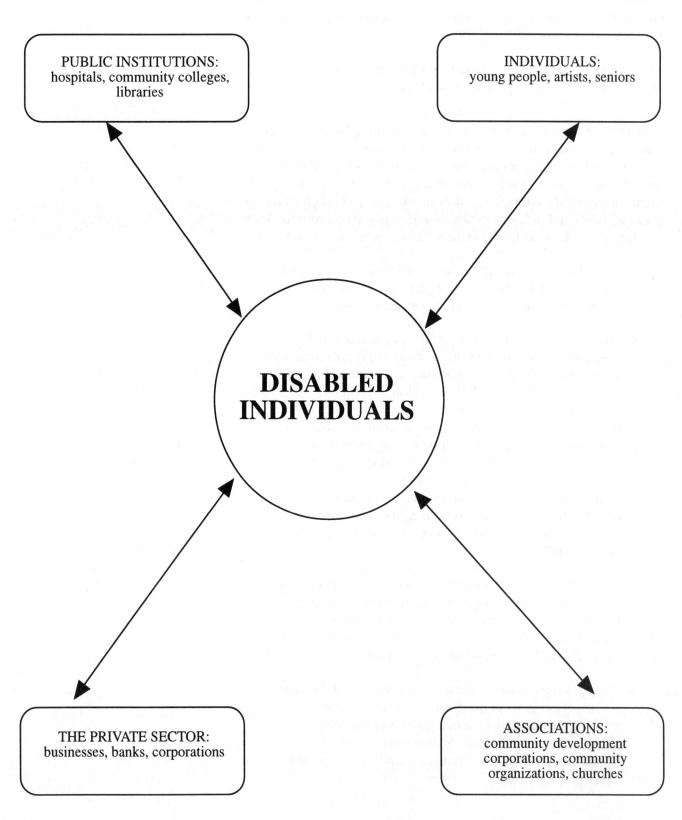

Chart Two on page 74 illustrates the kinds of relationships that can be built between disabled individuals and potential partners from within the community.

Building Productive Relationships Between Disabled Individuals and the Community

Many people who are labelled as being disabled have been marginalized and isolated from the mainstream of their communities. This is especially true of those who have been categorized as "developmentally disabled." In the past, well-intentioned representatives of the social service establishment have decided that the most humane and appropriate response to the needs of developmentally disabled people is to remove them entirely from their immediate community and surround them with a cadre of specially trained professionals. The immediate result of this process has been to further isolate those individuals who are already the most marginalized members of their own community. This increased (and often enforced) isolation can frequently lead to deterioration, stagnation, and even desperate personal actions which are frequently categorized as socially deviant behavior.

But, just as soon as developmentally disabled individuals are brought out of unnecessary isolation and put into normal, open, responsive and responsible social situations which are a part of the ongoing daily life of a real community, then we discover that the lives of developmentally disabled people can begin to change dramatically for the better—an outcome which social service agencies have been unable to accomplish with their traditional "service-based" methodology.

To document this nontraditional approach, as part of a research project initiated by the Center for Urban Affairs and Policy Research at Northwestern University, a coordinated effort was made to mainstream developmentally disabled adults into the community life of an inner-city neighborhood in Chicago. In response to this effort, a local community organization, the Logan Square Neighborhood Association, agreed to participate as host and coordinator.

Here are just a few of the stories that emerged from this systematic, cooperative effort to reintegrate the lives and potentialities of developmentally disabled individuals into the Logan Square community.

❧ Linda lives in a state institution and hates it. Linda's mother Maria asked the neighborhood organization for help. When it was discovered that Linda loves animals, the organization arranged to have Linda spend some time each week at a well-known local pet store. The arrangement was almost destroyed before it got started, however, when a professional at the institution told the pet store owner that Linda had problems that might

Chart Two: Strengthening Partnerships

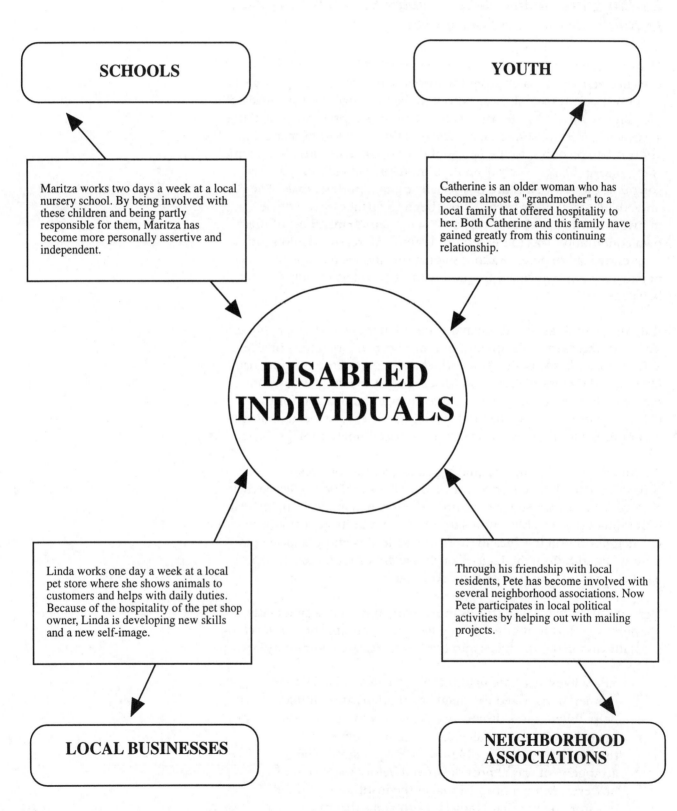

SCHOOLS

YOUTH

Maritza works two days a week at a local nursery school. By being involved with these children and being partly responsible for them, Maritza has become more personally assertive and independent.

Catherine is an older woman who has become almost a "grandmother" to a local family that offered hospitality to her. Both Catherine and this family have gained greatly from this continuing relationship.

DISABLED INDIVIDUALS

Linda works one day a week at a local pet store where she shows animals to customers and helps with daily duties. Because of the hospitality of the pet shop owner, Linda is developing new skills and a new self-image.

Through his friendship with local residents, Pete has become involved with several neighborhood associations. Now Pete participates in local political activities by helping out with mailing projects.

LOCAL BUSINESSES

NEIGHBORHOOD ASSOCIATIONS

interfere with her role at the pet store. The pet store owner and his wife discussed this and decided to go ahead anyway. Instead of being isolated in the institution, Linda spends her time surrounded by people. She shows animals to customers and helps with daily duties. Linda has a hard life inside the institution and desperately wants to get out. The people at the institution have told her she can only get out if she goes four months without displaying any aggression. Given the nature of the place and what goes on there that may be impossible. Linda, her mother, and a staff member of the neighborhood organization worked successfully to get Linda out of the institution for good.

❦ Harold is a man in his late 20s who loves to play games and has some uncanny abilities (immediately after he's introduced to you, he can spell your name forward and backward). Harold has been introduced to the local Boys and Girls Club where he helps out with the games and teaches them to the children. He's also involved with the Palmer Square Arts Festival. Staff at the Boys and Girls Club nominated him for a "volunteer of the year" award and he won.

❦ Bill, a man in his 30s who lives at home with his parents, has been introduced to the local hospital. He visits the hospital twice a week and volunteers in the mail room where he delivers the mail. This task is a tricky one for him since he can't read, so the mail room staff have worked out a special color-coding for him to follow and people in other departments have learned to expect him and watch out for him (and their mail). Bill loves being a volunteer. He loves wearing the vest and the volunteer badge and is convinced "this place couldn't run without me." Bill is a great talker and once prepared an elaborate report on how the mail room should be reorganized, which the mailroom supervisor took with calm consideration. The supervisor has driven Bill home from the hospital and stayed to dinner with his family, and he is willing to get involved in talking about Bill's future.

❦ Maritza, a woman in her mid-20s, lives with her family and was involved in a day program for people with disabilities where she spent her time on coloring books and pegboards to keep busy. She is a warm woman who loves little children. Staff of the local neighborhood association began bringing her to the local day nursery where the director was willing to see if Maritza could help out. At the beginning, the staff went with her each time; now Maritza goes by herself twice a week. She is called "Miss Maritza" by the children and staff. As any day care worker knows, little children need a lot of hugs (which sometimes the worker may be too busy or harassed to give). Miss Maritza is the one the children go to for comfort and affection; she is never too busy for a hug. The children understand that Miss Maritza is different in some ways from the other teachers—she is the one adult the children sometimes have to help. But children enjoy being able to help adults. Being around the children and being partly responsible for them has helped Martiza become more personally assertive and independent.

❧ Henry, who is 70, has lived in a group home for the last several years. He spends a lot of his time watching television. One thing he likes to do is go bowling. The association staff member, on a visit to the home, discovered a bowling ball among his things. She asked around and discovered that a local church has a Sunday afternoon bowling league, and that one of the teams would be willing to have Henry come bowl with them. The participants are all of Puerto Rican ancestry, many of whom speak mostly Spanish. Henry is Italian—but that doesn't matter as much as it might since Henry doesn't talk much anyway. While the team was initially willing to have Henry join them, they got worried when they discovered he isn't' all that good a bowler. This is a competitive sport after all, and they didn't want their average pulled down. However, they worked out an arrangement whereby he could bowl in rotation but his score wouldn't be added in with the rest. He is especially proud to wear the black and gold team shirt. At the end of the season, Henry attended the league banquet. He was delighted when the members awarded him a trophy and a black satin team jacket. He got up to thank them for making him part of their team.

❧ Mary Ellen was introduced to Pete by the neighborhod association staff. Mary Ellen is a lively, energetic woman, an artist and political activist, raising children and going to school full time. Pete has lived most of his life in a state mental hospital. Since it closed down he has lived with six other men, including his brother, in a group home. Pete is a man of few words but great enthusiasm. He especially loves good food and music. Mary Ellen has taken Pete to Cub games (another place where enthusiasm pays off: to Pete every hit is "a home run") and has involved him in her political activities, getting him to help out with mailing projects at the local office of SANE/Freeze.

❦ Clara was introduced to Alice. The original connection was simple enough: Alice loves jewelry—she wears rings on all her fingers—and Clara used to sell jewelry. Clara is a lively woman who works for a hospital, the president of her block club, politically active, smart and articulate. Alice is a gentle woman with a ready smile who lives at home with her elderly parents. Now Clara takes her shopping or invites her for dinner—simple things. Clara has a lot of demands on her time, but makes some time to spend with Alice. She also thinks about what other kinds of things Alice can be involved in—she's had her sign up as a deputy voter registrar, for example. She worries about what will happen when Alice's parents die.

❦ Connie and Julie were introduced to each other. Connie is a homemaker who loves gardening, a warm woman with beautiful long red hair who is a ready neighbor for many people in the community. Julie is a woman in her 30s who has lived in group homes since she was nineteen; until she met Connie, she had no friends outside the system, although her family lives in the suburbs and sees her regularly. Connie takes Julie out to dinner, to movies, museums and plays. Julie can be very articulate about the problems of life in a group home, and Connie has come to share those concerns— she has acted in some ways as an advocate for Julie.

❦ Lorraine is a woman in her 60s who lives in a group home. One thing she especially likes is going to church. She used to attend services with her mother, who died a few years ago; now going to church reminds her of her mother. The Episcopal Church welcomed Lorraine to its congregation—not a special service for disabled people but as a regular member. Lorraine loves liturgical rituals, especially exchanging the "kiss of peace." When the Bishop visited the parish for a special service and gave the blessing right by Lorraine's pew, Lorraine enthusiastically waved back at him. Lorraine has been welcomed by the pastor and the rest of the congregation. The Sunday services and other church activities have become a high point in her life and she is a valued member of the church.

❦ Nora has taken Catherine into her life—almost made her part of her family. The connection facilitated by the neighborhood association is important for both of them. Nora is a woman in her 30s with young children who is finishing her nursing education. Nora was born in Germany and both she and her husband live far away from their own families. Catherine is in her 70s and she too has been isolated from her family (though she remembers them vividly); she has lived almost her entire life in a large state institution. Catherine is a grandmotherly woman who loves being with Nora and especially her children, and the children respond with love as well. Nora explains it this way: "Because our parents and grandparents live very far from us Catherine represents a grandmother for our family. The love the children and she feel for each other is nurturing all of them. She not only fills a gap in the lives of our children but in ours as well. I have always been committed to community group work, but this relationship has taught me something new."

In each of these stories (and there are many more examples) a place in the Logan Square community has opened up space for a person with disabilities who would otherwise find most such public spaces closed. In some of these places—for example, the church, the bowling league—the developmentally disabled person is welcomed simply as another participant, as a member of the group. Other places in the community, most typically those where there is a specific job to do— have been able to create special valued roles or positions for people with disabilities with whom they have formed partnerships. For example, Maritza has become "Miss Maritza" to the children at Lutheran Day Nursery, and Bill takes great satisfaction in being the mailman at the local hospital. In all of these places, there has been a willingness to accept someone who may at certain times slow things down a bit or even create a few extra complications; in exchange for these few inconveniences, people in the neighborhood have come to recognize and appreciate the genuine skill, warmth, friendliness, and enthusiasm that each developmentally disabled person has been able to bring to their community.

This particular series of coordinated efforts to incorporate developmentally disabled individuals into one inner-city Chicago neighborhood, Logan Square, provides us with a powerful vision of the possibilities of creative community building. It brings marginalized people out of isolation and back into the community so that others can appreciate and benefit from their unique gifts and capacities.

The chart on the following page shows how local developmentally disabled individuals can become connected with actual partners residing within their own community.

Chart Three: One on One Relationships

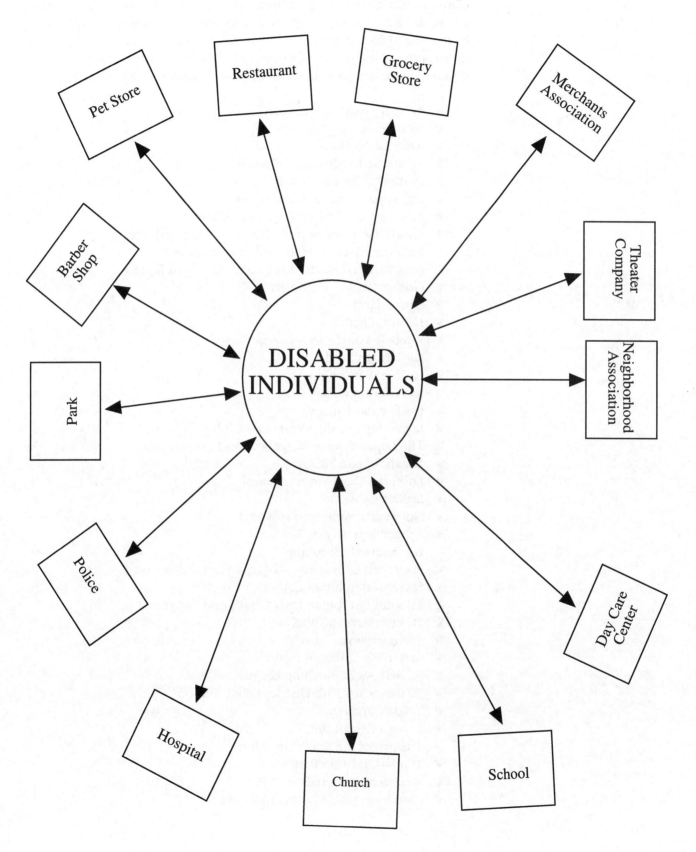

Even in our rapid-paced, competitive modern world, every local community always has a great number of potentially hospitable places where the gifts and capacities of developmentally disabled people can be mobilized for the process of community building. The following is a list of some of the places where people labeled developmentally disabled were connected by the local neighborhood association:

- Animal Kingdom Pet Store
- Arroyos Barbershop
- Association House
- Avondale Presbyterian Church
- Bethel Lutheran Church
- Episcopal Church of the Advent
- First Spanish United Church of Christ
- Fourth Congregational Church of Logan Square
- Fullerton Avenue Merchants Association
- Grace United Methodist Church of Logan Square
- Griffin Theatre Company
- Grocerland
- Holstein Park
- Kimball Avenue Evangelical Church
- La Caridad Produce
- La Nueva Borinquena
- La Progressiva Day Care
- Las Estellas Unisex
- Logan Square Boys and Girls Club
- The Logan Square Neighborhood Association
- Logan Square YMCA
- Lutheran Day Nursery School
- Lydia's Cafe
- Norwegian American Hospital
- Palmer Square Arts Festival
- B.J. Richards Preschool
- Roosevelt University—Logan Square Extension
- St. John Berchman Catholic Church
- St. John Berchman Early Childhood Center
- St. Elizabeth Hospital
- St. Genevieve Church
- St. Luke's Lutheran Church
- St. Sylvesters' Bowling League
- Shakespeare 15th District Police Station
- Tacos Garcia
- Tania's Restaurant
- Theatre of the Reconstruction
- TOPS—Holstein Park
- Wizard Auto Details
- Zion Evangelical Lutheran Church

Rather than being surrounded by social services that further isolate and exclude them, the next chart shows how developmentally disabled individuals can be placed into the very center of the community as the result of a series of partnerships in which their unique gifts and capacities have been fully received and actualized as parts of the community building process.

Sources for Further Reading About the Process of Creating Partnerships for People with Disabilities in the Process of Community Building

McKnight, John L. "Redefining Community," *Social Policy,* Fall-Winter, 1992: pp. 56-62.

O'Connell, Mary. "Community Building in Logan Square: How a Community Grew Strong with the Contributions of People with Disabilities," The Center for Urban Affairs and Policy Research, Northwestern University, Evanston, Illinois, 1990. $4.00

O'Connell, Mary. "The Gift of Hospitality: Opening the Doors of Community Life to People with Disabilities," The Center for Urban Affairs and Policy Research and the State of Illinois Department of Rehabilitation Services, Northwestern University, Evanston, Illinois, 1988. $4.00

Welfare Recipients and Community Renewal

Although they are frequently categorized as a group and labeled by the fact that they are all recipients of public assistance, "welfare recipients" include a wide variety of individuals whose specific assets can make significant contributions to community-building efforts. "Welfare recipients" are usually served by institutions of public assistance that focus on maintaining provider/client relationships and not on developing alternative relationships that are reciprocal and problem-solving. Thus those individuals receiving welfare often become defined by their role as clients of the institution rather than as participants in an on-going, ever-changing process. Moreover, as a labeled group, those individuals who are currently involved in the receipt of institutionalized services must now function with the additional handicap of being misunderstood and stigmatized by those members of the community who are not on welfare at the present time. As a result, welfare recipients frequently tend to become increasingly isolated and marginalized from the active life of the community. In other words, once individuals have been labeled as "welfare recipients" the talents and energies that they have to offer are usually left out of their community's inventory of assets, and their true ability to contribute in the present and future is systematically ignored.

Rediscovering Welfare Recipients as Assets Within the Community

What are the types of assets that welfare recipients may bring to the community in which they live? In spite of the fact that a particular individual is poor and has few economic resources, we must always remember that each person has a unique set of assets and attributes which the community can draw upon and develop.

Skills, Abilities and Experience

❧ Every person has some skill, ability or experience at doing something productive. It might be household skills or maintenance skills; it might be care-giving skills or interpersonal skills. In other words, each person, even those who have very little income at the present time, has acquired certain useful skills either through some form of formal training or through participation in informal economic activities and learning experiences. Everybody has these kinds of capacities, and skills such as these can be utilized as important resources for community-building.

Networking and Personal Relationships

ᴥ Every person has a group of other people with whom they interact, no matter how small or isolated that group may be. For example, the family unit almost always functions as one of the most important networks existing within a community. But in most instances each person also belongs to several other interconnective "networks" as well, and these informal networks represent just as much potential energy for the community as do those that are more formal in their structure. All the various kinds of both formal and informal connections that exist among people represent an important source of energy for community builders to tap into and should always be included in an inventory of the community's most valuable assets.

Desires, Dreams and Creativity

ᴥ Every person, no matter how poor, has certain specific ideas about where he or she wants to be and what one wants to be doing in the future, and each person also uses individual creativity to attempt to make these dreams a reality. When people are able to combine their dreams and coordinate their efforts with other members of the community, the entire community can be strengthened from the energies that are released.

Energy and Enthusiasm

ᴥ Welfare recipients want to have something better in their lives. As a result, they have a deeply felt enthusiasm for change, and, because of this, they represent a rich source of community-building power and potential.

Releasing the potential power of welfare recipients means identifying and connecting their special energy to the energies of others and to the assets of the specific community in which they live. Welfare recipients are perfectly capable of relating creatively to the various institutions, organizations and opportunities existing within their community in exactly the same manner as would any other individual. It is only because "welfare recipients" tend to be labeled and marginalized that their true potential as partners is often ignored. We must learn to think positively about the ways that individuals receiving publis assistance can connect productively with all the others who are actively engaged in developing and improving their community.

Mapping Community Assets to Discover Potential Partners for Welfare Recipients

Now that we have identified at least some of the assets that welfare recipients can bring to the process of community-building, we must go on to examine the means by which neighborhood leaders can most effectively mobilize these assets and turn them to valuable resources for community-building. This effort to "connect" local welfare recipients with the process of community-building involves the utilization of a specific four-step process:

❧ First, make a thorough "capacity inventory" outlining all the various skills and assets for each of the welfare recipients with whom you are currently working.

❧ Next, compile an inventory of the key assets and resources of the community as these are represented by local individuals, associations, organizations, and institutions. When this has been done, it will be discovered that these community assets fall into the following categories: (a) citizens associations and not-for-profit organizations of all types; (b) publicly funded institutions such as hospitals, parks, libraries, and schools; (c) the private sector including small businesses, banks and local branches of larger corporations; (d) local residents and special interest groups of "labeled people" such as "seniors," "youth," "disabled," and "artists."

❧ Then use the information that has been obtained from these inventories to build strong, concrete, mutually beneficial "partnerships" between local welfare recipients and the other individuals, organizations and associations that exist within the community.

❧ Finally, on the basis of these partnerships and the active participation of local welfare recipients in the community-building process, go on to build new relationships with resources that exist outside the immediate community.

Chart One on the next page illustrates the kinds of relationships that can exist between local welfare recipients and their potential community partners.

Chart One: Potential Partners

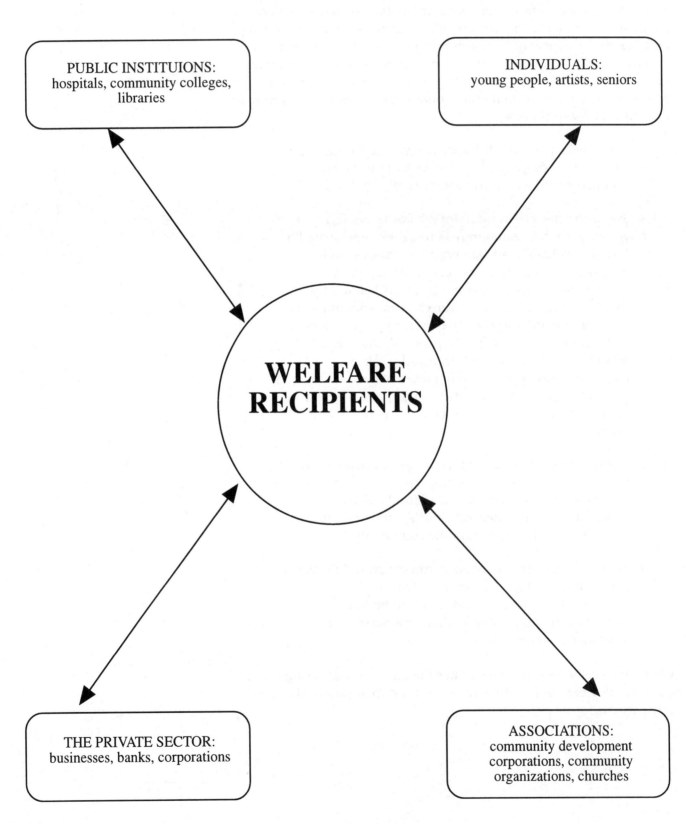

PUBLIC INSTITUIONS:
hospitals, community colleges,
libraries

INDIVIDUALS:
young people, artists, seniors

WELFARE RECIPIENTS

THE PRIVATE SECTOR:
businesses, banks, corporations

ASSOCIATIONS:
community development
corporations, community
organizations, churches

Building Productive Relationships Between Welfare Recipients and the Community

Let us now examine some of the means by which welfare recipients can be reintegrated into the ongoing life of the communities in which they live.

Welfare Recipients and Community Associations

Welfare recipients should be encouraged to connect with citizens associations of all kinds in order to plan how their community could be a more effective, safe and pleasant place for *all* the people who live within it. Thus, for example, a group of welfare recipients living in a Chicago public housing project organized a resident organization that enabled them to work effectively toward reducing the activities of gangs in their neighborhood and toward creating jobs for unemployed members of the community.

In many communities all across the country, local organizations and associations have been formed in order to provide small loans to welfare recipients who are interested in becoming self-employed and no longer dependent on public aid. The creative work of the Womens' Self-Employment Project in Chicago, along with its sister organization in othercities, has produced enterprise stories like these:

- A woman and her cousin open a dress shop as the culmination of a shared childhood dream of turning their sewing abilities into a business.

- A mother and daughter team start a small catering truck business to sell their homemade Mexican food around their community.

- A woman expands her home-based business making beaded jewelry and is enabled to reach a much larger market.

- A woman uses her experience in trucking to start a business in the transportation industry.

- A man is able to borrow the small amount of money necessary for him to be able to turn his upholstery skills into a small business.

- A woman uses her cooking experience to start a bake shop and catering business.

- A woman is able to start a business making silk flowers and dried flower arrangements which she distributes directly to neighborhood customers and retailers.

In all of the previous examples, welfare recipients have been able to work their way out of poverty with the help and support of community organizations, and, as a result, have not only improved the quality of their own lives but have also enriched the lives of many others and built the local economy.

Welfare Recipients and Public Institutions

There are many opportunities for connecting welfare recipients with public institutions such as schools, libraries, hospitals, and community colleges. Just as soon as reciprocal relationships are established, welfare recipients can begin to contribute their energies as effectively as anyone else to the on-going process of community development.

- In Chicago residents of a housing development work in close cooperation with citywide agencies to obtain contracts to maintain their own neighborhood housing.

- Residents of another Chicago housing development visit residents of a kibbutz in Israel in an effort to learn about cooperative life styles which might be transferable to their own community.

- The Pike Place Market in Seattle, after surviving the destruction that was planned in city redevelopment efforts, regenerates itself by offering a medical clinic, child care, a senior center, housing units, a food bank and food coupon program, and a home for street youth.

- The Portland Saturday Market lowers its vendors' fees so as to allow the participation of individuals from all income levels including the large homeless encampment that exists in the neighborhood.

- Informal markets like the Maxwell Street Market in Chicago generate income for the individuals who come together there on the weekends for a variety of different kinds of exchanges. Some of the vendors come to supplement their welfare checks through the invention of a product or service that they can sell or trade at the market. Individuals who set up booths at the market come to know each other, count on each other, and respect each other's informal rights to full participation.

Once community leaders have facilitated the release of the community-building power of welfare recipients into the local situation, productive relationships can be expanded beyond the scope of the local community itself. But the most important thing to remember is that active participation is the key. At each level the goal is to make welfare recipients into the producers of their own well-being by connecting them with other sources of power. Whether this activity is social, economic or political, in each and every instance an active producer and user of energy contributes much more to the future of the community than an isolated individual trapped in welfare dependency whose potential has not been developed or properly connected.

Welfare Recipients and the Private Sector

Welfare recipients can be profitably connected with businesses in the private sector by creating innovative ways to support and promote new enterprises that will provide the particular goods and services that they require.

- ❧ The East Side Market in Cleveland has a special relationship with the local community and its people. Because it is situated in a poor neighborhood, this market has made arrangements to accept food stamps in its produce stalls in order to encourage community residents to do their food shopping there. Vendors also regularly offer specials at drastically reduced prices to customers in the neighborhood.

- ❧ An organization in Hartford works with welfare recipients to help them move to a job or self-employment. Local banks provide small commercial loans to graduates of the self-employment program which they have established and also supply ongoing entrepreneurial support for the new ventures generated by this program.

Welfare Recipients and Other Individuals Within the Community

Welfare recipients should be encouraged to make mutually supportive connections with family members, neighbors and friends, as well as members of other specific groups such as seniors and youth.

- ❧ A group of homeless women with children are working together to create a housing cooperative in which they will provide care for each other's children and also share in community meal preparation several days a week. Their combined effort means that they will be involved in every aspect of planning, purchasing, remodeling, and maintaining their new home.

- ❧ Homeless men work together on a farm project which enables them to grow produce and receive the proceeds from their own labor. Combining the energies of these individuals and local farmers leads to the creation of new relationships which help to solve problems of homelessness and unemployment.

In ways such as these, mutual exchanges help people to manage their daily responsibilities and provide the strength and perspective that are required to overcome adversity and make a positive contribution to the community.

All of these stories present specific examples of how mutually beneficial partnerships can be established between local welfare recipients and community leaders who are active in both the public and private aspects of the community. Partnerships of these kinds are not only successful in themselves but also will usually lead to the discovery of other forms of linkage that will activate even more of the community's hidden assets for the purpose of constructive community-building.

Chart Two on page 91 shows how local welfare recipients can become connected with actual partners existing within the community in which those welfare recipients currently reside.

Chart Three on page 92 represents the complex network of actual partnerships that might exist for local welfare recipients who have been fully integrated as dynamic community assets.

Chart Two: Strengthening Partnerships

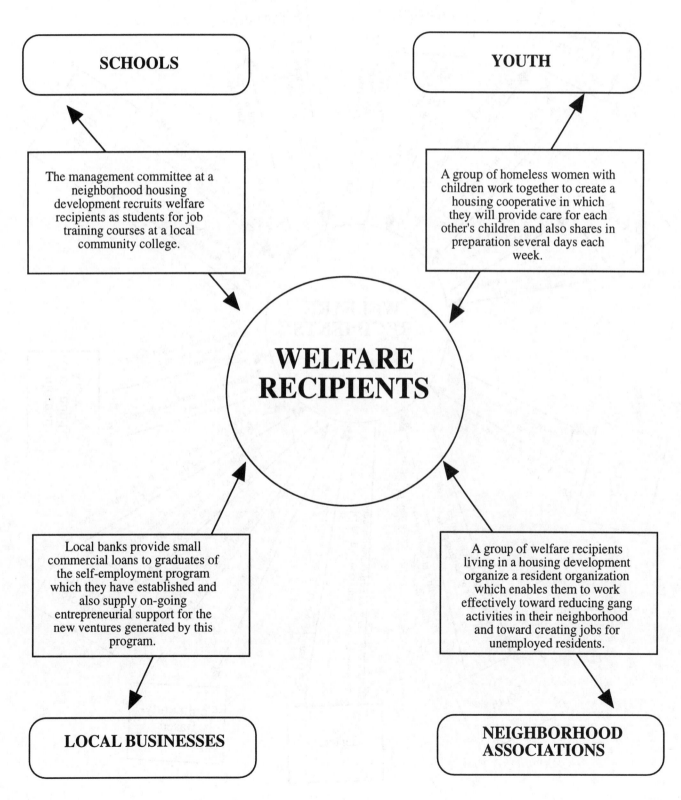

SCHOOLS

YOUTH

The management committee at a neighborhood housing development recruits welfare recipients as students for job training courses at a local community college.

A group of homeless women with children work together to create a housing cooperative in which they will provide care for each other's children and also shares in preparation several days each week.

WELFARE RECIPIENTS

Local banks provide small commercial loans to graduates of the self-employment program which they have established and also supply on-going entrepreneurial support for the new ventures generated by this program.

A group of welfare recipients living in a housing development organize a resident organization which enables them to work effectively toward reducing gang activities in their neighborhood and toward creating jobs for unemployed residents.

LOCAL BUSINESSES

NEIGHBORHOOD ASSOCIATIONS

Chart Three: One-on-One Relationships

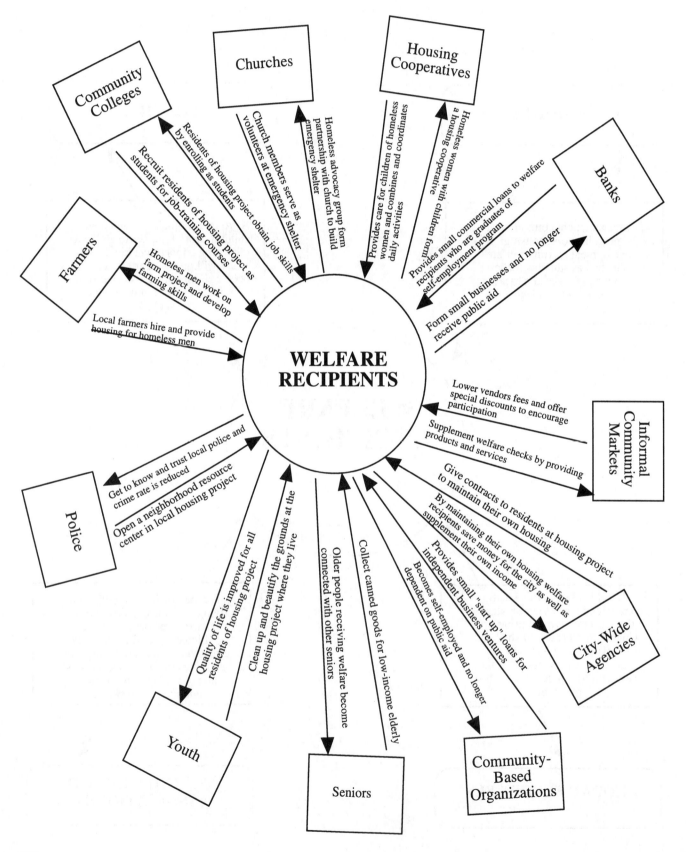

Sources and Contacts for the "Stories" in this Section

Chicago Coalition for the Homeless
1325 S. Wabash
Chicago, IL 60605
(312) 435-4548

Cleveland East Side Market
105th and St. Claire
Cleveland, OH
(216) 543-1144

Earthwise Education Center
Syracuse, NY

Good Faith Fund
1210 Cherry Street, Suite 9
Pine Bluff, AR 71601

Hartford College for Women
Programs for Women Interested in
  Self Employment
50 Elizabeth Street
Hartford, CT 06105
(203) 236-1215, ext. 234

The Homeless Women's Project and Women's
  Initative for Self Employment
201 Mission, Sixth Floor
San Francisco, CA 94105
(415) 624-3351

Institute for Social and Economic Development
1901 Broadway, Suite 313
Iowa City, IA 52240
(319) 338-5824

Maxwell Street Market
Maxwell Street and Sangamon
Chicago, IL

North Coast Opportunities
Bright Center Rural Economic Development
  Project
413 North State
Ukiah, CA 95482
(707) 462-1954

Pike Place Market
85 Pike Street, Room 500
Seattle, WA 98101

Portland Saturday Market
108 West Burnside
Portland, OR 97209
(503) 222-6072

Women's Self Employment Project
166 W. Washington Street, Suite 730
Chicago, IL 60602
(312) 606-8255

Artists and Community Renewal

If we start with the idea that art and culture can be found not only in museums and similar institutions but also in the everyday lives of ordinary people, we are already closer to uncovering the true artistic and cultural resources that can be found in local communities. Artists are still too often looked upon as members of a professional elite whose services are brought into a community by well-intentioned sponsors in order to beautify, enrich and enhance the quality of life in that community. Although cosmetic beautification of this sort has certain positive aspects, this process totally ignores the possibility of genuine artistic renaissance and revitalization that might be made possible through the development and utilization of the talents already existing *within* the community itself.

The problem is that many members of the community who have true artistic ability do not look upon themselves as "artists." They do not recognize the importance of the contributions that they might be able to make to the development of the cultural life of the community as a whole. These potential artists need to be encouraged to express themselves in ways that reflect the values, problems and traditions that are unique to their community. Direct response to creative work of this kind from their neighbors and other members of the community can create a greatly increased sense of social cohesion and help to shatter the poisonous myths that still exist of inner city "voicelessness" and apathy. In other words, local artists can help to create a revivified perspective from which can be derived the strength and vision that are required in order to heal sick, fragmented, internally divided neighborhoods and re-connect them with their genuine roots and uncompromised futures.

Rediscovering Artists as Assets Within the Community

In attempting to list the specific type of assets that artists can bring to the process of community-building, we must always remember that in terms of skill and talent each artist is absolutely unique and has a unique place within the configuration of the developing community. Nevertheless, certain qualities are common to all individuals who have artistic skills.

Tradition. Certain traditions may play the dominant role in a particular community, but, as a general rule, most communities are an amalgam of many specific traditions. In fact, it is the unique quality of this combination that provides a given community with its particular character and identity. The skills and visions of local artists are often linked to these traditions, and it is artists of this sort who keep these traditions alive and flexible enough to change in response to the on-going needs of the community.

Culture. The culture of a particular community is always unique to that community. It is composed of the many strands of history, experience and tradition that knit that community into a distinct entity. Artists are "weavers" whose skills help to keep this communal fabric intact. They also have the ability to create new patterns within it in response to current community needs and demands.

Skills. Some of the skills that an artist has may have been learned and developed formally in the home or neighborhood. Other skills may have been learned in more formal situations such as school or work. No matter how their skills have been acquired, artists are almost always eager to share the skills they have learned with others who are as yet untrained. These transmissible skills are an important part of a community's assets and should always be linked to the process of community-building.

Vision and Creativity. An artist's skills are the means through which a personal vision is expressed. But often these visions have much more than private significance. The personal visions that artists create can provide patterns through which a community can learn to relate to its past experience and present challenges. The artist's vision can even create new possibilities for community growth and further development.

Productivity. By expressing their personal visions through the skills they have acquired, artists create "products" that may have commercial as well as aesthetic value. Works of art and personal expression can become the basis for various cottage industries that will bring new sources of revenue into the community.

Self-Expression and Self-Esteem. Artists take pride in their work. This pride grows in proportion to the acceptance of their work within the community. Acceptance of this kind contributes not only to the artist's sense of self-esteem but also to the community's positive recognition of its own unique character and value.

Mapping Community Assets to Discover Potential Partners for Local Artists

Now that we have identified at least some of the assets that local artists can bring to the process of community building, we must go on to examine the means by which neighborhood leaders can most effectively mobilize these assets and turn them into valuable resources for community building. This effort to "connect" local artists with the process of community building involves the utilization of a specific four-step process:

❧ First, make a thorough "capacity inventory" outlining all the various skills and assets for each of the local artists with whom you are currently working.

❧ Next, compile an inventory of the key assets and resources of the community as these are represented by local individuals, associations, organizations, and institutions. When this has been done, it will be discovered that these community assets fall into the following categories: (a) citizens associations and not-for-profit organizations of all types; (b) publicly funded institutions such as hospitals, parks, libraries, and schools; (c) the private sector including small businesses, banks and local branches of larger corporations; (d) local residents and special interest groups of "labeled people" such as "seniors," "youth," "disabled," and other "artists."

❧ Then use the information that has been obtained from these inventories to build strong, concrete, mutually beneficial "partnerships" between local artists and the other individuals, organizations and associations that exist within the community.

❧ Finally, on the basis of these "partnerships" and the active participation of local artists in the community building process, go on to build new relationships with resources that exist outside the immediate community.

Chart One on the next page illustrates the kinds of relationships that can exist between local artists and their potential community partners.

Building Productive Relationships Between Artists and the Community

Listed below are exemplary cases of how the artistic assets of various communities have been linked with the other resources of these communities in order to create new possibilities for community development.

Local Artists and Community Associations

Citizens Associations

❧ Every neighborhood has a wide variety of citizens associations that promote and support the work of local artists. For example, here is a partial listing of the various community associations that promote the work of local artists in the Logan Square community of Chicago: Bucktown Arts Fest Committee, Copernicus

Chart One: Potential Partners

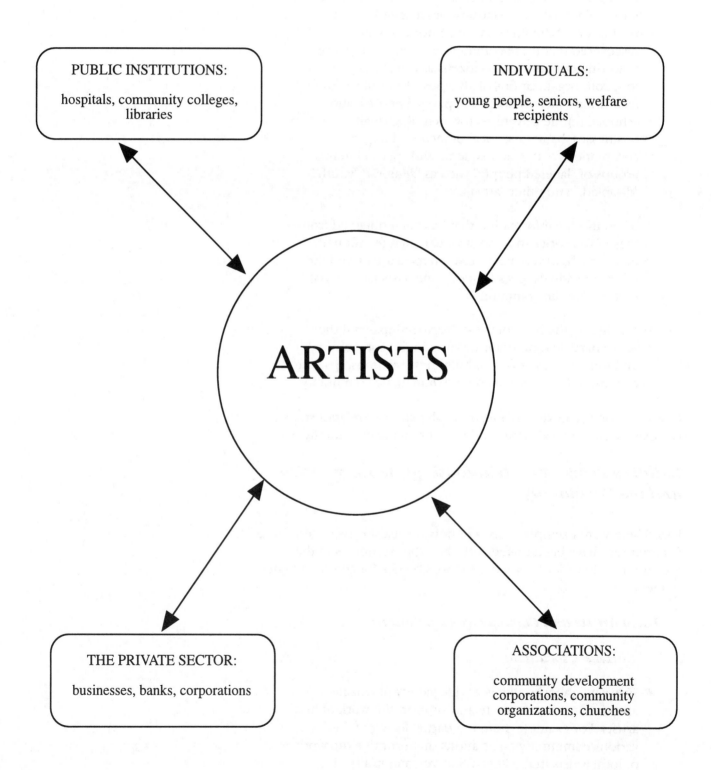

Center, Holstein Park Arts and Crafts Committee, Kosciuszko Park Arts and Crafts Committee, Logan Square Neighborhood Association, Palmer Square Fest Committee, and Ruiz Belvis Cultural Center.

Religious Institutions

❧ A group of local artists begin a program encouraging creative expression for youth through drama and music at a neighborhood church. As a result, the youth from the church and from the community put on a number of performances for the congregation and the community. (UCRP)

❧ A northside Chicago church allows a local theatre company to rehearse in its building in return for allowing the church's parishioners to attend its productions free of charge. (UCRP)

❧ A symphony orchestra is given free space at a local church for rehearsal, and in return members of the congregation enjoy the symphony during occasional worship services and are allowed to attend full performances free of charge. (North Shore)

Cultural Organizations

❧ Most museums are free on Tuesdays—so an art teacher at one park district decided to offer an art class that would meet in one of the community's art museums every Tuesday. As a result, students are now able to go through exhibits and obtain information that will encourage and strengthen their own art work. (Ekhert)

Local Artists and Public Institutions

Parks

❧ A community art gallery had more works of art that it could put on display, and in the neighborhood park one of the buildings had a large unoccupied room. As a result, the park agreed to let the gallery use this spare room for additional display space. Now the park has a cultural display area which is available to the public and discovers that some people now visit the park to see this display who might never otherwise have had a reason to use the park facilities. At the same time, the art gallery gets more display space, and the artists that this gallery represents get broader and longer lasting exposure for their work. (Beverly)

❦ A neighborhood park sponsored an art class for teens and adults that would provide them with the drawing and painting skills necessary for creating a community mural. Local artists were brought in to discuss their work as well as to demonstrate the techniques appropriate for mural work. The class also was placed in contact with a local historical society that could provide essential information about the evolution of the neighborhood. As a possible site for the mural they planned to paint, the group chose a park wall that was sprayed with graffiti. (Ekhert)

❦ Local artists display their work in park display cases and on blank, unused walls. (Orr, etc.)

❦ Local artists display and/or sell their work at neighborhood art fairs sponsored by community parks. (Wicker, etc.)

❦ A professional photographer whose child was active in local park activities allowed his child to borrow his equipment in order to photograph the activities happening in the park. (Wicker)

Libraries

❦ A local artist takes advantage of the library's display cases to exhibit her cross-stitching. (Scottsdale)

❦ A librarian arranges for the work of local Korean artists to be shown at suburban libraries in neighborhoods with large Korean populations. (Albany Park)

❦ A librarian invites a local Polish dance teacher to stage a performance with his students at the library. (Portage-Cragin)

Community Colleges

❦ A local community college has established an artist-in-residence program in which the purpose is to enable the artist to work on his personal style for a year without having to worry about income and also for the artist to "humanize and demystify the world of art for the everyday individual." As a part of this program, the artist visits civic, arts and community groups as well as local schools giving lectures, workshops and demonstrations. He works out of a donated storefront in town and encourages the public to drop by and watch him work. (Central Florida)

❧ A community college hires a neighborhood artist to lead an art tour of the community in which the students will visit various art and sculpture museums as well as the studios of other local artists. (Long Island)

❧ A community college hosts a concert of performances by young music students enrolled in a Suzuki program. (Queensborough)

Schools

❧ A city-wide organization that finds work for local artists provides an artist-in-residence for an elementary school where this artist spends six months making murals with the students over the walls of the school. (Johnson)

❧ A school decides to sponsor a community arts festival in which entries are accepted from students at the high school and all the elementary schools, as well as from community artists. (Orr)

Police

❧ In many communities local police departments have worked with neighborhood artists to create crime prevention posters and to organize the painting of murals on walls and fences formerly covered with gang grafitti.

Hospitals

❧ A hospital employee who is on the board of the neighborhood arts council photocopies fliers for a community arts fair and circulates these flyers to all other employees of the hospital. (Lutheran)

❧ A local artist spends a sabbatical as artist-in-residence at a community hospital where he uses an old kitchen as his studio and employs other local artists to paint murals and graphics and to put on performances at the hospital. He stimulates patients and staff to make art themselves, "negating the feeling that art has been imposed on them." (Senior)

Local Artists and the Private Sector

❧ Local banks and merchants associations frequently sponsor and provide exhibition space for the work of local artists. Sometimes monetary awards and/or scholarships are also supplied by these representatives of the private sector in order to encourage and improve the artistic standards of the community.

101

Local Artists and Individuals Within the Community

Local Residents

❦ The work of local artists has as its source and inspiration the daily lives of local residents of the community. By giving expression to shared values and aspirations, local artists in turn inspire local residents to participate in projects, mural painting and neighborhood craft fairs.

Persons with Disabilities

❦ Local artists often contribute to the lives of disabled people in the community by creating works of art that are accessible to them and by teaching informal classes that encourage disabled people to participate in various modes of self-expression.

Welfare Recipients

❦ The work of local artists can be a source of genuine inspiration to the most economically disadvantaged members of the community. Activities such as mural painting and arts and craft fairs offer opportunities for even the poorest residents to make meaningful and inspiring contributions to their community.

Youth

❦ Local companies donate paint for young artists and youth to collaborate on the designing and painting of murals in the community. (Tacoma)

❦ Youth become involved with a local youth shelter by doing some cooking. Then they decide to make a promotional video for the shelter. They write the script, film the video, and make connections with a local cable company to edit and market it. (Snohomish)

❦ At a community-based youth center, youth hang out and eventually come together as groups to design their own artistic projects. A youth is on the board of directors, and youth visit schools to lead workshops on the issues addressed by their performances. (Aunt Martha's)

Seniors

❦ Seniors learn traditional Greek fabric art and cross-stitching and then display their works at a senior center operated by the Department of Aging. (Greek)

❧ An 85-year-old Mexican-American woman teaches a six-week traditional art and pottery course to other senior citizens at the Mexican Fine Arts Museum. (Mexican)

In all of these stories we have seen how local artists have been able to become active in the community building process by entering into a series of successful "partnerships" with neighborhood organizations, institutions and/or groups of people with special interests. In partnerships like these, both partners in the relationship win, and when this happens, a strong incentive is created to build even further on these relationships and establish new projects that will continue to enhance the strength and solidarity of the entire community.

Chart Two on the next page shows how a local artist can become connected with actual partners existing within the community in which that particular artist currently resides.

Chart Three then represents the complex network of actual partnerships that might exist for a local artist whose talents have been fully utilized as a dynamic community asset.

Chart Two: Strengthening Partnerships

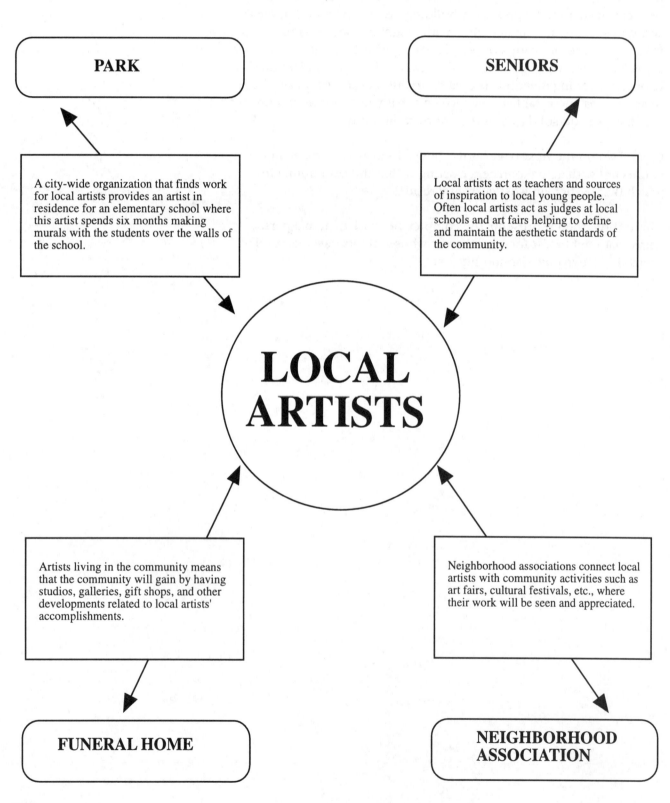

Chart Three: One-on-One Relationships

Sources and Contacts for the "Stories" in This Section

Albany Park   Albany Park Library
5150 N. Kimball Avenue
Chicago, IL 60625
(312) 744-1933 (Chahee Stanfield,
Branch Head)

Aunt Martha's   Aunt Martha's
4343 Lincoln Highway, Suite 340
Matteson, IL 60443
(708) 747-2701 (Jennifer Kneeland)

Ekhert   Ekhert Park
1330 W. Chicago Avenue
Chicago, IL
(312) 294-4710 (Mickey Maher)

Greek   Greek-American Community Service Center
3940 N. Pulaski
Chicago, IL 60641
(312) 545-0303 (John Pstharis)

Johnson   Johnson Elementary School
1420 S. Albany
Chicago, IL 60623
(312) 534-1830 (Mattie Tyson, Principal)

Lutheran   Lutheran Medical Center
150 55th Street
Brooklyn, NY 10467
(718) 630-7000 (Mary Theresa McKenna,
Assistant Director of Community Relations)

North Shore   North Shore Baptist Church
5244 N. Lakewood
Chicago, IL
(312) 728-4200 (Pastor Marcus Pomeroy)

Orr   Orr Community Academy
730 N. Pulaski
Chicago, IL 60624
(312) 265-5000

Portage-Cragin   Portage-Cragin Library
5108 W. Belmont
Chicago, IL 60641
(312) 744-0152 (Carol Tarsitano, Branch Head)

Scottsdale

Scottsdale Library
4101 W. 79th Street
Chicago, IL 60652
(312) 747-0193 (Bernadette Nowakowski,
Children's Librarian)

Senior

Peter Senior
Department of Architecture & Landscape
Manchester Polytechnic
Manchester
M15 6HA

Snohomish

Snohomish Youth Initiative
917 134th Street SW, #A6
Everett, WA 98204
(206) 742-5911 (Laura Putnam)

Tacoma

Washington Leadership Institute
Tacoma-Pierce County Office
P.O. Box 377
Tacoma, WA 98401
(206) 596-2501 (Jennifer Kurkoski)

UCRP

United Church of Rogers Park
Ashland & Morse Avenues
Chicago, IL 60626
(312) 761-2500 (Rev. Kerm Krueger)

Wicker

Wicker Park
1500 N. Wicker
Chicago, IL
(312) 276-1723 (Greg Chrobak)

RELEASING THE POWER OF LOCAL ASSOCIATIONS AND ORGANIZATIONS

The Nature of Associations

The basic community organization for empowering individuals and mobilizing their capacities is the association. An association is a group of citizens working together. An association is an amplifier of the gifts, talents and skills of individual community members.

This section focuses on local associations because they are the basic American tool for:

- ❧ empowering individuals

- ❧ building strong communities

- ❧ creating effective citizens

- ❧ making democracy work.

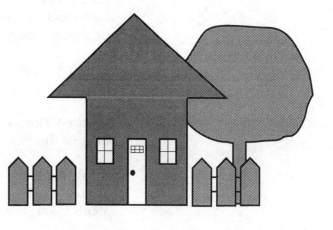

For purposes of local community-building, an association is usually a group of local citizens joined together with a vision of a common goal. To achieve that goal, they usually take on three powers:

- ❧ they decide on a common problem

- ❧ they share in developing a plan to solve the problem

- ❧ and they take action to implement the plan and solve the problem.

Sometimes, associations may have a *small* staff to assist the members. However, the members always create the vision and are the key people in doing the work to solve the problem or achieve the goal.

Types of Associations

A powerful community is a place where all kinds of different work is being done by local citizens. Therefore, they create many kinds of associations to do the work. These associations may be very formal groups with elected officers and paid members. Other associations may be very informal groups with no officers or formal memberships. The group may have boundaries larger than the neighborhood, but it involves, empowers and impacts the citizens of the neighborhood.

One way to identify many of the various working associations in local communities is to use the following map as a guide.

A Neighborhood Map of Associations

Artistic Organizations:	musical, theatrical, writing
Business Organizations:	Chamber of Commerce, neighborhood business associations, trade groups
Charitable Groups & Drives:	Red Cross, Cancer Society, United Way
Church Groups:	service, prayer, maintenance, stewardship, acolytes, men's, women's, youth, seniors
Civic Events:	July 4th, art fair, Halloween
Collectors Groups:	stamp collectors, flower dryers, antiques
Community Support Groups:	"friends" of the library, nursing home auxiliary
Elderly Groups:	Senior Citizens
Ethnic Associations:	Sons of Norway, Black Heritage Club, Caballeros de San Juan
Health & Fitness Groups:	jogging, exercise, dieting
Interest Clubs:	recycling, antique car owners, book groups
Local Media:	community radio and newspaper, local access cable TV
Men's Groups:	cultural, political, social, educational, vocational
Mutual Support (Self-Help) Groups:	Alcoholics Anonymous, sweat equity housing, La Leche League
Neighborhood:	crime watch, block clubs, neighborhood organizations
Outdoor Groups:	garden clubs, Audubon Society, conservation clubs
Political Organizations:	Democrats, Republicans, caucuses
School Groups:	printing club, PTA, child care
Service Clubs:	Zonta, Kiwanis, Rotary, American Association of University Women, fraternities, sororities
Social Cause Groups:	peace, rights, advocacy, service
Sports Leagues:	bowling, basketball, baseball, fishing, volleyball
Study Groups:	literary clubs, bible study groups
Veteran Groups:	American Legion, Amvets, Veterans of Foreign Wars, their Auxiliaries
Women's Groups:	cultural, political, social, educational, vocational
Youth Groups:	Future Farmers, Scouts, YM/YWCA

These associations, together with the capacities of individuals, are the basic community-building tools of local neighborhoods. As described later in this manual (see Chapter 6), an effective process of regenerating local communities requires an organization that identifies and involves as many of these associations as possible in creating *and* implementing a vision for the local community.

Associations in Lower Income Neighborhoods

There are associations of citizens in every neighborhood. However, the number of associations and amount of participation varies by neighborhood. For example, in a newly built suburban neighborhood there may be very few associations because people don't know each other yet. In a well-established stable middle-class neighborhood there may be many associations. In older, lower income neighborhoods there is often an assumption that associations are not common. While this may be the case in some of these neighborhoods, others are rich in associations. For example, researchers in one lower income Chicago neighborhood found over 150 associations. These included such different kind of groups as:

- 32nd Ward Democratic Party
- 3600 W. Dickens Block Club
- Act Now
- Alcoholics Anonymous
- American Legion FDR Post
- Amistad Spanish Speaking Youth
- Artists Coalition
- Boy Scouts and Girl Scouts
- Computer Club
- Crime Prevention Committee
- Damen Avenue Revitalization Effort
- Familias Hispanas
- Fullerton Avenue Merchants Association
- Golden Agers
- Greater North Pulaski Development Corporation
- Guardian Angels
- Habitat for Humanity
- Holy Name Society
- Inner City Impact
- Jefferson Park Lioness Club
- La Leche League
- League of Americans of Ukranian Descent
- Logan Square Ministerial Association
- Logan Square Neighborhood Association
- Luther League
- Moniusko Choir
- Mothers Juvenile Protection Association
- Neighbor to Neighbor
- Northwest Council of Senior Citizens
- Odd Fellows
- Our Lady of Grace Basketball Team
- Painters Local #147
- Palmer Square Art Fair
- Shamrock Club
- Summer Tent Camping Club

    ❦ Task Force Against Gangs
    ❦ Ukranian Youth Group
    ❦ United Methodist Women
    ❦ United Neighbors in Action
    ❦ Women's Moose Club

This rich diversity may not be reflected in every low-income neighborhood. However, no one should assume that these powerful associational tools are absent unless they have carefully "inventoried" their neighborhood.

It is especially important to note that in lower income neighborhoods, there are many associations that are informal groups without officers or even a name. However, they do vital community work. These groups include:

    ❦ five women who watch over the children on the street,

    ❦ three public housing residents who create a garden on a lot beside their building,

    ❦ and four church members who transport older members to the grocery store to shop.

The fact that these associations don't have a formal name should not keep us from recognizing what a powerful community force they are. Therefore, any serious inventory of local associations must include these informal groups as vital assets.

An Inventory of Local Associations

An important part of the community development process involves the identification of all the neighborhood's assets. Therefore, an inventory of local associations is a basic step in mobilizing the power of the community.

One way to start is to ask a group of local citizens to identify all the associations to which they belong and the names of all the others they know about. Often, the participants will be surprised to see how many local groups they know.

This beginning list can then be shared with other associations and their members asked to add groups they find missing. This process, itself, will help inform and interest local associations in their number, diversity and significance.

A Guide to Finding Out About Neighborhood Groups

A neighborhood is more than just streets and buildings and the people who live there. Underneath the surface is a complex network of connections, of people relating to each other in different ways that make up the "stuff" of community life.

Some residents belong to the same extended family; others work together. Some go to the same church on Sunday mornings; others play softball in the park on Saturday afternoons or bowl on Tuesday nights. Young families organize childcare co-ops; other people form book clubs or bridge groups. There may be local school councils, block clubs, historical societies, theater groups, gardening clubs, Alcoholics Anonymous meetings, and a thousand other groups. Formality ranges from three neighbors meeting over coffee to plan a block party, to a full-fledged community meeting with gavels and microphones and *Robert's Rules of Order.*

How can you inventory the diverse groups and associations in your neighborhood? The following is a guide to several methods for identifying them.

The research staff of the Community Studies Program of the Center for Urban Affairs at Northwestern University set out to identify as many groups as possible that people belong to within one Chicago neighborhood. (The staff worked in an older Chicago neighborhood, measuring approximately 24 square blocks and housing 85,000 people; a neighborhood rich in diverse ethnic and socioeconomic groups.) We wanted a way that was simple, inexpensive, quick, and productive.

We found three ways that worked:

   ❧ using newspapers, directories, and other printed
       sources,

   ❧ talking to people at local institutions—such as parks
       and churches,

   ❧ conducting a telephone survey of a sample of local
       residents.

In Appendix 1, beginning on page 120, we list all the different groups we identified in one neighborhood after using these three methods.

Getting Started: Using Printed Sources

Newspapers and Magazines

If you came to an area and knew nothing about it, a simple way to find out something fast is to look through the local newspaper. Community newspapers vary in size from mimeographed monthlies to sophisticated full-size papers published once or twice a week. Almost all cater to local readers by publishing community calendars, announcements, and news about local organizations.

We reviewed four consecutive issues of the weekly community newspaper published for the neighborhood we were studying. We circled any mention of events, club, meetings, sports, and recreational groups, and anything else people could join. This effort yielded 25 groups; time expended was relatively small (1/2 hour per issue).

We also reviewed the Sunday arts section of a citywide paper, the *Chicago Tribune*, which included information on events and cultural groups around the city. While not targeted to the neighborhood, this listing did give some additional groups in which local people might be involved.

Another useful resource was the citywide monthly magazine, *Chicago*. The magazine publishes a quarterly "Involvement" section listing volunteer and self-help programs in various areas around the city.

Special-purpose newspapers—published by a local political party, community organizations, environmental group, or church group—can also be helpful.

Directories

Often someone has already published a listing of the community's organizations, and you can shorten your work by using it. Such directories may be published by the community newspaper; the alderperson's office (or other local political leaders); the public library; United Way (we used a citywide directory, but it identified local groups); churches; and community organizations.

Other information is available in more general directories:

- *The Phone Book.* In the yellow pages, check the listings under Associations and Organizations, Fraternities. In the white pages, look under the name of the neighborhood (e.g., Rogers Park Historical Society, Chatham Businessmen's Association); or, if you know what ethnic groups predominate in the neighborhood, you can look under that name (e.g., Polish-American Congress) to see if there's a local branch.

- *Encyclopedia of Associations* (published by the Gale Research Company, Book Tower, Detroit MI 48226) is usually available in public libraries. The newly published Regional Editions, which list regional, state, and local organizations, can be helpful.

❦ *Self-Help Directories.* Hospitals often publish lists of self-help groups (for new mothers, widows or widowers, people who've had various operations or chronic diseases, families of Alzheimer's victims, etc.). *Directory of Self-Help Mutual Aid Groups in Illinois* (published by The Self-Help Center, Evanston, IL) lists a broad range of self-help groups operating in Illinois, including art and poetry groups, women's groups, and the like.

Contacting Local Institutions

Libraries

A good way to track down local groups is to go to the places where they meet. From our newspaper search, for example, we discovered that many groups met at the local library. We contacted the librarian and obtained information about groups meeting there as well as the library's self-published directory of local organizations.

Parks and Recreational Facilities

Another popular meeting place is the local park. Not only recreational groups, but other general purpose groups—community organizations and local school councils—often use park facilities for meetings. Calls to local park directors yielded information on groups that met there; some park directors sent along detailed listings.

Other recreational sites might also provide information; for example, a call or visit to local bowling alleys should produce information about leagues or other groups that use the lanes.

Churches

By far the most important meeting places in many neighborhoods are local religious institutions. Churches, mosques, and synagogues not only provide meeting space for outside groups like Alcoholics Anonymous, but they also organize their own membership in a variety of ways (women's groups, youth groups, etc.). For a good many people, their only formal membership is in or through their church.

For this reason, we decided to make a special effort to identify church-related organizations by obtaining a list of neighborhood churches from a local community organization; similar lists can also be obtained from local hotels or hospitals.

We began with a letter to the local churches (see Appendix 2, Part 1 on page 126) explaining what we were trying to find out and why we thought it would be useful. Along with the letter we included a list of different types of organizations (see Appendix 2, Part 2 on page 127).

We followed this up with phone calls to the pastor or other staff member. Sometimes, the pastor simply went through the list; others had forgotten (or not received) the list, but willingly provided information anyway.

We asked:

- ❧ What groups does the church sponsor? (If necessary, we added a prompting question, e.g.: What about Bible study?) Is the purpose of this group social, spiritual or recreational? How often does it meet? Is it open to anyone in the community or only church members?

- ❧ What [other neighborhood] groups use the church as a meeting place? (We often added a prompt, e.g.: What about block clubs?)

- ❧ How else is the church used by the community? (We usually added a prompt, e.g.: How about informal classes in aerobics or photography?)

We received cooperation from the pastors we spoke to, but there were also many whom we were never able to reach by phone. We sent those pastors a follow-up letter with a list of organizations (Appendix 4, Part 1 and Part 2) and a form (Appendix 5) to fill out identifying groups sponsored by or meeting at the church, with information about each. Several additional pastors provided information in this way.

Many pastors were interested in what we were doing and asked for a copy of the finished product, which we promised to provide. We sent every pastor a second follow-up letter giving them an opportunity to review the information about their church before we published it (see Appendix 6).

Church contacts were extremely helpful. From them, we obtained the names of 340 church-sponsored groups and an additional 110 groups using churches as a meeting place, for a total of 450 groups from the 43 responding churches. Appendix 1 identifies which groups in our total neighborhood list were provided through church contacts—those with "church" after the group's name.

Contacting Individuals

The most obvious way to find out which groups people belong to is to ask them personally. But this is harder than reading newspapers or asking the local clergyman or librarian. You have to identify which people to survey, find an efficient way to contact them, and ask the right questions so that people will cooperate without feeling their privacy is being compromised.

We asked the local neighborhood organization to identify residential blocks they considered "typical" of the neighborhood: where different ethnic groups and income levels were represented. From these, we chose three streets—six blocks in all—that had a mix of housing types.

We consulted the Chicago-area *Criss-Cross Directory* (published by Haines, Schaumburg, IL). This directory provides names and phone numbers corresponding to street addresses. Thus, if you have addresses for the building on a given block, you can find the names and phone numbers of the people who live there. If you need to find the publisher of a criss-cross directory for your area, you may contact Haines and Company, 8050 Freedom Avenue, NW, North Canton, OH, 44720, telephone (216) 494-9111.

We sent letters (Appendix 6) to each resident of the chosen blocks. We explained the project and enclosed The Association Map (Appendix 2) suggesting different kinds of associations they might know about.

Within a week, we followed up the letters with phone calls. Aware that some people might be suspicious of being asked what groups they belong to, we stated immediately that we were working under the auspices of a university-sponsored project. You may want to identify your research with some respected local institution or organization.

We began each phone call by saying:

> Hi, my name is _____ and I'm with the Center for Urban Affairs and Policy Research at Northwestern University. Did you receive our letter? I'm interested in any clubs and organizations you've heard of, participated in, or are a member of.

We also called some people "cold" (without sending the letter first), saying:

> Hi, my name is _____ and I'm with the Center for Urban Affairs and Policy Research at Northwestern University. We're conducting a very brief survey on clubs and organizations in your neighborhood. We don't need your name, we're only interested in the names of clubs and groups you know. Would you be able to answer the questions now?

We quickly learned it was too tedious to go through our list asking about each kind of organization individually. Instead, we learned to ask a few open-ended questions:

- Can you name any groups you've heard of or participated in? Does it meet in your neighborhood?

- Is there a local neighborhood organization in your area? What about a book club?

❦ Is there any church or religious organization you're
involved with? If yes, within the church, are there any
other groups or clubs that you're a part of?

❦ Are there any other special interest groups that you or
people in your family are in—such as women's or men's
groups, veterans organizations, artistic clubs, or other
clubs?

❦ What about informal groups? Do you get together or
associate with your neighbors?

❦ How else do you feel a part of the community? How else
do you get involved in your neighborhood?

Not everyone is willing to answer such questions (we found that it
didn't make much difference whether people had received the letter
first or not). Some people didn't speak English; some we were never
able to reach; and others were willing to talk but said they were not
members of any organizations. Those who were cooperative and said
they did belong to different groups provided us with the names of 100
different organizations (as well as 49 repeats). This worked out to an
average of 10 organizations per hour spent making phone calls.

Of course, some of this information overlapped. Many people, for
example, mentioned church groups of which we were already aware.
But the calls gave us a good general idea of the neighborhood and
how involved its residents were. We also found two or three people on
each block who were exceptionally well-connected to local groups and
organizations, and who could clearly serve as an informal guide to
their neighborhood.

Appendix 1 lists organizations we identified by telephoning with the
word *phone* after the group's name.

Conclusion

Using the methods we've described here, we were able to identify 575
groups which were either located in the neighborhood or which had
neighborhood residents as members.

The most productive method for us was contacting local leaders, like
church pastors or librarians. These people were generally cooperative
and were able to provide a good deal of very useful information about
neighborhood groups.

The other two methods also provided useful (though more general)
information for a relatively small expenditure of time.

We were studying a city neighborhood, and our conclusions are drawn from that urban area. In a different type of community—a small town or suburb, for example—the conclusions might be different; churches might be a less important source of information than, say, the local newspaper.

Not reflected in the tables was the *wealth* of information we learned, especially from personal calls and conversations with pastors. For example, several church leaders spoke of strong church membership in earlier years, which had dwindled when new ethnic groups moved into the neighborhood. Other people mentioned that because most parents are employed, there is less time available for community involvement. We also came across some people who are clearly very involved in the neighborhood and who would be excellent contacts for getting acquainted with other local residents.

APPENDIX 1

LOGAN SQUARE NEIGHBORHOOD ASSOCIATIONS

(IDENTIFIED FROM LOCAL RESOURCES)

KEY:

book	=	phone book
church	=	church responses
word	=	discussions with neighborhood leaders
sulzer	=	Sulzer Library Directory of Associations
paper	=	*Logan Square Times* newspaper
local	=	local community newspapers
phone	=	phone calls to neighborhoods

32ND WARD ADVISORY COUNCIL (sulzer)

32ND WARD CRIME COMMITTEE (sulzer)

32ND WARD DEMOCRATIC PARTY (sulzer)

32ND WARD REPUBLICAN PARTY (sulzer)

33RD WARD DEMOCRATIC PARTY (sulzer)

40TH WARD REPUBLICAN COMMITTEE (sulzer)

3600 W. DICKENS BLOCK CLUB (word)

ACT NOW: neighborhood group (church)

ACTION CLUB: neighborhood food to senior citizens (church)

AIRCRAFT OWNERS AND PILOTS ASSOCIATION (phone)

AL-ANON (church)

ALCOHOLICS ANONYMOUS (phone)

ALL PEOPLE'S CONGRESS (book)

ALTAR AND ROSARY SOCIETY (church)

AMERICAN LEGION FDR POST #923 (book)

AMERICAN LEGION LAFAYETTE POST #159 (book)

AMERICAN LEGION (SKOKIE POST) (phone)

AMERICAN SOCIETY OF CIVIL ENGINEERS (phone)

AMISTAD SPANISH-SPEAKING YOUTH (church)

ANGLERS (word)

ANIN ART PUPPET THEATER (local)

ANTIOCH PROJECT: coalition to improve the neighborhood (church)

ART THERAPY GROUP (phone)

ARTISTS COALITION (phone)

ATHLETIC ASSOCIATION (church)

AUTOHARP LESSONS (church)

AVONDALE COMMUNITY CENTER (local)

AVONDALE COMMUNITY TOGETHER IN OUR NEIGHBORHOOD (word)
BLOCK CLUB (phone)
BOY SCOUTS (CUB SCOUTS) OF AMERICA (phone)
BOY'S CLUB (phone)
BROTHERHOOD (church)
CBS SENIOR CITIZENS GROUP (church)
CADETS (church)
CAMERA CLUB (church)
CAMPBELL BLOCK CLUB (phone)
CAMPING/FISHING CLUB (church)
CASA CENTRAL (book)
CATHOLIC CHARITIES: mother/child program (church)
CENTER FOR COMMUNITY AND LEADERSHIP DEVELOPMENT (word)
CENTRO PARA DES ARROLLO (church)
CENTRO UNIDAD LATINA (sulzer)
CHARISMATIC PRAYER GROUP (church)
CHICAGO COMMONS ASSOCIATION (word)
CHICAGO CULTURAL COLLABORATIVE (phone)
CHICAGO NORTH NEIGHBORHOOD ARTISTS (phone)
CHICAGO PUBLICITY GROUP (phone)
CHINA/BURMA/INDIA ORGANIZATION (phone)
CHRISTIAN THEATER COMPANY (paper)
CHRISTIANS IN ACTION: Spanish social group (church)
CHURCH OF LATTER DAY SAINTS (phone)
COCAINE ANONYMOUS (church)
COMMITTEE IN SOLIDARITY WITH PEOPLE OF EL SALVADOR (CISPES) (word)
COMMUNITY SERVICE THRIFT SHOP (church)
COMPUTER CLUB: also called the MS-DOS GROUP (church)
COPERNICUS CENTER (phone)
CRETAN FRATERNITY OF CHICAGO (book)
CRIME PREVENTION (phone)
CS&A (phone)
DAISYS: kids group (church)
DAMEN AVENUE REVITALIZATION EFFORT (DARE) (word)
DANISH ROSARY GROUP (church)
DAUGHTERS OF MERCY (church)
DAUGHTERS OF MARY (church)
DEMOCRAT CLUB (phone)
DISTRICT COUNCIL (phone)
DULCINEA (word)
EARLY CHILDHOOD CENTER (church)
EMOTIONS ANONYMOUS: self-help group (church)
ENOW TUTORING (phone)
EQUAL RIGHTS CONGRESS (book)

FAMILIAS HISPAÑAS: family group (church)

FAMILY CAMPING GROUP (church)

FIRESIDE BOWLING (book)

FRIENDSHIP CLUB: senior citizens club (church)

FULLERTON AVENUE MERCHANTS ASSOCIATION (church)

FUTURE AVIATION PILOTS OF AMERICA (phone)

GABRIEL RICHARDS: Hispanic public speaking group (church)

GIRL SCOUTS (BROWNIES) OF AMERICA (church)

GOLDEN AMERICANS (local)

GOLDEN AGERS (church)

GOLDEN DINERS CLUB (church)

GREATER NORTH PULASKI DEVELOPMENT CORPORATION (book)

GUADALUPANA SOCIETY (church)

GUADALUPARES (church)

GUARDIAN ANGELS (church)

HABITAT FOR HUMANITY (church)

HEAD START (church)

HEALTH AND FITNESS GROUP FOR FILIPINOS (phone)

HEALTH CLUB (phone)

HERMANAS (church)

HERMANOS (church)

HERMOSA COMMUNITY ORGANIZATION (church)

HERMOSA CRIME PREVENTION ORGANIZATION (church)

HOLY NAME SOCIETY (church)

HOMEOWNERS ASSOCIATION OF PALMER SQUARE (word)

HUMBOLDT BOULEVARD HOMEOWNERS (church)

INDEPENDENT POLITICAL ORGANIZATION (phone)

INNER CITY IMPACT (church)

INTERNATIONAL FEDERATION OF POLICE (book)

IRISH THEATER GUILD (paper)

JEFFERSON PARK LIONESS CLUB (word)

JEHOVAH EVANGELICAL LUTHERAN CHURCH (phone)

JUNIORS (church)

KOSCIUSZKO PARK SENIOR CITIZENS CLUB (phone)

LADIES OF FATIMA (church)

LADIES OF CHARITY (church)

LADY JOSÉ DIEGO PTA (church)

LALECHE LEAGUE (church)

LATIN DRAMA CLUB: Northwest Community Drama Club (local)

LATIN AMERICAN STUDY GROUP (church)

LEAGUE OF AMERICANS OF UKRANIAN DESCENT (book)

LEGION OF MARY (church)

LIFELINE PILOTS (phone)

LOCAL 25 SERVICE EMPLOYEES UNION (phone)

LOCAL 102808 AMERICAN FEDERATION OF MUSICIANS (phone)
LOGAN BOULEVARD ASSOCIATION (local)
LOGAN SQUARE BOYS AND GIRLS CLUB (local)
LOGAN SQUARE LIBRARY (paper)
LOGAN SQUARE LION'S CLUB (word)
LOGAN SQUARE MINISTERIAL ASSOCIATION (church)
LOGAN SQUARE NEIGHBORHOOD ASSOCIATION (phone)
LOGAN SQUARE PRESERVATION SOCIETY (church)
LOGAN SQUARE SUMMER OLYMPICS (church)
LOGAN SQUARE YOUTH DEVELOPMENT PROGRAM (church)
LOYOLA ALUMNI CLUB (phone)
LUNCH (church)
LUTHER LEAGUE: youth group (church)
M&M CLUB: for little kids (church)
MAPLE LANES BOWLING (book)
MAPLE AVENUE BLOCK CLUB (church)
MEDIEVAL PLAYERS: performing Medieval plays (church)
MEDILL AVENUE BLOCK CLUB (church)
MILWAUKEE-DIVISION MERCHANTS ASSOCIATION (word)
MISSION COUNCIL #4 OF UNITED CHURCH OF CHRIST (church)
MONIUSKO CHOIR (church)
MOODY MEMORIAL (phone)
MOTHER AND CHILD NUTRITION CLASSES (church)
MOTHERS CLUB (church)
MOTHERS JUVENILE PROTECTION ASSOCIATION (church)
NEAR NORTHWEST NEIGHBORHOOD NETWORK (sulzer)
NEIGHBOR TO NEIGHBOR (church)
NEIGHBOR INTER-CITY IMPACT (church)
NEIGHBORHOOD VOLUNTEER GROUP "W3" (church)
NEIGHBORHOOD WATCH (phone)
NETWORK FOR YOUTH SERVICES (book)
NORWEGIAN WOMEN'S GROUP (church)
NORTH PARK COLLEGE EXTENSION (church)
NORTHWEST NEIGHBORHOOD FEDERATION (paper)
NORTHWEST COMMUNITY ORGANIZATION (church)
NORTHWEST COUNCIL OF SENIOR CITIZENS (paper)
NORTHWEST GAY AND LESBIAN ASSOCIATION (church)
ODD FELLOWS IOOF NORTHWEST (book)
OUR LADY OF GRACE (phone)
OUR LADY OF GRACE BASKETBALL TEAMS (church)
P.R.C.O. OF S. DANCERS (church)
PAINTER'S LOCAL #147 (phone)
PALMER SQUARE ARTS FAIR (phone)
PALMER SQUARE HOMEOWNERS (church)

PARENTS AGAINST STREET VIOLENCE (church)

PARKS, ZOOS, MUSEUMS (phone)

PHILIPPINE NATIONAL BASKETBALL ORGANIZATION (phone)

PIKA WOMEN'S MISSION GUILD (church)

PIONEERS (phone)

POLICE SOCIETY #911 OF POLISH NATIONAL ALLIANCE (paper)

POLISH MUSEUM OF AMERICA LIBRARY (sulzer)

POLISH MUSEUM OF AMERICA (sulzer)

POLISH-AMERICAN POLICE ASSOCIATION (book)

PORTIS PARK CHURCH (phone)

PRINCE OF PEACE LUTHERAN SCHOOL (church)

PSYCHIC DEVELOPMENT CLASSES (church)

PUERTO RICAN CHAMBER OF COMMERCE & INDUSTRY OF CHICAGO (sulzer)

PURCHASING ASSOCIATION (phone)

QUEEN/KING CLUB (church)

REPUBLICAN NATIONAL COMMITTEE (phone)

RETIRED CITIZENS GROUP (phone)

ROCKWELL AVENUE BLOCK CLUB (church)

RUIZ BELVIS CENTER (book)

SELSA: block club (church)

SCOUT MOTHERS' ASSOCIATION (church)

SEA SCOUTS (church)

SENIOR CITIZENS GOLDEN DINERS CLUB (local)

SENIOR CITIZENS DINERS CLUB (church)

SHAMROCK CLUB (phone)

SID SAKOWITZ FAN CLUB (phone)

SISTERHOOD (church)

SOFTBALL: through park district (phone)

SPAULDING-WRIGHTWOOD BLOCK CLUB (CLARA LYLE) (word)

ST. LOUIS BLOCK CLUB (church)

ST. LUKE'S SENIOR CITIZENS NUTRITION GROUP (phone)

ST. ANNE'S CITADEL (phone)

ST. VINCENT DE PAUL (church)

ST. HYACINTH'S (phone)

ST. FRANCIS (phone)

ST. JOHN BERCHMAN'S (phone)

SUMMER TENT CAMPING GROUP (church)

TAILWAGGERS: dog training class (church)

TASK FORCE AGAINST GANGS (church)

TED KNUSSMAN VFW (phone)

THE ORGANIZATION OF PALMER SQUARE (TOPS) (word)

THE ESTONIAN LUTHERAN CHURCH (church)

THEATRICAL HISTORICAL SOCIETY (book)

TOASTMASTERS (phone)

UKRAINIAN YOUTH GROUP (church)
UNA NUEVA ESPERANZA (book)
UNION OF MACHINE OPERATORS (phone)
UNITED NEIGHBORS INVOLVED TEAM EFFORT (local)
UNITED NEIGHBORS IN ACTION (sulzer)
UNITED METHODIST WOMEN'S GROUP (church)
USHERS CLUB (church)
VFW CHICAGO BLACKHAWK POST #7975 (book)
VFW #300 (phone)
VIETNAM VETERAN'S MUSEUM (paper)
WEST TOWN SHELTER (church)
WEST TOWN WILDCATS: youth group (church)
WICKER PARK NEIGHBORHOOD COUNCIL (church)
WICKER PARK ARTISTS GROUP (church)
WILSON AVENUE CIVIC ORGANIZATION (paper)
WOMEN'S MOOSE CLUB (phone)
YMCA (phone)
YMCA SENIOR CITIZENS CLUB (phone)
YOUNG/OLDTIMERS CLUB (church)
YOUNG PEOPLE'S DRAMA GROUP (church)

APPENDIX 2
PART 1

Center for Urban Affairs and Policy Research

Northwestern University

2040 Sheridan Road / Evanston, Illinois 60208
(312) 491-3395

February 16, 1988

St. Matthew's Episcopal Church
3333 Bayside
Chicago, IL 60000

Dear Reverend:

The Northwestern University Center for Urban Affairs and Policy Research is working on a project involving local communities. We believe that clubs and organizations are vital parts of communities, and as such we are trying to gather information and compile a list of local community clubs and organizations.

We see the church as a primary focal point of community activity, both through the groups that are sponsored by the church, and through groups that utilize the church as a meeting place. As part of our project, we would like to document the various groups that are connected, in any way, to your church. During the week of February 22-29, I will be calling to ask you a few questions about the clubs and organizations your church sponsors and about any other groups that simply meet at your church. It will only take five to ten minutes of your time.

Before our call, we would appreciate your looking over the enclosed list of different types of groups. Could you please note the groups that are connected with your church? Then, when we call, we will simply go over the list with you.

We greatly appreciate your time and cooperation. If you should have any questions, please feel free to give me a call.

Sincerely,

Kathy Nakagawa
Research Assistant

encl.

APPENDIX 2
PART 2

AN ASSOCIATION MAP

ARTISTIC ORGANIZATIONS:	choral, theatrical, writing
BUSINESS ORGANIZATIONS:	Chamber of Commerce, neighborhood business associations, trade groups
CHARITABLE GROUPS & DRIVES:	Red Cross, Cancer Society, United Way
CHURCH GROUPS:	service, prayer, maintenance, stewardship, acolytes, men's, women's, youth, seniors
CIVIC EVENTS:	July 4th, art fair, Halloween
COLLECTORS GROUPS:	stamp collectors, flower dryers, antiques
COMMUNITY SUPPORT GROUPS:	"friends" of the library, nursing home, hospital
ELDERLY GROUPS:	Senior Citizens
ETHNIC ASSOCIATIONS:	Sons of Norway, Black Heritage Club, Hibernians
HEALTH & FITNESS GROUPS:	bicycling, jogging, exercise
INTEREST CLUBS:	poodle owners, antique car owners
LOCAL GOVERNMENT:	town, township, electoral units, fire department, emergency units
LOCAL MEDIA:	radio, newspaper, local access cable TV
MEN'S GROUPS:	cultural, political, social, educational, vocational
MUTUAL SUPPORT (SELF-HELP) GROUPS:	Alcoholics Anonymous, Epilepsy Self-Help, La Leche League
Neighborhood & Block Clubs:	crime watch, beautification, Christmas decorations
Outdoor Groups:	garden clubs, Audubon Society, conservation clubs
Political Organizations:	Democrats, Republicans, caucuses
School Groups:	printing club, PTA, child care
Service Clubs:	Zonta, Kiwanis, Rotary, American Association of University Women
Social Cause Groups:	peace, rights, advocacy, service
Sports Leagues:	bowling, swimming, baseball, fishing, volleyball
Veterans Groups:	American Legion, Amvets, Veterans of Foreign Wars & Auxiliaries
Women's Groups:	cultural, political, social, educational, vocational
Youth Groups:	4H, Future Farmers, Scouts, YWCA

127

APPENDIX 3
PART 1

Center for Urban Affairs and Policy Research

Northwestern University

2040 Sheridan Road / Evanston, Illinois 60208
(312) 491-3395

April 19, 1988

All Saints Church
31 W. Reston Street
Chicago, IL   60000

Dear Reverend:

We are planning to produce a booklet on information about groups and clubs associated with neighborhood churches. We feel this booklet would be very useful to persons in the community as a way of knowing what's happening in neighborhoods and how they may get involved. The document will be made available to any interested community organizations, individuals, and churches.

In our previous phone calls, we were unable to gather information from your church. We still hope to include your church in our document, and if you would like to be included, please fill out the enclosed questionnaire and return it to us by Friday, May 6, 1988. We are interested in both groups sponsored by your church (e.g., Bible study, choirs, or prayer groups) and groups which just use your church as a meeting place (e.g., neighborhood block clubs, recreation classes). Please also include any annual events you may sponsor (like rummage sales, bazaars, or carnivals) and any other information on the way you feel the church is utilized in your community.

If you should have any questions, please contact me at 491-7767. Thank you very much for your time and help.

Sincerely,

Kathy Nakagawa
Research Assistant

encl.

APPENDIX 3
PART 2

FOLLOW-UP LIST

Listed below are different types of associations and examples of each. Please note the names of any groups you have heard of or participated in.

ARTISTIC/CULTURAL:	neighborhood artists, Theatrical Historical Society
CIVIC/COMMUNITY\SUPPORT:	PTA, Chamber of Commerce, Merchants Association, Friends of the Library
CHURCH:	Bible study, choir, St. Anne's Citadel, prayer group
ELDERLY:	Golden Diners Club, senior citizens' club
ETHNIC:	Polish-American Congress, Black Heritage Club
HEALTH & FITNESS:	Baseball league, aerobics class, YMCA
MEN'S :	Fraternal Order of Police
MUTUAL SUPPORT (SELF-HELP):	La Leche League, marriage encounter
NEIGHBORHOOD/BLOCK CLUBS:	Northside Neighbors, Crime Watch
POLITICAL:	Republican Committee, Ward Office, local fire department
RECREATION:	ceramics classes, dog training classes
SOCIAL CAUSE/SERVICE:	Zonta, Kiwanis, Sierra Club
SPECIAL INTEREST:	stamp collectors, dog owners, car club
VETERAN GROUPS:	American Legion, Amvets, VFW
WOMEN'S GROUPS:	Women in Government
YOUTH/CHILDREN:	4H, Future Farmers, Boy and Girl Scouts, YWCA

APPENDIX 4

Please list the names of groups and provide information on when they meet (e.g., Wed. evenings 1/week, 1/month) and who may join (anyone in the community or just parish members). Please see enclosed list for ideas and examples of groups.

	When does it meet?	Who may join?

I. GROUPS SPONSORED BY THE CHURCH.

_____   _____   _____

_____   _____   _____

_____   _____   _____

_____   _____   _____

II. GROUPS THAT USE CHURCH AS A MEETING PLACE.

_____   _____   _____

_____   _____   _____

_____   _____   _____

_____   _____   _____

III. OTHER INFORMATION, COMMENTS, SUGGESTIONS?

_____

_____

_____

_____

APPENDIX 5

Center for Urban Affairs and Policy Research

Northwestern University

2040 Sheridan Road / Evanston, Illinois 60208
(312) 491-3395

April 19, 1988

Reverend Richard Barnes
St. Peter's Lutheran Church
1000 W. Kensington
Chicago, IL   60000

Dear Reverend Barnes:

Thank you very much for taking the time to answer our questions about the groups and clubs associated with your church. We are planning to put together a booklet of this information and would like to include the information from your church. We feel such a document would be very useful to persons in the community as a way of knowing what's happening in neighborhoods and how they may get involved. It would be made available to any interested community organizations, individuals, and churches.

Enclosed please find the listing we have for your church. If you wish information to be changed or added, or if you do not want to be included in our booklet, please contact me at 491-7767 by Friday, May 6, 1988. If we do not hear from you, we will assume the information is correct and that you approve of your inclusion in our document.

Again, thank you for your time and help. If you should have any other comments or questions, please contact me.

Sincerely,

Kathy Nakagawa
Research Assistant

encl.

APPENDIX 6

Center for Urban Affairs and Policy Research

Northwestern University

2040 Sheridan Road / Evanston, Illinois 60208
(312) 491-3395

December 30, 1987

Mr. James Brown
3000 W. Barnack Street
Chicago, IL   60000

Dear Mr. Brown:

I am writing to ask for your help in a project being conducted by our Center for Urban Affairs and Policy Research.

We believe that local clubs and organizations are important parts of local communities. Therefore, we are trying to compile a list of the kinds of clubs and organizations in which people in Chicago's neighborhoods participate.

As part of this project, we have chosen your name at random and would like to ask you about the various groups and clubs with which you are involved. Therefore, during the week of January 6 through January 13, one of my research associates will telephone and ask you a few questions for our survey. It will only take ten or fifteen minutes of your time.

Before our call, we would appreciate your looking over the enclosed list of many kinds of clubs and organizations. Could you note the groups you are involved with? Then, when we call, we will simply go over the list with you.

I appreciate your cooperation. If you should have any questions, feel free to give me a call.

Sincerely,

John L. McKnight

encl.

The Powerful Kinds of Community Work Performed by Associations

An inventory of local associations will not necessarily reveal the nature of all the community work the groups may do. Nor will it indicate the work the groups might do if called to action. Therefore, an effective inventory must also identify the various *kinds* of activities undertaken by local associations—formal and informal.

In this section of the guide, there are stories of many kinds of associations and the differing work they do. Then, there are two sections specifically focused on the work of two particular types of associations—churches and cultural organizations.

- In a small rural community, a group of citizens formed an association and created a locally owned and operated radio station. The station is available to local individuals and associations to broadcast debates, announcements, performances. The station is the "voice" of the community. (KAXE)

- A group of unemployed residents of public housing formed an association to seek jobs. They created a job service that helped prepare members for jobs and referred residents to permanent and part-time job opportunities. Over 75 residents have secured jobs through their mutual efforts (Dearborn Homes).

- A group of neighborhood block clubs came together in an informal association to inventory the skills and capabilities of the residents of the area. As a result, the group has been able to initiate self-help, mutual support and exchange networks. They have also created a property management cooperative that employs the skills of local residents to provide services to landlords in the neighborhood. (ACE)

- An association of people organized to practice Olympic style rowing has expanded its activities to include classes for beginners, organizing local regattas, supporting rowing programs at local colleges and maintaining two public boathouses. The group has also become a public advocate for keeping a beautiful natural gorge from becoming a marina site. (Rowing)

- A local chapter of the National Association of Black Accountants has offered free accounting services to local community groups and businesses. They have begun to play a critical role in the start-up of several local businesses and nonprofit groups. (National)

❧ An association of people involved in recreating the era of the fur traders sponsors a series of "rendezvous" each summer in their local community. This annual event recreates the life of fur traders and their camps in the 1700s. The "rendezvous" is part history, part theater and part festival. It has grown so that it is held for several weekends each year and draws many people from outside the community. The event teaches history, boosts the local economy and draws the local community together. (White Oaks)

❧ A group of public housing residents formed an association to take responsibility for managing their building. This Resident Management Corporation has developed a vision for the future embodied in current plans to convert their building to a mixed income development fully managed by the residents (Dearborn Homes).

❧ A group in a small town created a hospitality center in a local church. They put in a shower and supplies for visitors. Volunteers also operate an office that serves as a contact point for community events. Space is available for gatherings of all kinds. They began to run "community fundraisers" to raise money for local groups or individuals with creative ideas. Sometimes when outsiders come to the area, they convene a community meeting where local people and visitors can talk. (Lawron)

❧ A group of African-American men of middle age and older created an association to work with young men in order to help them to come of age in constructive, historically rooted and community-supported ways. The association has created workshops, presentations, classes and a network of ready and willing mentors. (Rites)

❧ Family members of people experiencing mental illness formed a local self-help association. In addition to providing mutual support, the group has become a connecting place between its members and other associations and businesses in the community. The group identifies supportive employers, suggests useful local services and helps guide people with mental illness to groups or activities where they can participate in the life of the community. (Family)

❧ A neighborhood resident, troubled by the behavior of local young men, began to talk with them about their abilities and found they were interested in making things. He then suggested that, as an informal group, they make something that would help neighborhood people live together more effectively. After considerable discussion, they decided to make some wooden lawn chairs so neighborhood people could enjoy the outside and be available to talk with each other. Without telling anyone, two adults and 11 youth produced 90 chairs and painted them green. Then, early on a Sunday morning in spring, they set the chairs out in each front yard of all the buildings in a two-block area. The neighbors "discovered" the chairs, talked about them, came out in the evening and sat in them, visited, shared and made new friendships or renewed old ones. Subsequently, new crews of local young people have produced more chairs for local residents. (Chair)

❧ A local neighborhood association initiated a youth affiliate to try to stimulate more community involvement by local young people. A group of young people responded and created an association called the Youth Express. The group has created some youth-run enterprises, set up a youth skill bank that identifies what they can do and initiated a job finding club that checks out employment leads and promotes greater involvement of young people in local community projects. (Lexington)

❧ A local neighborhood organization became the connecting organization between neighbors who could help and neighbors who could use help. They identified homebound people (seniors or disabled people) who needed assistance in clearing snow from their sidewalks or digging up their gardens. Then the association found local neighbors willing to do these tasks and connected them to the homebound. In return, some of the homebound people offer daily prayers for the neighborhood people who are providing help. The neighbors who shovel sidewalks and dig gardens are called "The Earthmovers" by the local association. Those who pray for community workers are called "The Prayer Warriors." The association's newsletter reports each month on the number of hours the Earthmovers have contributed and the number of hours the Warriors have prayed. (Southwest)

❧ More than 15 years ago, a group of neighbors created a cooperatively operated child care program. The child care association relies on nonpaid parent time and has survived because of the attractiveness of small-scale, near-home, well-run, nonprofessional child care. (Seward)

❧ In an inner-city neighborhood where over half the land was vacant or abandoned, the remaining neighbors formed an association to create a vision for renewing the area. They hired their own planner and developed a plan that captured their vision. In order to implement their plan, they needed to gain control over owners of the vacant land. They skillfully approached the Mayor and he agreed to grant the association the city's power of eminent domain so the neighbors could gain control of their land. (Dudley)

❧ A group of recently graduated college students created an association that collected information from the people in their neighborhood who were willing to teach others what they knew either for pay or for free. The group identified thousands of things local people could teach from how to play a guitar to the works of Aristotle. This "library" of community knowledge became a major new resource for local learning, discussion and recreation. (Learning)

Each of these stories tells how a group of citizens used the power of association to do the work of community—work as vital and varied as:

❧ creating a local radio station
❧ preparing people for jobs
❧ exchanging the skills of neighbors
❧ preserving a beautiful riverfront
❧ assisting in starting new businesses
❧ organizing an annual community celebration
❧ managing an apartment complex
❧ raising money for community projects
❧ initiating young people into adulthood and community life
❧ finding employers willing to hire local people
❧ making lawn furniture to promote neighborliness
❧ creating youth-run businesses
❧ connecting neighbors needing help with those who can help
❧ establishing a neighborhood day care cooperative
❧ designing a major plan to renew the community
❧ creating a library of community experts available to everyone.

Local Associations and Their Community Building Work

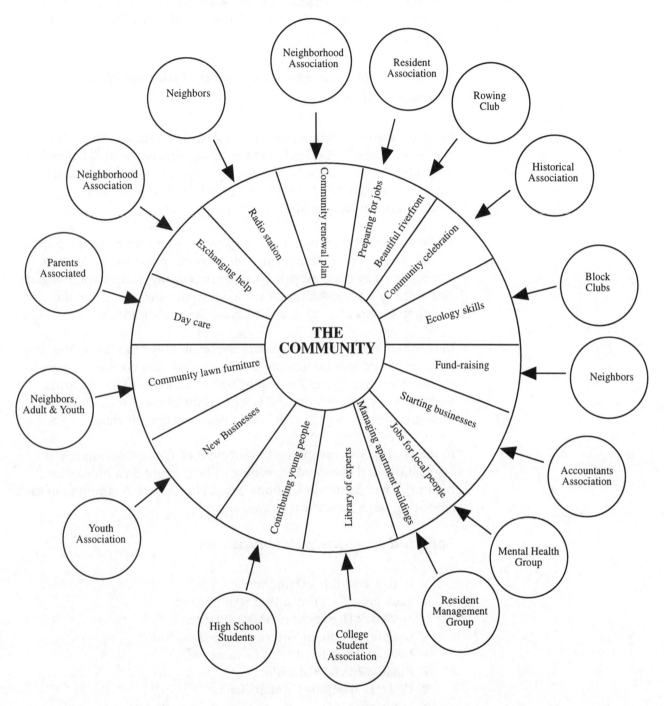

This work of local citizen associations represents a community-building agenda. In combination, the associations empower the members and the community so that the neighborhood looks like the chart on the previous page.

The Potential for Associations to Take on New Responsibility

Most associations were created to do a particular thing. The Boy and Girl Scouts were associated to teach young people the skills of outdoor life. The Veteran's Association is designed to provide mutual support and advocate for veterans' interests. The Volunteer Firefighters are organized to stop fires.

While each of these functions is empowering for members and for the community, each of these groups also has the potential to do more. The Scouts may take responsibility for organizing a community parade. The Veteran's Association may raise money for the affair. And the Firefighters may give rides at the parade to local children.

In communities where local assets are being fully mobilized, one vital function is asking local groups to take on new functions or responsibilities. One example of the willingness of all kinds of local associations to take on new functions is a program in many states that asks local groups to "adopt" a mile of highway and keep it clean.

In the state of Wisconsin, the Department of Transportation asked associations if they would be willing to help maintain a mile of local highway. Over 2,000 associations have volunteered. A sampling of the kinds of groups are shown below.

Selected Wisconsin Associations

- Bethel #44 Job's Daughters
- Sauk Prairie Optimist Boy Scout Troop
- Fall River High School SADD Chapter
- League of Women Voters of Dane Co., Inc.
- Lomira Area Chamber of Commerce
- Rotary Club of Platteville
- Country Womens Homemakers
- TOPS #WI, 552
- Wyona Wildcat 4-H Club
- OKEE Community Associations
- Chapter 221 Vietnam Veterans of America
- Southwest Wisconsin Auto Club
- Senior High Youth Group
- Cuba City National Honor Society
- Girl Scouts of Badger Council

- Beaver Dam Jaycees
- Trailblazers Snowmobile Club
- Dodge County Tavern League
- Southwestern Izaak Walton League
- Rock River Radio Club
- Moravian Church
- Knights of Columbus Council 765
- Four Lakes Metal Detector Club
- Monroe Volunteer Firefighters, Inc.
- National Association of Retired Federal Employees
- Wisconsin Morgan Horse Club, Inc.
- Baraboo Bassmasters
- Portage Education Association
- Bear Valley Wildlife Group
- Mineral Point Odd Fellows Iowa #1
- Black Hawk Future Farmers of America
- Darlington High School Student Council
- Belleville Memorial VFW Post 5461
- Green County Pilots Association
- Calvary Baptist Youth Group
- Phi Kappa Psi Fraternity
- Badgerland F-100 Truck Club
- Fennimore Junior Women's Club
- Marshall High School National Honor Society
- Wisconsin Trappers Association
- Employees of Shirley's Village Diner
- Telephone Pioneers of America
- Hobbit Outdoor Club
- Sun Prairie Hockey Team
- Special Adults Athletic Club
- Verona Aquatic Club
- Janesville Homeschoolers
- National Wild Turkey Federation
- Bluffview Civic Association

Not one of these associations was organized for the purpose of maintaining highways, but the citizens in all these associations agreed to work for the well-being of society when they were asked.

Therefore, a vital role for local leadership is to make certain that as many associations as possible are involved in creating new plans, visions and projects and that they are asked to reach out to do new work in community-building.

Religious and Cultural Organizations: Exemplary Associations

While the chart of community associations describes many kinds of groups at work to build their community, the following sections describe the community work of two special kinds of associations in detail: religious and cultural associations.

Churches, temples and mosques are present in every community serving people of diverse incomes, races and ethnicity. While their basic purpose is the spiritual care of their members, they have demonstrated incredible capacity to undertake community work of every kind. The diversity of this work is described in the following section.

Cultural organizations and their work are described in the subsequent section. These groups are often overlooked in the community-building process because their contributions aren't as obvious as a new building or business or youth project. However, their ability to mobilize the spirit of the community is historic and it is this spirit of community that is the foundation of effective community building work.

Sources and Contacts for the Stories in This Section

A.C.E.   A.C.E. Block Clubs
                      (612) 871-6553 (Flo Green)

Chair   Green Chair Project
                      Joel Sisson
                      3118 Pleasant Avenue South
                      Minneapolis, MN 55408
                      (612) 649-4546

Dearborn   Dearborn Homes Resident Management Corp.
                      2710 S. State Street, Suite 208
                      Chicago, IL 60616
                      (312) 326-3730

Dudley   Dudley Street Neighborhood Initiative
                      513 Dudley Street
                      Roxbury, MA 02119
                      (617) 442-9670

Family   Family Support Group
                      (218) 245-3994 (Joan Huge-Beech)

KAXE   KAXE Radio
                      Michelle Johnson
                      (218) 326-1234

Lawron   Lawron Presbyterian Church
                      (218) 245-3888 (Dee Talley)

Learning   Learning Exchange
                      Attn: Alice Murray
                      Center for Urban Affairs and Policy Research
                      Northwestern University
                      2040 Sheridan Road
                      Evanston, IL 60208

Lexington   Lexington-Hamline Community Council
                      (612) 645-3207 (Ted Benson)

Rites   Rites of Passage
                      (612) 374-9339 (Antar Soleem)

Rowing   Minneapolis Rowing Club
                      (612) 333-4555 (Chip Magid, President)

Seward   Seward Child Care Cooperative
                      (612) 724-3030

Southwest   Southwest Improvement Council, Inc. (SWIC)
Jan Marie Belle, Director
1000 South Logan Blvd., #200
Denver, CO 80219-3339
(303) 934-2181

White Oaks   White Oaks Society
(218) 246-9393

Introduction—Local Religious Institutions and Community Renewal

Neighborhood religious institutions have an abundance of resources that can contribute directly to the process of rebuilding communities. As a matter of fact, many churches and synagogues have already begun to utilize their resources within the community in extremely creative and innovative ways and thus have become centers for interaction between local individuals, groups, associations, and institutions. In other words, at the present time many contemporary religious leaders have come to understand that they cannot continue to remain viable within their community unless they learn to develop vital links to the development and improvement of that community. This understanding has led to an astounding variety of creative approaches to community-building by religious institutions. This guide will point to only a few of these and will outline only one set of strategies. (For more ideas, see the wonderful resource, "Economic Home Cookin': An Action Guide for Congregations on Community Economic Development," by Kim Zalent, available from the Community Workshop on Economic Development, 100 S. Morgan, Chicago 60607.)

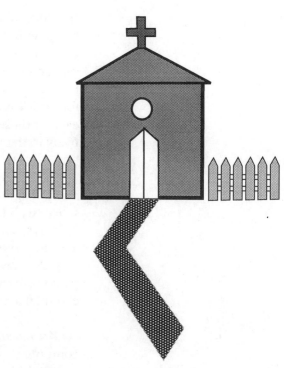

So how can religious institutions more fully utilize the abundance of resources that are available to them in the process of building better communities? The answer to this question can be discovered through the creation and continuing development of a wide-ranging series of "partnerships" with other associations, institutions, organizations, and individuals that also exist within their community. By uniting the resources of local religious institutions with those that already exist in other aspects of the community, churches, synagogues and other religious institutions can become actively connected to the most vital issues of their community and can be empowered to build a series of strong relationships through whose combined perspective these issues can be confronted and most effectively resolved.

Rediscovering Local Religious Institutions as Assets Within the Community

Almost every neighborhood contains a wide variety of religious institutions. Each particular religious institution offers a unique configuration of specific resources which can be utilized in the process of community building. Yet *every* religious institution, whether large or small, urban or rural, Protestant, Catholic, Jewish, Muslim, Buddhist, or other always offers certain common sets of resources which can be mobilized effectively to assist in community renewal.

Personnel. Churches and other religious institutions are staffed by people who are not only well trained and educated but also who have many special skills and interests. These skills and interests can often be harnessed to help build communities in many different ways. For example, many churches have recently become actively involved in home-building programs in cooperation with non-profit housing developers. Other religious institutions are choosing to develop their interest in certain specific aspects of the community such as "youth," "seniors," and/or the arts.

In addition, those who are members of local religious institutions bring with them a wide variety of special skills, interests and concerns that can be of value to the entire church community. For example, carpenters, plumbers, doctors, nurses, teachers, writers, scientists, business leaders, and artists, all of these individuals can usually be found within the membership of most local religious institutions, and each of these members has particular skills that can be utilized effectively in the process of community building.

Space and Facilities. No matter what their size or denomination, many religious institutions have at least one large meeting room, a sanctuary, classroom space, office space, a basement, a lobby, walls, hallways, a kitchen, a parking lot, and some open unused space. In addition, other larger, more fully equipped churches and synagogues may also have a stage, a gymnasium, a library, a school, and even a parsonage or dormitory rooms. All of these resources can become essential assets in the on-going process of community building.

Materials and Equipment. Many local religious institutions have computers, photo copiers, fax machines, musical instruments and materials, landscaping equipment, educational supplies, tools, kitchen utensils, and furniture such as tables and chairs. Other larger churches and synagogues may also have sports equipment, a bus or van, video and/or audio taping equipment, and various art supplies. If closely examined, each religious institution will be found to have available a unique collection of material resources that can be utilized for improving the community.

Expertise. Religious leaders often provide the community with a visionary framework for the development of programs promoting greater social and economic justice. While at the present time all too many organizations and institutions are placing their major emphasis on competition and "self-interest," religious institutions almost always stress altruism and doing good deeds for the sake of others and the entire community.

Religious institutions also bring a relevant understanding of and appreciation for the necessity of ritual in the life of the community. Ritual, a symbolic re-enactment of tradition, pulls the myriad strands of

144

community life together and allows each member of the religious community to participate as a valued part of the body. This means that even in a divisive era ritual expresses to the community the sense that "we are a whole fabric; we share a common history; we belong together in both the past and the future." In other words, religious ritual is the expression of the deep human need to participate fully in the spiritual life of the community.

Because of their stress on altruism and their understanding of the necessity for ritual, religious institutions also are recognized as having the moral authority to speak directly concerning social issues that negatively impact the life of the community. For example, in Chicago a coalition of local churches rallied together to address the negative ramifications of proposed casino gambling in the city. In other cities, churches and synagogues have addressed the morality of factory closings and the type of neighborhood development which does not take into proper consideration the basic interests of local residents.

Economic Power. Neighborhood churches and synagogues not only may purchase supplies and materials locally, but they also have the capacity to hire residents of the community for renovation projects or on-going programs and activities which they sponsor. They may even have had endowment funds which can be invested in local community development projects. In addition, local religious institutions may often be able to pool their own resources with those of other community organizations in order to create opportunities for local businesses to start up or expand their activities.

The various resources which have just been listed are only a few of the many that can be found in local religious institutions. But in order for these resources to become assets for the purpose of community building, they must be linked actively to the other major resource centers of the community. This means that local religious institutions must be prepared to enter into a series of mutually beneficial "partnerships" if they are going to realize their full potential in the process of building a better community that is stronger both materially and spiritually.

Mapping Community Assets to Discover Potential Partners for Local Religious Institutions

Now that we have identified at least some of the many resources that local religious institutions can offer to the process of community building, we must go on to examine the means by which neighborhood leaders can most effectively mobilize these resources and turn them into valuable assets for community building. This effort to "connect" local religious institutions with the process of community building involves the utilization of a specific four-step process.

❦ First, make a thorough inventory of the specific resources of each local religious institution.

❦ Next, compile an inventory of the key assets and resources of the community as these are represented by local individuals, associations, organizations, and other institutions. When this has been done, it will be discovered that these community assets fall into the following categories: (a) citizens associations and not-for-profit organizations of all types; (b) publicly funded institutions such as hospitals, parks, libraries, and schools; (c) the private sector including small businesses, banks and local branches of larger corporations; (d) local residents and special interest groups of "labelled people" such as "seniors," "youth," "welfare recipients," and "artists."

❦ Then, use the information that has been obtained from these inventories to build strong, concrete, mutually beneficial "partnerships" between local religious institutions and the individuals, organizations and associations that exist within the community.

❦ Finally, on the basis of these partnerships and the active participation of local religious institutions in the community building process, go on to build new relationships with resources that exist outside the immediate community.

Chart One illustrates the relationships that can exist between a local religious institution and the potential partners that can be found within the community in each of these four specific categories that have just been mentioned.

Building Productive Relationships Between Local Religious Institutions and the Community

When the true assets of both the local religious institution and the community within which that religious institution is located have been properly mapped and identified, then religious leaders can begin to work together with other community leaders to develop a series of new partnerships that will connect the local religious institution with the on-going process of building a stronger, more fully integrated community.

Chart One: Potential Partners

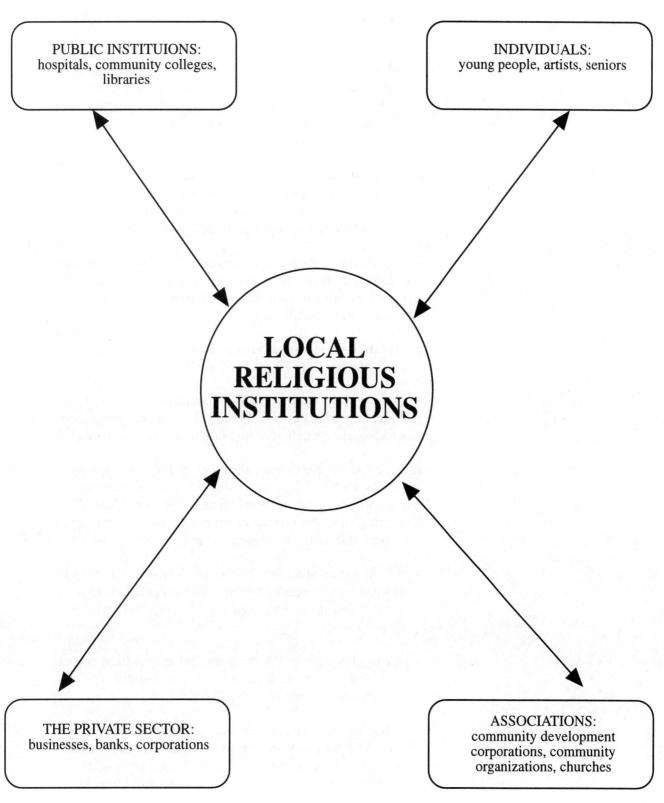

Let us note just a few examples of this process in action as it has occurred in a variety of communities:

Local Religious Institutions and Community Associations

Citizens Associations

❧ Several local block clubs now meet at a church on the south side of Chicago where the congregation works with them to inculcate family values into the community. This church is working toward hosting all of the block clubs in the neighborhood in order to create a greater sense of community. (Zion)

❧ A Catholic parish is a member of a local and national network of groups that addresses the problem of tobacco and alcohol billboard advertising targeted toward low-income communities. (St. Sabina)

❧ A minister's alliance works together to address issues of concern to the local community such as local hiring practices, appropriate merchandise for sale in the community, etc. (Zion)

❧ A church shares its photocopy machine with several local non-profit organizations. (UCRP)

❧ A community center creates a relationship with a local church in order to enable members of its congregation to advocate on behalf of individuals in crisis situations.

❧ A Catholic congregation allows neighborhood groups to use its main hall for fundraising events. This church occasionally receives user fees and gets more deeply connected to the community through the wide variety of groups now using the space. (Pius V)

❧ A staff person at a Catholic church develops a directory of local human service facilities and organizations for general distribution throughout the entire community. (Pius V)

❧ A church's community development corporation works with seven community groups in a community development credit union. (Bethel)

❧ A Baptist congregation establishes a partnership with a local YWCA in order to create a day care center which this church sees as an opportunity for ministry and greater contact with the community. (North Shore)

❧ A parish grants the local YMCA the use of its parking lot and basement for a special summer program. In exchange for this, the youth of this congregation are permitted to use the facilities of the YMCA after school. (Pius V)

Other Religious Institutions

❧ A cluster of Catholic congregations develops a community organization in order to address the issues of local policing, youth programs, adequate city services, and public housing. (Pius V)

❧ Several Lutheran churches combine resources to begin an inner-city volunteer corps program which is staffed by an executive director and which receives local volunteers to work with neighborhood non-profit organizations. (First)

❧ A coalition of neighborhood congregations develops a housing corporation to build a 130-unit complex with an emphasis on creating intentional community space. (Fourth)

❧ Six local congregations work together to provide a community meal on separate days during the week. (Fourth)

❧ A network of local churches coordinate several shelter programs targeting different ethnic populations. The shelters and churches make referrals back and forth to each other in order to make the most efficient use of their combined resources. (Uptown)

❧ An interfaith coalition of churches responds to the planned building of a stadium by garnering enough community support and activism to shake some major concessions for the neighborhood from the developers. These concessions include guaranteed replacement housing, a major grant from the city for local development, a new public library, and access to parking. (First Baptist)

❧ A coalition of local churches provides sanctuary for refugees from Central America. (UCRP)

❧ A local church allows other congregations without their own worshiping space to utilize its own sanctuary. These "guest" congregations in turn pay modest fees which help the host church to pay its utility bills. The host church's participation in the community is enriched through the presence of numerous different ethnic groups now using its facilities. (North Shore)

Cultural Organizations

❦ A local congregation creates a partnership with a non-profit immigrant's support program and the local immigration service in which this church provides a non-threatening atmosphere for recent immigrants while gaining greater contact with the various ethnic groups in the community. (Uptown)

❦ An African-American congregation establishes a support relationship with African nations by signing and supporting a document which outlines productive policy measures toward these nations. This church builds on its relationship with African churches to imbue its members with a sense of their African heritage. (Trinity)

❦ A congregation establishes links with several development and relief agencies in Nicaragua in order to raise the consciousness of its members about the poverty and social conditions in Central America. (Fourth)

Local Religious Institutions and Public Institutions

Parks

❦ Churches can provide not only space for religious activities but also take part in events sponsored by the local park that are important to all members of the community. (Fuller)

❦ A local park honors teens who earned first and second place in the Park District Junior Citizen Competition by taking them on a trip to the University of Illinois at Champaign/Urbana. This trip is paid for by donations from local churches. (Foster)

Libraries

❦ In order to make better contact with the Hispanic residents of the neighborhood, a librarian attends the local Catholic Church and sets up a table outside the church where information about the library is distributed. (Albany Park)

❧ The local pastor asks the community librarian to recommend performers for church programs. (Austin)

Community Colleges

❧ A parishioner teaching English As a Second Language classes at a community college recommends that these classes be transferred to a local church where these classes will be much more accessible to members of the community. (North Shore)

❧ A community college holds some of its GED classes at a local Catholic church. (Pius V)

Schools

❧ The Urban League connects churches with schools through an "adopt-a-school" program in which churches provide tutoring for neighborhood school children. As a result, the church gains an opportunity to become better connected to its neighborhood. (Chicago Urban League)

❧ A church forms a relationship with a local school through students who are allowed to use the church's youth center. (St. Sabina)

Law Enforcement System

❧ A local church starts a construction company in order to bring affordable housing to the community. Because this church cannot afford to pay standard wages, it forms a partnership with the local prison in which prisoners are released each day to a local community college, and they get college credit for their construction work. (Christian)

Hospitals

❧ A parish in Chicago develops a partnership with a local hospital through which three staff persons are hired by the church (funded by the hospital) to organize the community around health care issues and develop health-related programming. (Pius V)

❧ Two neighborhood churches share a community nurse who spends twenty hours per week at one church and another twenty hours at the other. One of these churches houses a shelter and the other a senior citizens program. (Lakeview)

Local Religious Institutions and the Private Sector

❧ A Catholic parish provides space for the meetings of a local business association. Then this relationship goes a step further when the church advocates for fair hiring practices in the community and the establishment of a local code of business ethics. (St. Sabina)

❧ A pastor establishes a relationship with a local business association that wants to provide scholarships for neighborhood youth. The reason that this happened is that this pastor is so well-connected with the community that he is the one who can best provide the association with the information that they need. (Uptown)

❧ A large church publishes a monthly newspaper and actively solicits local minority businesses to advertise in this publication. In this way the church supports the local economy and the businesses get lower rate advertising to reach a wide audience. (Trinity)

❧ A congregation contracts with city agencies and local businesses to provide labor support through its Manpower program. (Christian)

❧ A congregation always hires out to local contractors when construction or repair projects are undertaken. (UCRP)

Local Religious Institutions and Individuals Within the Community

Local Residents

❧ A Chicago church houses a 24-hour "hotline" service in which this church promotes training events in the community. (UCRP)

❧ Several churches are developing relationships with Habitat for Humanity in which they assist in the construction of affordable housing for their communities. (Fourth, Uptown)

❧ A church is at the center of a coalition of local groups and organizations which establish a commemoration of the 20th anniversary of Black Panther leader Fred Hampton's assassination. (UCRP)

People with Disabilities

❧ Seniors are involved in the Visiting Important Persons program sponsored by a local church in which they visit less mobile elderly and try to assist with any practical problems. Seniors are trained to be able to provide CPR, to recognize drug abuse, to give bed baths and first aid, and to help with practical daily matters like budgeting and food selection and preparation. The oldest participant is an 82 year old woman. (Little Brother's)

❧ A local church welcomes a developmentally disabled older woman to become a regular member of its congregation, and now participation in Sunday services and church activities have become an important part of her life. (Logan Square)

Welfare Recipients

❧ A congregation establishes a three-way partnership with a homeless advocacy group and a shelter provider to build an adjunct emergency overnight shelter for homeless men. This project is funded largely by the church, and church members are given an opportunity to volunteer in fulfillment of the church's vision of social justice. (Fourth)

❧ A women's group at a local church develops a partnership with a neighborhood shelter in which these women provide volunteer support. (Trinity)

❧ A community development corporation created from a neighborhood church works with another congregation to turn its rectory into transitional housing for twenty families. The parish leases their old rectory to the community development corporation for one dollar per year. (Bethel)

❧ An alliance of local congregations works with the Chicago Housing Authority to rehab vacant apartments in the public housing complex in the neighborhood. (Fourth)

Youth

❧ A church invites a children's nursery school to become a tenant in its building. This newly expanded children's program helps the church to meet its bills and provides an opportunity for leadership by placing church members on the school's board. (UCRP)

❧ A church serves a hot lunch to children at the school that is located across the street. In return, the school allows church members to use its parking lot. (First)

❧ A youth service organization helps a church to establish a youth program at the church. (UCRP)

❧ A local pastor who is also an accomplished artist establishes a relationship with the service organization of a local high school in which the school gains from the murals and art projects that are created by students under the tutelage of the pastor. (Uptown)

Seniors

❧ High school students who are members of a local congregation establish an "adoption" program with seniors who are living in the affordable housing which was created by the church's development corporation. (Trinity)

❧ A congregation invites the city's Department on Aging to establish a senior nutrition site at the church. (North Shore)

Artists

❧ A group of local artists begin a program encouraging creative expression for youth through drama and music at a neighborhood church. As a result, the youth from the church and from the community put on a number of performances for the congregation and the community. (UCRP)

❧ A northside Chicago church allows a local theatre company to rehearse in its building in return for allowing the church's parishioners to attend its productions free of charge. (UCRP)

❧ A symphony orchestra is given free space at a local church for rehearsal, and in return members of the congregation enjoy the symphony during occasional worship services and are allowed to attend full performances free of charge. (North Shore)

In all of these stories we have seen how religious institutions which are active in the community building process have been able to enter into successful partnerships with local organizations, institutions (including other churches and synagogues) and/or groups of people with special interests. In partnerships like these, *both* partners in the relationship win, and when this happens, a strong incentive is created to build further on these relationships and establish new projects that will continue to enhance the strength and solidarity of the community.

Chart Two on page 157 shows how a local religious institution can become connected with actual partners existing within the community in which that particular religious institution is located.

Chart Three on page 158 represents the complex network of actual partnerships that might exist for a local religious institution that has fully developed itself as a dynamic community asset.

Building Bridges Between Local Religious Institutions and Resources Outside the Community

Having built solid "partnerships" within the immediate community, a local religious institution is now well-situated to act as a bridge-builder to outside resources. In many cases, these relationships to "outside" resources already exist and only need to be modified and refined in order for the community to achieve the maximum possible benefit from their utilization.

For example, although there is often a chasm that exists between city and suburb and between suburb and rural areas, churches can be at the very forefront of bridging these chasms because churches have ready-made partners from their own denominations in each of these areas. Thus many inner-city congregations have established links or partnerships with suburban parishes and have even gone on to create more broadly-based coalition efforts with religious institutions from surrounding communities. These efforts serve to funnel new resources into the community and serve to focus the utilization of these re- sources in the most effective manner:

  ❦ A CDC organized by a neighborhood church works with individuals from outside the community who can provide specialized expertise. One of these working relationships utilizes the skills and experience of a suburban home builder who knows how to construct energy-efficient homes. (Bethel)

  ❦ A consortium of congregations, both city and suburban, establishes a pool of financial resources in order to enable the poorer congregations within the coalition to take out no-interest loans for renovation or enhanced space utilization projects. (North Carolina)

Beyond a church's "religious" connections, it can also attract public and private philanthropic support. For example, many churches have been able to leverage public funds for the development of affordable housing. A few churches have even incorporated their own foundations to support community outreach programs.

Chart Two: Strengthening Partnerships

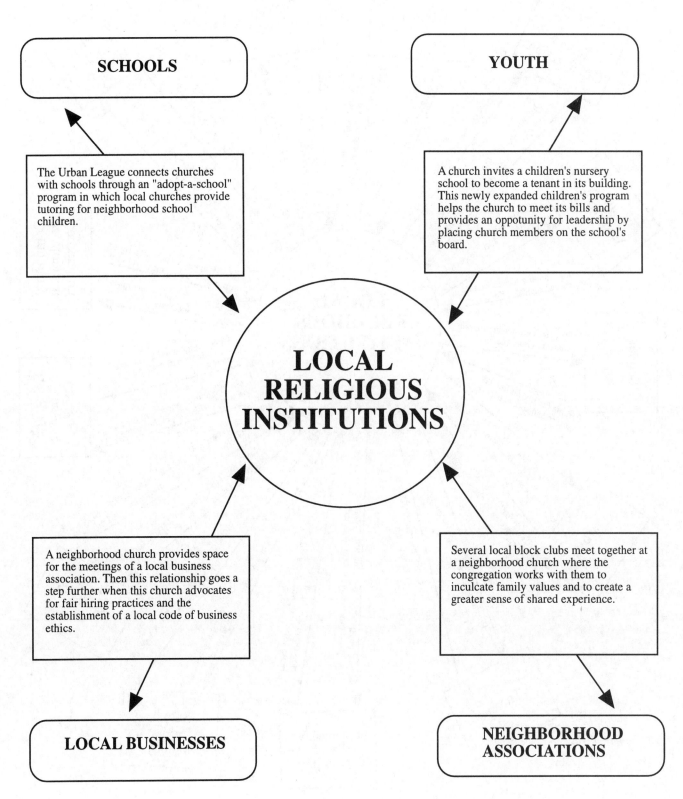

SCHOOLS

The Urban League connects churches with schools through an "adopt-a-school" program in which local churches provide tutoring for neighborhood school children.

YOUTH

A church invites a children's nursery school to become a tenant in its building. This newly expanded children's program helps the church to meet its bills and provides an oppotunity for leadership by placing church members on the school's board.

LOCAL RELIGIOUS INSTITUTIONS

A neighborhood church provides space for the meetings of a local business association. Then this relationship goes a step further when this church advocates for fair hiring practices and the establishment of a local code of business ethics.

Several local block clubs meet together at a neighborhood church where the congregation works with them to inculcate family values and to create a greater sense of shared experience.

LOCAL BUSINESSES

NEIGHBORHOOD ASSOCIATIONS

Chart Three: One on One Relationships

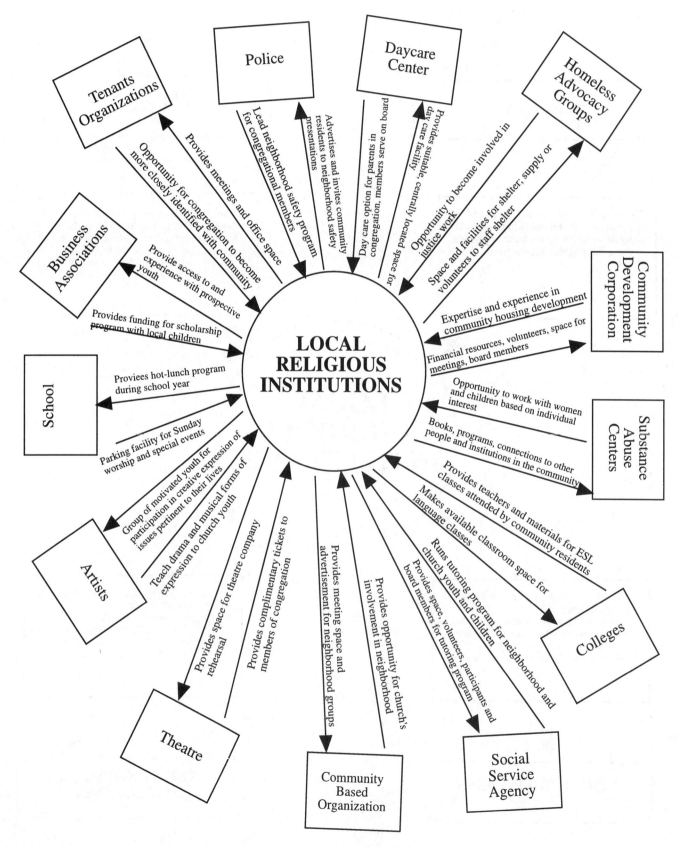

Sources and Contacts for the "Stories" in This Section

Albany Park   Albany Park Library
5150 N. Kimball Avenue
Chicago, IL
(312) 744-1933 (Chahee Stanfield,
Branch Head)

Austin   Austin Library
2121 W. 95th Street
Chicago, IL 60644
(312) 746-5038 (Donna Kanapes, Branch Head)

Bethel   Bethel New Life, Inc.
367 N. Karlov
Chicago, IL 60624
(312) 826-5540 (Mary Nelson, President)

Christian   Christian Family Center Church
1800 W. Bradley Avenue
Peoria, IL 60606
(309) 673-2600 (Rev. Tony E. Pierce)

First Baptist   First Baptist Congregational
1613 W. Washington Blvd.
Chicago, IL
(312) 243-8047 (Rev. Arthur Griffin)

Foster   Foster Park Church of Christ
12814 S. Lowe
Chicago, IL
(312) 821-5797

Fourth   Fourth Presbyterian
126 E. Chestnut
Chicago, IL
(312) 787-4570 (Rev. Ted Miller)

Fuller   Fuller Park
331 W. 45th Street
Chicago, IL
(312) 268-0062 (Fred Toler)

Lakeview   Lakeview Presbyterian
716 W. Addison Street
Chicago, IL
(312) 281-2655 (Rev. John Scott)

Little Brother's — Little Brother's Friends of the Elderly
1658 W. Belmont
Chicago, IL
(312) 477-7702 (Jamie Hirsch)

Logan Square — Logan Square Neighborhood Association
3321 W. Wrightwood
Chicago, IL 60647
(312) 384-4370 (Rosita De La Rosa)

Mars Hill — Mars Hill Missionary Baptist
5916 W. Lake Street
Chicago, IL 60644
(312) 287-3535 (Rev. Clarence Stowers)

North Shore — North Shore Baptist
5244 N. Lakewood
Chicago, IL
(312) 728-4200 (Pastor Marcus Pomeroy)

Pius V — St. Pius V Church
1919 S. Ashland
Chicago, IL 60608
(312) 226-6161

St. Sabina — St. Sabina Church
1210 W. 78th Place
Chicago, IL
(312) 483-4300 (Rev. Michael Pfleger)

Trinity — Trinity United Church of Christ
532 West 95th
Chicago, IL 60628
(312) 962-5650 (Rev. Jeremiah Wright)

UCRP — United Church of Rogers Park
Ashland & Morse Avenues
Chicago, IL 60626

Uptown — Uptown Baptist Church
1011 W. Wilson
Chicago, IL
(312) 784-2922 (Pastor Brian Bakke)

Zion — Zion Hill Missionary Baptist Church
1460 W. 78th Street
Chicago, IL 60620
(312) 651-2622 (Rev. George Waddles)

Introduction—Cultural Organizations and Community Renewal

People in communities have always come together to celebrate, to sing and dance and play music, to tell each other stories, to produce and share things of beauty. All of this activity is sometimes called "culture," and it is the glue which holds people together and helps to form strong communities.

Every community has people who "produce" culture, who paint, write, sing, tell stories, make jewelry and pottery and quilts. As individual artists and craftspeople, these residents represent invaluable contributors to community building, as this guide noted in Chapter One. When these creative energies come together in local organizations, they belong squarely at the center of the community development process.

What do we mean by "local cultural organizations?" Certainly those institutions which are more professional, formal and visible are important parts of the local cultural landscape—community theaters, galleries, museums, musical groups. But equally important are those less formal, more amateur groupings which local people create together—the range of musical groups from large church choirs to street-corner rappers, from Gospel singers to occasional jazz, blues and rock bands, to ethnic heritage musicians playing everything from mariachi to polkas. And they include the groups which come together as neighbors or church members to dance the old dances, sing the old songs, produce beautiful crafts in the old ways. And they also encompass all of the special projects and events which are organized to introduce younger people to their ethnic and community roots, and which pass along a love of beauty to the next generation.

Rediscovering Cultural Organizations as Assets Within the Community

Community builders in every neighborhood have a range of cultural assets with which to work. Finding the more formal groups will not be difficult; locating the informal and occasional musical, dance, theatrical, story-telling, or crafts groups might take more persistence.

The larger and more formal groups may well have significant material assets to contribute to the community building process. For example, local theater groups or larger church-related musical groups might have:

Space and Facilities. Often the theater, auditorium or rehearsal space can become a focus not only for the activities of the groups which own it or control its uses, but for less formal and occasional programs involving young people, older folks, or groups which would not normally have access to it.

Materials and Equipment. Larger cultural organizations often have a wide range of valuable materials which can be made available for wider community use. For example, community groups and school children use paints and brushes, clay and other potting equipment, costumes, instruments and sheet music—all made publicly accessible by local cultural organizations.

People. Obviously it is the local residents who produce culture themselves who represent the most valuable community building resource. Too often, particularly in lower income communities, those who make part or all of their living by producing art are not asked to contribute their skills and vision within their own neighborhood. When given opportunities to read, perform, direct, play and teach with their neighbors, many artists have done so with great enthusiasm, and have begun to develop new skills and to open up new possibilities among community people.

But beyond the more professional groups, community builders focus on those who produce "culture" simply because they love to do so. These are the local individuals and groups who are eager to teach what they do, to tell stories about the community's history to younger people, to add music and poetry and dance to local meetings. These are the people who can contribute the spirit and vision to the community building project.

Economic Power. Local cultural organizations may represent significant economic development potential. They may have resources with which they can purchase supplies locally, or hire local residents, or even spin off related businesses. In Chicago, for example, retail shops and tourism campaigns are being fashioned around local craftspeople, an ethnic heritage museum is sparking local redevelopment, and a community theater company has acted as a magnet for other arts-related businesses.

Mapping Community Assets to Discover Potential Partners for Cultural Organizations

Now that we have identified at least some of the assets that cultural organizations can bring to the process of community building, we go on to examine the means by which neighborhood leaders can most effectively mobilize these assets and turn them into valuable resources for community building. This effort to connect cultural organizations with the process of community-building involves a four-step process.

❧ First, make a thorough capacity inventory outlining all the various skills and assets for each of the cultural organizations which you can discover the community.

❧ Next, compile an inventory of the key assets and resources of the community as these are represented by local individuals, associations, organizations, and institutions. These community assets fall into the following categories: (a) citizens associations and not-for-profit organizations of all types; (b) publicly funded institutions such as hospitals, parks, libraries, and schools; (c) the private sector including small businesses, banks and local branches of larger corporations; (d) local residents and special interest groups of labelled people such as "seniors," "youth," "disabled people," and "artists."

❧ Then use the information obtained from these inventories to build strong, concrete, mutually beneficial partnerships between cultural organizations and the other individuals, organizations and associations that exist within the community.

❧ Finally, on the basis of these partnerships and the active participation of cultural organizations in the community-building process, go on to build new relationships with resources that exist outside the immediate community.

Chart One on the next page illustrates the relationships that can exist between cultural organizations and their community partners.

Building Productive Relationships Between Local Cultural Organizations and the Community

When the assets of both the local cultural organizations and the community within which these cultural organizations are located have been identified, then the leaders of these cultural organizations can begin to work together with other community leaders to develop a series of new partnerships. Let us now note a few examples of this process as it has occurred in a variety of communities.

Local Cultural Organizations and Public Institutions

Parks

❧ A group of seniors that forms the East Side Historical Society works with a local high school in space provided by the park system, to develop a museum which documents the history of four Chicago neighborhoods. (East Side)

Chart One: Potential Partners

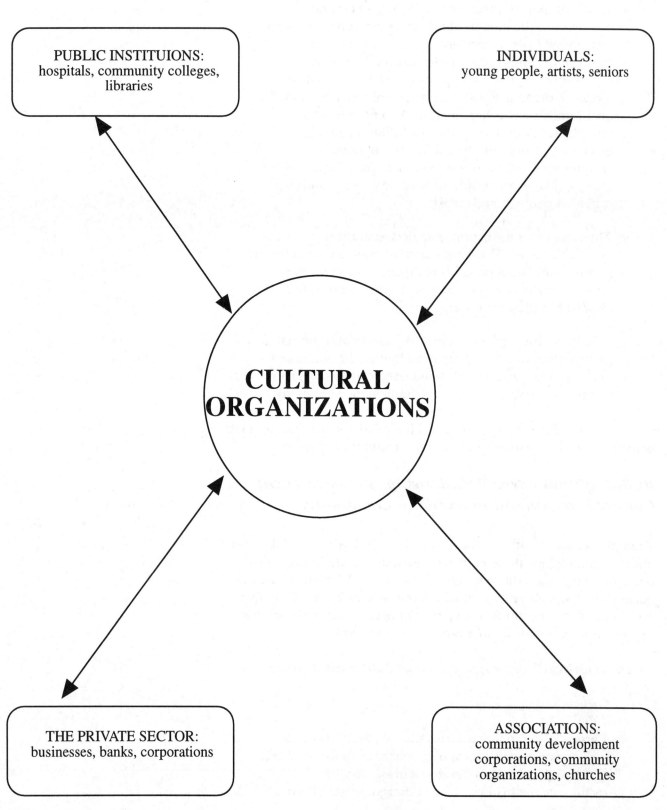

❦ A community art gallery had more works of art than it could display, and in the neighborhood park one of the buildings had a large unoccupied room. The park agreed to let the gallery use this spare room for additional display space. Now the park has a cultural display area which is available to the public. Some people now visit the park to see this display who might otherwise have never had a reason to use the local park. At the same time, the art gallery gets more display space, and the local artists get broader and longer lasting exposure for their work. (Beverly)

❦ Because a local art museum did not charge admission on Tuesday, an art teacher at a park district decided to offer an art class on Tuesday in the museum. As a result, park students are now able to go through museum exhibits and obtain information that will encourage and strengthen their own art work. (Ekhert)

❦ A park worked out an arrangement with a local museum so that courses offered by the museum could be taught in park facilities when space was not available at the museum. As a result, the park has hosted classes on mask-making and applique quilting. In return the park has been given free xeroxing privileges at the museum. (Harrison)

Libraries

❦ A local historical society holds its meetings and houses all of its records at a local library. In collaboration with a local theater company, the historical society sponsored a Shakesperean play at the library. (Rogers Park)

❦ A representative from a nationally known museum visits a neighborhood library bringing a series of "experience boxes," collections of materials which invite hands-on involvement on the part of children, and now the local librarian presents similar programs on an ongoing basis for the children of the neighborhood. (Marshall Square)

❦ A library and a local community college work together to organize booths and programs for a Korean Cultural Day in which traditional Korean storytelling, singing and dancing, as well as discussions of current social issues, are included. (Albany Park)

Community Colleges

❦ A community college hires a neighborhood artist to lead an art tour of the community in which the students visit various art museums as well as the studios of local artists. (Long Island)

Schools

❦ The Hispanic Club at an urban high school brings a sense of the importance of Latino culture to the community by hosting a Latino Cultural Week and organizing a food festival. (Boston)

Police

❦ Local police create a hotline focussing on breakins and theft, and this hotline is publicized by a local African-American broadcasting coalition. (Youngstown/NNFPC)

Hospitals

❦ A local hospital sponsors a Chinese health fair in which local volunteers provide translations of relevant information, doctors donate prizes, and students from a local school perform. (Arcadia)

Local Cultural Organizations and Individuals Within the Community

❦ A group of seniors presents skits, songs, historical presentations and cooks southern-style food at local churches, synagogues and senior centers during Black History Month. (Lincoln Park)

❦ An 85-year-old Mexican-American woman teaches a six-week traditional art and pottery course to other senior citizens at the Mexican Fine Arts Museum. (Mexican)

❦ Seniors from the community help on the Day of La Posadas during which children go from house to house asking for shelter (as did Mary and Joseph in the Bible). (Pilsen)

❦ A group of seniors active in the Vietnam Association of Illinois organize an annual celebration in honor of the founding father of Vietnam. (Vietnam)

❦ Elderly people from the Vietnamese community in a Chicago neighborhood contribute poetry to the Vietnamese Association's monthly publication. (Vietnam)

This very brief selection of stories illustrates how cultural organizations which are active in the community-building process have been able to enter into successful partnerships with other local organizations, institutions and/or groups of people with special interests. In partnerships like these, both partners in the relationship win, and when this happens, a strong incentive is created to build further on these relationships and establish new projects that will continue to enhance the community.

Chart Two on page 168 shows how local cultural organizations can become connected with actual community partners.

Chart Two: Strengthening Partnerships

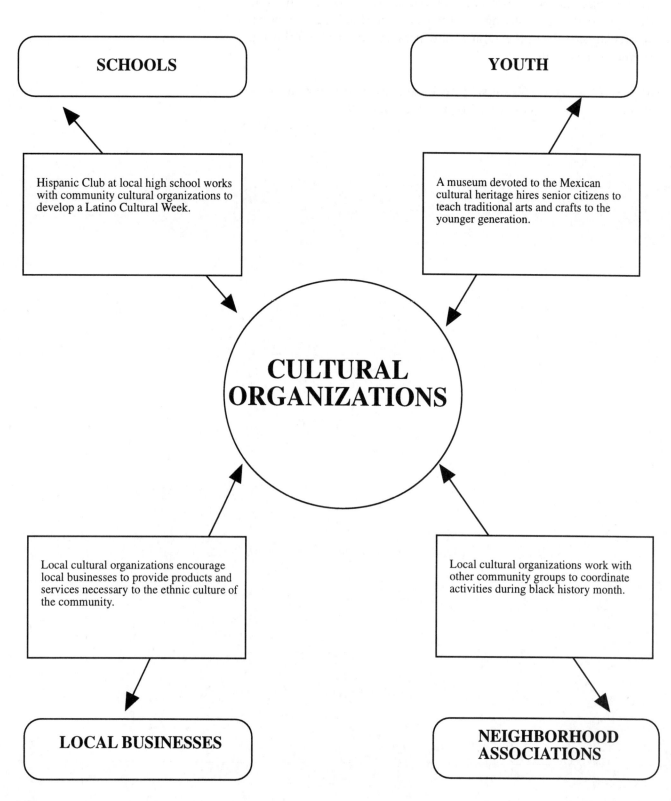

Sources and Contacts for the Stories in This Section

Albany   Albany Park Library
5150 N. Kimball Avenue
Chicago, IL 60625
(312) 744-1933 (Chahee Stanfield,
Branch Head)

Arcadia   Arcadia Methodist Hospital
300 Huntington Drive
Arcadia, CA 91007
(818) 445-4441 (Nancy Baillie, Director of
Volunteer Services)

Beverly   Beverly Park
2460 W. 102nd Street
Chicago, IL

Boston   Boston Technical High School
55 New Dudley Street
Roxbury, MA 02120
(617) 445-4381 (Yolanda Pinto)

East Side   East Side Historical Society
10833 Avenue D
Chicago, IL 60617
(312) 221-7349 (Frank Stanley)

Ekhert   Ekhert Park
1330 W. Chicago Avenue
Chicago, IL
(312) 294-4710 (Mickey Maher)

Harrison   Harrison Park
1824 S. Wood
Chicago, IL
(312) 294-4714

Lincoln Park   Lincoln Park Senior Center
2111 Halsted Street
Chicago, IL
(312) 543-6776 (Lorraine Myers)

Long Island   Long Island Community College
Long Island, NY

Marshall Square	Marshall Square Library 2724 W. Cermak Chicago, IL 60608 (312) 747-0061 (Julie Lockwood, Branch Head)
Mexican	Mexican Fine Arts Center Museum 1825 W. 19th Street Chicago, IL 60608 (312) 738-1503
Pilsen	Pilsen Resurrection Project 1641 S. Allport Chicago, IL 60608 (312) 226-7887
Rogers Park	Rogers Park Library 6907 N. Clark Street Chicago, IL 60626 (312) 744-0156 (Angie Spataro, Branch Head)
Vietnam	Vietnamese Association of Illinois 4842 N. Broadway Chicago, IL 60640 (312) 728-3700 (Qua Dran)
Youngstown/NNFFC	National Neighborhood Foot Patrol Center School of Criminal Justice Michigan State University 560 Baker Hall East Lansing, MI 48824-1118 (800) 892-9051)

CAPTURING LOCAL INSTITUTIONS
FOR COMMUNITY BUILDING

Along with the assets represented by its individual residents and its citizens associations, every community hosts some combination of more formal public, private and not-for-profit institutions. Since these institutions represent significant concentrations of resources, local neighborhoods have begun to capture them for community-building purposes. In turn, creative leaders of these institutions have begun to realize their own stake in the well-being of their local community, and their own, often unused capacity to contribute to the social, physical, and economic health of their neighborhood.

The number, size and nature of institutions present will obviously vary from neighborhood to neighborhood. Some local communities are "institution rich," while others are not. But even the most devastated community is the site of at least some business activity, along with a combination of public and nonprofit institutions such as schools, parks, libraries, police stations, social service agencies, community colleges, and hospitals.

Since an important step in the development process involves the identification of all of the neighborhood's assets, a complete inventory of local institutions will provide vital information. Though the institutions themselves will not be difficult to locate and list, an inventory which is to prove useful for community-building purposes will usually contain more than a barebones identification. This is because local institutions, especially larger ones, are complex and multidimensional. In order to accomplish their purposes, they bring together people with different skills, buildings, equipment, budgets, relationships with other institutions, etc. Institutions, then, are themselves collections of assets. And different parts of each institution's unique "asset collection" might prove useful for particular community-building purposes.

For example, neighborhood leaders who were working to involve a local school in the community-building process began by listing all of the assets that the school represented. Their list included:

- *Facilities.* Schools are places where community groups can meet. They also can serve as places that "incubate" community activities—from small businesses to neighborhood festivals to social service programs.

- *Materials and Equipment.* The computer, communication and duplicating equipment in schools can be used in support of, or shared with, community groups. Similarly, the books and library can be used by local people as a resource.

- *Purchasing Power.* The materials, commodities, and services purchased by schools can be directed to initiate, support, or expand neighborhood enterprises, including those created by young people.

❧ *Employment Practices.* As a major employer in most neighborhoods and towns, the school's hiring practices can focus upon local residents.

❧ *Courses.* Through existing classes or newly created evening courses, schools can provide education and training for residents or groups that seek to participate in the area's development efforts.

❧ *Teachers.* In every neighborhood the teachers are a concentrated pool of highly trained and specialized adults with critical skills and essential knowledge that they can contribute to the efforts of local groups involved in development activities.

❧ *Financial Capacity.* Schools have the power to generate and receive special funds through bond issues and proposals to government agencies, corporations, and foundations not usually accessible to community groups. This special capacity can be an important resource in a community development strategy.

❧ *Young People.* The students with ideas, energy and idealism can become important actors through classes and internships in the local community development process.

(NOTE: See section on "Schools," and "A Primer for a School's Participation in the Development of Its Local Community" (Center for Urban Affairs and Policy Research, Northwestern University, $1) for more ideas about a local school's role in the community-building process.)

In this case, then, an institutional inventory included a detailed listing of many of the institution's internal assets, since creative neighborhood and school leaders recognized that the school could help build the community in a variety of ways. Similar internal asset inventories can provide the starting point for community-building projects involving parks, libraries, social service agencies, police and fire stations, hospitals, community colleges, even local businesses.

Capturing Local Institutions for Community Building

Though every neighborhood has at least some institutions that are physically present, many are frustrated by these institutions' lack of connection to local community-building agendas. Unlike local residents and citizens associations, which are clearly responsive to local conditions, challenges and plans, the local institutions are often directed and controlled by forces and relationships outside the neighborhood. In larger cities especially, leaders of the local school, park, library, and police station answer first to the larger systems of which they are a part, not to local residents. Furthermore, those institutions that employ professional staff owe loyalty to their organized professions before their local neighborhood. And finally, many local institutions find their employees outside the immediate area.

For all of these reasons, the first challenge facing neighborhood leaders is to capture these local institutions for community development purposes. In some instances, this process has involved simply building or rebuilding relationships between local community residents and their associations on the one hand, and local institutions on the other. Both resident leaders and the professionals in charge of local institutions understand their mutual interest in a healthy community, and find that building cooperative relationships can benefit everyone. The result can be a park which hosts a wide range of activities initiated by clubs and churches and youth groups and schools, and which benefits as members of those groups contribute time, energy and ideas to the park's programming. Or the relationship building might produce a library which functions not only as the neighborhood information center but as the hub around which community discussion and planning happens. In case after case, as the following sections will reveal, local residents have joined with institutional leaders to explore and create powerful new partnerships for community-building.

But in other cases, reestablishing the links between local residents and institutions that are physically present in the neighborhoods has proved more difficult. Big city bureaucracies of the kind that dominate schools, parks, police and fire departments, community colleges and some social service outlets, for example, are seldom responsive to neighborhood generated agendas. Thus it is significant when local citizens can assemble the political power necessary to reroot these institutions in their neighborhood. Chicago's school reform thrust, which lodges considerable authority in a parent and community-based Local School Council, provides one example of the reassertion of local responsibility for a significant neighborhood institution. Once community interests assume some measure of responsibility for the well-being of the institution, that institution, in turn, becomes accountable in new ways to those same community interests. Successful schools and healthy neighborhoods become two sides of the same coin, as leaders recognize the ways in which each contributes to the other.

Once an institution such as a local school has become at least partly accountable to neighborhood leadership, many opportunities for new relationships between the school and its surroundings begin to emerge. The section on schools will provide examples of the growing number of ways in which local schools are becoming the center of a web of relationships which can drive the community-building process. Similar possibilities open up for other branch institutions such as parks, libraries, etc., once the local community has established its right to regard those organizations as an integral part of the neighborhood, and has established some ways to hold them accountable.

The following sections introduce somewhat more thoroughly the ways in which six very different local institutions can be rediscovered and mobilized as community-building assets. In each instance, the suggested path involves four common-sense steps:

❧ Rediscovering the local institution as an asset within the community. This initial step involves both the establishment of local accountability and the process of developing an inventory of the collected assets that make up the institution.

❧ Mapping the community assets that are potential partners for the institution in its community-building task. These include individuals and citizens associations, as well as other public, private and nonprofit institutions within the community.

❧ Building productive relationships between the institutions and a wide range of other community groups and individuals. This concrete, mutually beneficial relationship building lies at the center of the asset-based development process.

❧ Building bridges between local institutions and resources outside the community. This final challenge takes advantage of the local institution's links with larger systems, and its potential as a magnet for financial and other resources.

Though each institution contributes its own unique set of assets to the community-building task, these simple steps appear to be common elements of successful participation in the asset-based development process. The sections that follow should be read simply as introductions to the possibilities, not as exhaustive and authoritative summaries of the one true way.

Introduction—Parks and Community Renewal

The local park is a rich neighborhood treasure which can be a powerful tool for rebuilding the community. In many cultures, the park has been the center of community life, the common space in which people find each other and build their lives together.

Working with park officials, creative neighborhood leaders are discovering a wide variety of ways to strengthen the community-building power of the park by connecting it to individuals, associations and institutions throughout the entire community, and by rebuilding vital relationships around this unique asset.

Here are a few examples of local energies released by an imaginative use of the resources of the local park:

ꙮ Parks mobilize young people into Advisory Councils which, for example, plan fundraisers and manage a bank account for youth activities, publish a neighborhood newsletter, design and plant gardens, and organize themselves as mentors and teachers for younger children from the community.

ꙮ Parks provide leadership and space for community-wide projects and events. They host, for example, local music and arts festivals, "international dinners" which reflect the ethnic diversity of the community, home-improvement and neighborhood history fairs, and even a "community circus."

ꙮ Parks build strong working relationships with other local groups and institutions in the community. Schools and churches are natural partners, but a wider range of allies might also include, for instance, art galleries, restaurants, bakeries, police and fire departments, local businesses, community development corporations, and local social service agencies.

But just how do community leaders discover the best ways to release the potential community-building power of the local park? In its simplest terms, this process involves four steps.

ꙮ Leaders begin by making an inventory of all of the elements that combine to make up the asset we call a "park."

ꙮ Then community builders construct a similar inventory of the associations and institutions that make up the specific assets of the community.

❧ Next, the program of community-building begins to take concrete shape as strong reciprocal relationships are continuing to be built between the assets of the park and those that are unique to the community itself.

❧ Finally, as a result of these strong interconnections, the park's community-building power is further enhanced as bridges are constructed to additional resources that exist outside the community.

Rediscovering Parks as Assets Within the Community

When we say that a local park represents "a rich community asset," what exactly do we mean? It is clear that parks come in all shapes and sizes, from tiny packets of green to multiacred expanses with full facilities. So it is very important to begin with a thorough inventory of each particular park's unique resources. Such a resource inventory might uncover a list of assets such as these.

Personnel. A park represents a concentrated pool of skilled and trained adults. These are people who can teach, work well with children (and therefore with everyone else as well), and may also have certain particular skills in art, music and/or athletics.

Space and Facilities. Inside the walls of a park are spaces of all kinds: large and small meeting rooms, auditoriums with stages, gyms, art studios, glass display cases, and kitchens. Parks often also have basketball courts, sandboxes, open space, playgrounds, drinking fountains and decorative/playing fountains, baseball diamonds, duck ponds, and various kinds of gardens. In many cases the architecture of the park buildings and even blank exterior walls represent potential opportunities for further community development.

Materials and Equipment. In most parks a wide range of sports equipment is available for community use. Art and woodcraft materials and equipment are also commonly available. Even music equipment ranging from pianos to sheet music is often found and can be used by interested members of the community.

Expertise. Most parks offer classes for all ages of people at all kinds of levels in many fields including (but not limited to) the arts, woodcraft, athletics, and even music and drama.

Economic Power. Parks often have budgets with certain built-in flexibilities. Parks also have the ability to sponsor various fundraising activities on behalf of the community in which they are located. In addition, parks frequently are able to hire local residents on a full- or part-time basis.

Mapping Community Assets as Potential Partners for Parks

A wide array of people and groups can be found at the community end of potential park/community partnerships. As parks begin to act as powerful community-builders, they should always start by making a thorough inventory of the specific assets of the community in which they are located. In all communities these assets include:

- ❧ Citizens associations and not-for-profit organizations of many various kinds.

- ❧ Publicly funded institutions such as schools, libraries, or the police and fire departments.

- ❧ The private sector which ranges from small businesses to banks and larger corporations.

- ❧ Individuals and groups of people, such as youth, seniors, artists, and others with special interests and abilities.

Chart One on the next page shows the relationship of a park with the potential partners that exist within the community in which the park is located.

Building Productive Relationships Between Parks and the Community

Having identified both the resources of the park itself and the assets of the surrounding community, the community-building agenda turns next to the challenge of building new relationships and strengthening old ones. In every instance, the most vital and powerful parks are those that have formed strong, concrete partnerships with the widest range of individuals, associations and institutions in the neighborhood. Specific connections to schools and churches are a natural place for this process to start, but in many communities the local parks are learning to cooperate with a much wider range of partners:

Parks and Community Associations

Citizens Associations

- ❧ A neighborhood park annually holds a "Back to School" community parade during the last week of August. People from the local Post Office, the Department of Human Services, and the Police Department all march in this parade as well as Boy Scout troops, principals, teachers and hordes of kids. This is a full-scale parade

Chart One: Potential Partners

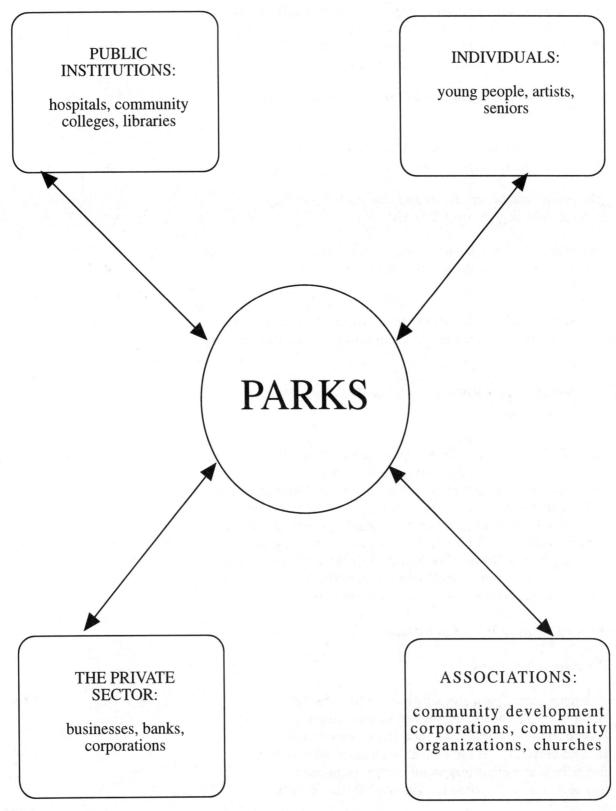

PUBLIC INSTITUTIONS:

hospitals, community colleges, libraries

INDIVIDUALS:

young people, artists, seniors

PARKS

THE PRIVATE SECTOR:

businesses, banks, corporations

ASSOCIATIONS:

community development corporations, community organizations, churches

with floats and lots of community participation at various levels. After the parade, everybody goes to the park for a splash party. (Ogden)

❧ When the boiler system breaks down, this park gets quite cold, and the pool becomes unusable. But this park has an extremely active and competitive swimming team and so it made an arrangement with a local Boys and Girls Club to use its pool when the boiler is not functioning properly at the park. In return for this service, the Boys and Girls Club is able to use outdoor space provided by the park for its summer activities. (Harrison)

❧ Recognizing that a nearby seniors' program was in need of more space, a local park decided to offer a good-sized room to this group for as long as they needed it. This park already had a senior program of its own, but since it had plenty of space to spare, it felt it could also host a senior program that was not its own. (Columbus)

❧ Residents living near a park were very interested in getting other residents actively involved in starting a neighborhood watch program. They went to a community organization specializing in organizing around local issues and got professional advice on expanding their ranks. Now they have a successful, park-centered neighborhood watch program and also an ongoing relationship with an important local community organization. (Galewood)

❧ This same group decided they wanted to use the facilities of the park in order to offer young people alternatives to drug use and trafficking. In order to accomplish this, they had discussions with a local social service agency. As a result, both the park and the agency formed a partnership in which the park offered recreation to the young people and the agency provided education and leadership training. (Galewood)

❧ Another park loaned its outdoor space to a neighborhood settlement house for a day so the settlement house could give a health fair. By doing this, the park got patrons from the settlement house to see its facilities, and the settlement house got parkgoers involved who might otherwise not have attended a "fair" where they were able to obtain free testing and important health-related information. (Ekhert)

Religious and Cultural Institutions

❧ A local park honors teens who earned first and second place in the Park District Junior Citizen Competition by taking them on a trip to the University of Illinois at Champaign/Urbana. This trip is paid for by donations from local churches. (Foster)

Cultural Organizations

❧ Most museums are free on Tuesdays—so an art teacher at one park district decided to offer an art class that would meet in one of the community's art museums every Tuesday. As a result, students are now able to go through exhibits and obtain information that will encourage and strengthen their own art work. (Ekhert)

❧ Another park worked out an arrangement with a local museum so that courses offered by the museum could be taught in park facilities when space was not available at the museum. As a result, the park has hosted classes on mask-making and applique quilting, and in return the park has been given free xeroxing privileges at the museum. (Harrison)

Parks and Public Institutions

Libraries

❧ A librarian arranges with the local police department for them to provide transportation for a group of senior citizens from the library to a local park where the seniors like to have summer picnics. (Stateway Gardens)

Schools

❧ Since many schools and day care centers do not have their own outdoor space, many of the parks in the community allow their outdoor space to be used on a regular basis for everything from nature walks to playtime and sports activities. (Wicker, Ogden, etc.)

❧ A public school which does not have adequate gym facilities works out an arrangement with a neighborhood park to use the park facilities before the park is open to the public. During these early hours, the school staff is responsible for the students and for the proper use and maintenance of the park facilities. (Ogden)

❧ Representatives of the local parks went to community PTA meetings in order to explain the programs they were currently offering to the community. As a result, young people from four neighborhood schools—three parochial and one public—turned out in large enough numbers to generate nine volleyball teams which now compete in park-sponsored competitions. (Graver, Fuller)

❧ A public school works out an arrangement to use the facilities of its local park for after-school tutoring in math. (Sheridan)

Community Colleges

❧ In a park in a largely Latino neighborhood, a nearby city college uses a park facility to offer its programs in English as a second language. After these classes have started, the park supervisor notices that the families who initially came to the park for classes now also are beginning to utilize the recreational programs that the park offers to the community. (Ekhert)

Police

❧ One park decided to inform the local police department that a number of volunteer coaching positions were open, and now they have many of the officers spending some of their free time coaching teams in a wide variety of sports activities. (Loyola)

❧ Many parks have discovered their local police departments can be very supportive of their efforts to make their parks safe and drug-free. Representatives from the local police station have attended community meetings initiated by the park staff to discuss these problems and have helped the community set up their own "neighborhood watch" program. (Galewood)

❧ A park invited representatives of the local post office and police department to use its gym with the result that now each of these groups has its own team with regularly scheduled playing hours. When these two teams had a playoff, players and members of the audience had to bring three cans of food as their ticket for admission to the game. The food that was collected was then donated to a local church for their food drive and distribution program. (Ogden)

Hospitals

- A community art gallery had more works of art than it could put on display, and one of the neighborhood park buildings had a large unoccupied room. The park agreed to let the gallery use this spare room for additional display space. Now the park has a cultural display area which is available to the public. It has discovered that some people now visit the park to see this display who might otherwise never have had a reason to use the park facilities. At the same time, the art gallery gets more display space, and the artists whom this gallery represents get broader and longer lasting exposure for their work. (Beverly)

- A local park wanted to offer a complete range of sports activities, including bowling, but since it could not afford to set up a bowling alley of its own, representatives of the park worked out an arrangement with a neighborhood commercial bowling alley allowing their team regular weekly practice time. Now the park has a regular bowling team with twenty-five members. (Loyola)

- Many parks have discovered the advantages of having a direct relationship with local businesses that deal in food. For example, one park held its Local Advisory Council elections at a poolside breakfast with orange juice, scrambled eggs, grits, bacon, and biscuits contributed by local merchants. (Ogden)

- Another park has established a relationship with a local restaurant that allows it special discounts for staff parties and other events. (Wicker)

- When planning festivals and other community events, many local parks have worked together with local hospitals to set up public information booths and displays that deal with health issues of particular importance to the community. (Ekhert)

Parks and Individuals Within the Community

Local Residents

- A neighborhood park hosts an international dinner where local residents can each bring a dish representative of their own ethnic or national heritage. (Wicker)

❦ A park hosts a special event where local residents who have the skills necessary to do their own home repairs can run workshops to teach these skills to other members of the community. (Wicker)

❦ A park sponsors a neighborhood fair, which includes a walking tour of the gardens, homes and historic sites of the neighborhood, as well as live music from local bands and displays of art produced by local artists. (Wicker)

❦ One park decided to sponsor a "potluck" picnic with each person bringing a dish of food and local bakeries and restaurants providing the "extras." (Fuller)

Youth

❦ Local bands formed by young people in the neighborhood provide the music for a festival in the community park. (Wicker)

❦ At dances held in a neighborhood park the music for younger teens is provided by older teens who have already formed local bands. (Wicker)

❦ A community decided to redevelop two local parks by organizing one to fit the needs of teens and the other for grade-school-age young people. They then held a meeting at the designated teen park and invited the teens playing there to provide them with ideas. As a result of these discussions, the teens and adults worked together toward the same goals, and the parks have been redeveloped. (Bethel)

A number of parks have started youth advisory councils:

❦ One teen advisory council meets in a local park where they hold their own fundraising activities. As a result, they have built up their bank account and now are able to sponsor horseback riding and a trip to visit the state legislature. (Columbus)

❦ Another park starts a teen council to provide innovative ideas for developing park policy and programs. (Galewood)

❦ Park leaders have worked with teens to design and plant a garden and helped them start their own community newsletter. (Ogden)

❧ A neighborhood park discovers that it gets teenagers involved in park activities by using them as volunteer assistants, helping the instructors of younger children. (Ogden)

Seniors

❧ Senior citizens who lived in a local high rise wanted to use their expertise in gardening. They worked out an arrangement with a neighborhood park to provide space and with local businesses to donate bulbs and perennials. The result of this cooperation was that the seniors planted flowers all around the perimeter of the park. They continue to rake and trim the park and even plan meetings with guest speakers who give them further tips on improving their gardening skills. (Wicker)

Artists

❧ A neighborhood park sponsored an art class for teens and adults that would provide them with the drawing and painting skills necessary for creating a community mural. Local artists were brought in to discuss their work as well as to demonstrate the mural techniques. The class also was placed in contact with a local historical society that could provide information about the evolution of the neighborhood. As a site for the mural, the group chose a park wall that was sprayed with graffiti. (Ekhert)

❧ Local artists display their work in park display cases and on blank, unused walls. (Orr, etc.)

❧ Local artists display and/or sell their work at neighborhood art fairs sponsored by community parks. (Wicker, etc.)

❧ A professional photographer whose child was active in local park activities allowed his child to borrow his equipment to photograph the activities happening in the park. (Wicker)

What all of these relationships have in common is that they benefit everyone who is involved. A school that uses park facilities expands its own offerings, while at the same time the park gains new users. Local artists who exhibit, teach or perform in the local park are expanding their own audience and reputation by enhancing the park's programming and cultural contributions to the community. The neighborhood restaurants discover that they can reach a wider public and improve public relations by helping the local park to become a more inviting gathering place for the members of the community.

In other words, these are all examples of "win-win" partnerships, which are established on a clear understanding of the different strengths and interests represented by both the local park and its particular community partner. In situations like these in which everyone wins, a strong incentive develops to extend these partnerships even further in order to create new joint projects and to plan together for the future. A series of solid and lasting relationships such as these, constantly involving more and more local people and organizations in an ever-growing web of connectedness and accomplishment, lie at the very center of an "asset-driven" community development process.

To illustrate this process, Chart Two on the next page shows a typical series of these mutually beneficial relationships between a park and its community partners.

Chart Three on the following page represents the complex network of possibilities for a park that has fully developed itself as an essential community asset.

Building Bridges Between Parks and Resources Outside the Community

Having established strong relationships within its immediate community, the local park can now be mobilized as a "bridge-builder." These new bridges will serve to connect the local park and its neighborhood partners with a wide range of resources that are located outside the immediate community.

One of the first bridges that should be constructed, or at least strengthened, is the one that solidifies the local park's relationships with its own governing authority. Especially in larger cities, local parks that approach their system's leadership with proposals demonstrating broad community support are much more likely to be given an increase in the resources that will be made available for their work.

But even beyond their own structures and systems, parks can also leverage significant outside institutional interest and resources:

- Parks are often able to attract both public sector and philanthropic support for park-sponsored activities targeting "youth," "seniors," and other marginalized members of the community.

- Larger arts organizations and even museums have begun to find ways to utilize local parks as hosts and venues for events that will attract participants from far beyond the neighborhood community.

Chart Two: Strengthening Partnerships

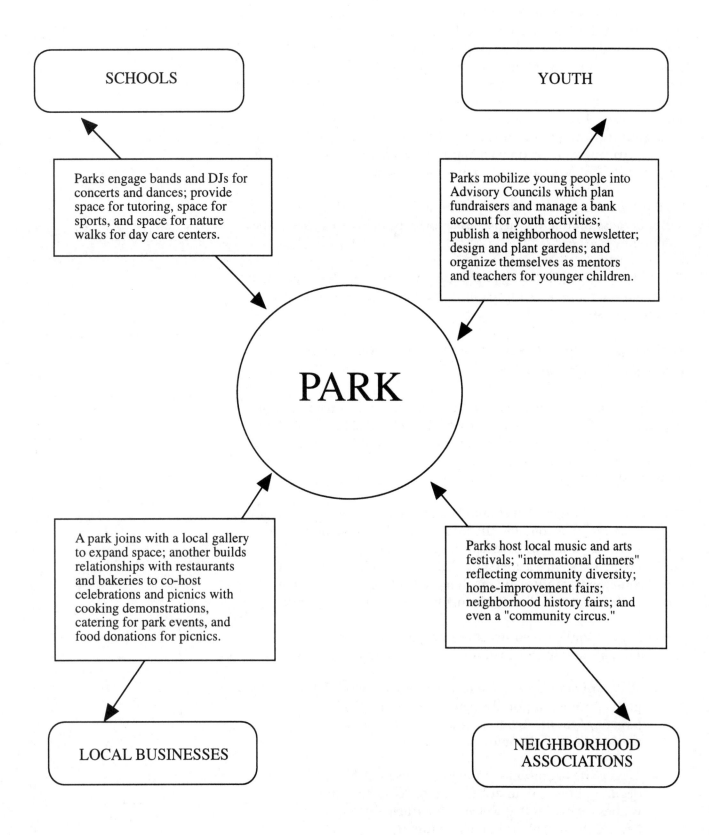

SCHOOLS

Parks engage bands and DJs for concerts and dances; provide space for tutoring, space for sports, and space for nature walks for day care centers.

YOUTH

Parks mobilize young people into Advisory Councils which plan fundraisers and manage a bank account for youth activities; publish a neighborhood newsletter; design and plant gardens; and organize themselves as mentors and teachers for younger children.

PARK

A park joins with a local gallery to expand space; another builds relationships with restaurants and bakeries to co-host celebrations and picnics with cooking demonstrations, catering for park events, and food donations for picnics.

Parks host local music and arts festivals; "international dinners" reflecting community diversity; home-improvement fairs; neighborhood history fairs; and even a "community circus."

LOCAL BUSINESSES

NEIGHBORHOOD ASSOCIATIONS

Chart Three: One-on-One Relationships

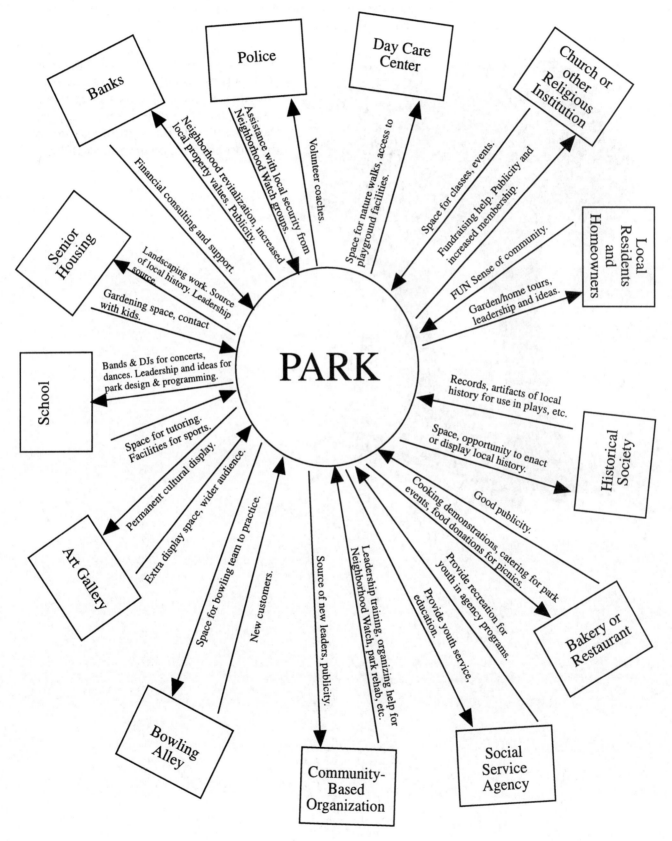

❧ Creative uses of park space for festivals, fairs, exhibits, concerts, and other events can help make the entire community a destination for visitors from outside the community as well as local residents.

In short, a fully mobilized local park can act as a powerful magnet for attracting outside resources. When this happens, a strongly interconnected community can then direct these new resources toward the most effective community-building uses.

Sources and Contacts for the "Stories" in this Section

Bethel   Bethel New Life
        367 N. Karlov
        Chicago, Illinois
        (312) 826-5540 (Mary Nelson)

Beverly   Beverly Park
        2460 W. 102nd Street
        Chicago, Illinois
        (312) 445-5443 (John MacAskill)

Columbus   Columbus Park
        500 S. Central Avenue
        Chicago, Illinois
        (312) 378-0643 (Andrew Walton)

Ekhert   Ekhert Park
        1330 W. Chicago Avenue
        Chicago, Illinois
        (312) 294-4710 (Mickey Maher)

Fuller   Fuller Park
        331 W. 45th Street
        Chicago, Illinois
        (312) 268-0062 (Fred Toler)

Galewood   Galewood Park
        5729 W. Bloomingdale Avenue
        Chicago, Illinois
        (312) 622-3877 (Joseph Laws)

Graver   Graver Park
        1518 W. 102nd Place
        Chicago, Illinois
        (312) 238-6913

Harrison   Harrison Park
        1824 S. Wood
        Chicago, Illinois
        (312) 294-4714

Loyola   Loyola Park
        1230 W. Greenleaf
        Chicago, Illinois
        (312) 262-0690

Ogden	Ogden Park 6500 S. Racine Chicago, Illinois (312) 873-1038 (Mary Smith)
Orr	Orr Park 730 N. Pulaski Road Chicago, Illinois (312) 826-3713
Sheridan	Sheridan Park 910 S. Aberdeen Chicago, Illinois (312) 294-4717 (Bud Patti)
Stateway Gardens	Stateway Gardens Library 3618 S. State Street Chicago, IL 60609 (312) 747-6872 (Leanna Newson, Branch Head)
Tilton	Tilton Park c/o Bethel New Life 367 N. Karlov Chicago, Illinois (312) 826-5540 (Mary Nelson)
Wicker	Wicker Park 1500 N. Wicker Chicago, Illinois (312) 276-1723 (Greg Chrobak)

Introduction—Libraries and Community Renewal

Libraries are natural community centers that do much more than just lend books to interested readers. Because the purpose of libraries is to make various resources available to the members of their local communities, they are usually eager to encourage community participation and often are able to provide safe and welcoming places for community people to congregate and engage in activities that will be of benefit to the entire community. This means that libraries can play an essential role in the process of community-building and should be seen as vital assets that exist at the very heart of community life.

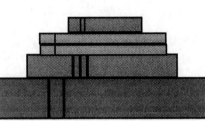

Imaginative librarians and neighborhood leaders can find innovative ways to work together so as to maximize the utilization of the local library's resources for the benefit of the entire community. The potential community-building power of the neighborhood library can be most effectively released by connecting its inherent resources with local individuals, associations and institutions. Here are some examples of how this can be done:

- ❧ Libraries are natural meeting places for the young people of the community. In the library, free from the pressures of school, young people are able to make valuable connections with each other. Furthermore, creative librarians are often able to channel the free time and talents of young people into avenues that can make significant contributions to the entire community. Examples of this process include encouraging young people to form advisory councils for the library, to read their stories and essays at library-sponsored community events, to design programs to introduce younger children to the resources of the library, and to act as tutors and mentors for other students in literacy or language programs.

- ❧ Libraries are also natural meeting places for various community groups, and local librarians often become active participants in community coalitions. Libraries are community centers, and librarians are able to facilitate neighborhood events and celebrations by providing space and materials, as well as knowledgeable help in planning and publicizing these events.

- ❧ Most school systems have long-established, mutually beneficial relationships with the libraries in their district. This sort of relationship can serve as a model for libraries to form new "partnerships" with other organizations and institutions in their community.

How can neighborhood leaders learn to maximize and expand the effective utilization of the resources of their local libraries? Here are four steps in a process through which neighborhood leaders can effectively engage libraries and their librarians in building a stronger, more fully integrated community:

❧ First, neighborhood leaders compile lists of the specific resources that exist in each of the neighborhood libraries. In this process it should always be remembered that books and related materials are only one of the many types of resources that local libraries contain.

❧ Next, leaders can take an inventory of local assets—such as associations, institutions and groups of people with special talents or interests—that currently exist in the same neighborhood as each library.

❧ Now, by connecting the assets of these libraries with the various assets of the surrounding neighborhoods, local leaders can facilitate a series of mutually beneficial "partnerships" that will serve to strengthen the entire community.

❧ Finally, having established a network of successful partnerships for the library within the local community, leaders can work together with librarians to create new connections to additional resources that exist outside of the community.

Rediscovering Libraries as Assets Within the Community

Libraries are more than storehouses for books. From tiny storefronts to large modern multimedia centers, all libraries contain a variety of resources which can be used as community-building material. Some of these resources include:

Personnel. Librarians are people who have many talents that go far beyond their traditional booklending duties. For example, one librarian might be able to lead an aerobics class, while another might be able to use research and writing skills to write extensive community histories or help community leaders in writing grant proposals. Since librarians are often local residents themselves, they are often eager to be involved in activities such as these that will improve the quality of life in the neighborhood.

Space and Facilities. Although these resources will vary depending on the size and operating budget of each library, nevertheless all libraries have windows, walls, display cases and bulletin boards. In addition, many libraries have large auditoriums, smaller classrooms and meeting rooms, kitchens, lobbies, parking lots, and playrooms.

Materials and Equipment.. One of the main purposes of a library is to make books and other related materials available to interested members of the community. Libraries also have many other types of resources that are available for community use, and these other resources might include:

Video cassettes

Computers

Board games

Toys and stuffed animals

Tools

Financial information for small business owners

Telephones for the hearing impaired

"Culture" kits

Artwork

Literacy and GED materials

Community files containing information about the history
    of the community

Pianos and other musical instruments

Information about other organizations and events taking place in
    the neighborhood

Expertise. Libraries often offer free classes for people of all ages. Many libraries have established GED, literacy and language classes—and increasingly they are beginning to offer educational workshops on topics such as immigration, crime prevention, and computer literacy, as well as arts and crafts, theater, ethnic dancing, exercise, storytelling, and family writing seminars (in which participants compile their poems and stories into anthologies).

Economic Power. Although some libraries are forced to operate on extremely restricted budgets, most libraries have at their disposal funds which allow them to purchase supplies locally. Some librarians also have the capacity to hire local residents on at least a part-time basis. Moreover, librarians are frequently able to use their skills to help community organizations and others write and submit grant proposals for projects that will benefit the community as a whole.

Mapping Community Assets as Potential Partners for Libraries

Who are the people and the groups that can be found in the community that will best be able to serve as partners in the development of the resources of local libraries? Librarians will discover the answer to this question by "mapping" the assets of the neighborhoods in which their libraries are located. As a result of this "mapping" process, librarians will discover potential partners in four specific areas of the community.

- Citizens' associations and not-for-profit organizations of many specific kinds.

- Publicly funded institutions such as schools, parks, and police and fire departments.

- The private sector, which ranges from small businesses to banks and branches of larger corporations.

- Individuals and groups of "labeled" people such as "youth," "seniors," "artists," and others with special interests and abilities.

The chart on the next page shows the relationship of a local library to the potential partners that exist within the community in each of these four specific categories.

Building Productive Relationships Between Libraries and the Community

When the assets of both the local library and its neighborhood have been "mapped" and identified, then librarians can work together with community leaders to connect their library in a vital web of mutually beneficial relationships. Although most libraries already have solid relationships with local schools, now they will also be able to form creative partnerships with parks, artists and cultural institutions, police departments, senior citizens organizations, and a wide variety of other local individuals, organizations and institutions. Examples of each of these kinds of relationships follow.

Libraries and Community Associations:

Citizens Associations

- A librarian suggested that a series of community forums be held at the library in which leaders of different community groups would present information about their organizations and consult with librarians and local

Chart One: Potential Partners

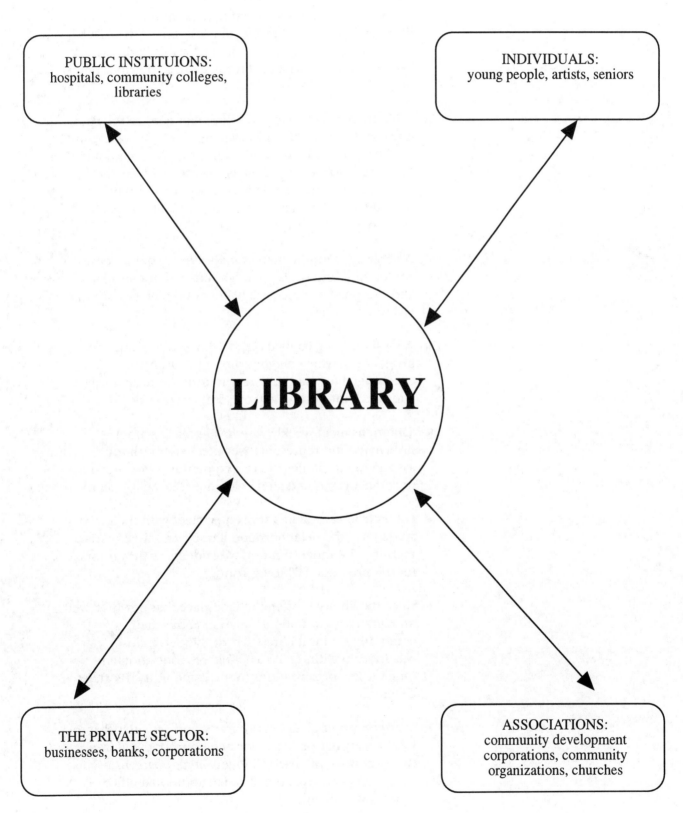

PUBLIC INSTITUIONS:
hospitals, community colleges, libraries

INDIVIDUALS:
young people, artists, seniors

LIBRARY

THE PRIVATE SECTOR:
businesses, banks, corporations

ASSOCIATIONS:
community development corporations, community organizations, churches

residents about how the library could help these organizations become more effective. (Rudy Lozano)

❧ As a result of allowing a Community Development Corporation to hold its meetings at a local library, the librarian has been asked by the president of the CDC to be on their executive board, and now this librarian has been given a special award for making a contribution to the community. (Kelly)

❧ A librarian at a Housing Development goes to the Local Advisory Council meetings every month, and, as a result, the library has an increased visibility in the community. Now this librarian coordinates a summer picnic for seniors at the local park and also arranges for children from the day care center to come to the library for storyhours. (Stateway Gardens)

❧ A librarian, with the help of the secretary of the local community council, collected a series of oral histories and compiled an extensive history of the neighborhood. (Whitney Young)

❧ A local building council organizes a series of summer programs in which neighborhood children are encouraged to visit the library in order to hear stories and watch interesting videos. (Stateway Gardens)

❧ Librarians meet weekly with local police, school principals, and representatives of a neighborhood association to participate in a community-wide initiative to combat gangs and street violence. (Portage-Cragin)

❧ Tutors from a local literacy center meet with their students at the neighborhood library, and the librarian recruits additional community residents as new tutors for the program. (Whitney Young)

❧ Since the library is often the first place that newly arrived immigrants go to find information about their community, a local library has developed a close relationship with the Polish Welfare Association and other ethnic organizations in the community. (Portage-Cragin)

❧ In appreciation of all the programs and activities that the local library has provided for neighborhood children, the local Boys and Girls Club lets library patrons use its computers and gives the librarian additional office space. (McKinley)

❧ The local Boy Scout troop uses the window of their neighborhood library to present displays for special events that they sponsor. (McKinley)

❧ A YMCA chapter sends a local library listings of available jobs in the community for posting on the library's bulletin board. (Rudy Lozano)

Religious Institutions

❧ To make better contact with the Hispanic residents of the neighborhood, a librarian attends the local Catholic Church and sets up a table outside the church where information about the library is distributed. (Albany Park)

❧ In another neighborhood the local pastor asks the community librarian to recommend performers for church programs. (Austin)

Cultural Organizations

❧ A local historical society holds its meetings and houses all of its records at a local library. At this library, in collaboration with a local theater company, this group also presented a performance of a Shakespearean play. (Rogers Park)

❧ A representative from a nationally known museum visits a neighborhood library bringing a series of "experience boxes," and now the local librarian presents similar programs on an ongoing basis for the children of the neighborhood. (Marshall Square)

❧ A library and a local community college work together to organize booths and programs for a Korean Cultural Day in which traditional Korean storytelling, singing and dancing, as well as discussions of current social issues, are included. (Albany Park)

Libraries and Public Institutions:

Parks

❧ A librarian arranges for the local police department to provide transportation for a group of senior citizens from the library to a local park where the seniors like to have summer picnics. (Stateway Gardens)

Schools

❧ A children's librarian encourages school principals in the neighborhood to make a workshop about the library compulsory for all the teachers in the district. (Scottsdale)

❧ Teachers from a neighborhood school arranged for the local library to display the artwork of their students and also to participate in a grant which sponsored a program for local students to write and "publish" their own books. (Rudy Lozano)

❧ A children's librarian creates a space at the library where local teachers can put together collections of stories for their classrooms, and then organizes a workshop for these teachers on the importance of storytelling. (Marshall Square)

❧ A substitute teacher at a local school calls the neighborhood library and volunteers to tutor students after school. (Robert Taylor Homes)

❧ The principal of a local school, who had worked with the head librarian on an anti-gang initiative, agrees to speak at the opening of the library's new computer center. (Portage-Cragin)

❧ Librarians attend a local music school to learn about culturally specific instruments so they can properly present programs to the children of the community about their ethnic heritages. (Logan Square)

Community Colleges

❧ A local librarian works with the local community college to bring a self-employment training program to the library. (Austin)

❧ A librarian is able to set up an after-school tutoring program for the young people of the neighborhood by using students from the local university. (Blackstone)

❧ A neighborhood librarian helps the local community college develop a Korean Studies Program in response to the needs of the neighborhood. (Albany Park)

Police

❦ A representative from the local police precinct comes to the library to give workshops on crime prevention. (Whitney Young)

❦ A farewell luncheon held just before a local library closed for renovation becomes a real community event when members of the police department, a hospital director, members of the senior center, and a representative of Volunteers for Housing are among the guests. (Kelly)

Hospitals

❦ A children's librarian in a rural area makes regular visits to the waiting room at the County Health Department in order to do a reading program with the children who are there waiting to be seen. (Aiken)

Libraries and the Public Sector

❦ A librarian sends the local business association a bibliography of materials that the library has collected for the use of small business owners in the community. (Whitney Young)

❦ Another library offers a course for small business owners (in Korean) on how to use computers in their businesses. (Albany Park)

Libraries and Individuals Within the Community

Local Residents

❦ A local librarian develops the resources for a "tool-lending library," and two neighborhood residents start an informal business using the tools they have borrowed. (Austin)

❦ Another librarian assembles a list of students needing help in reading and math and then encourages a former employee of the library to start a tutoring service in response to these needs. (Whitney Young)

❦ A library sets up a family literacy program with several local families and helps them complete an "anthology" of all the poems they have written together during the program. (North Austin)

❦ A library patron learns that the Department of Education is funding literacy grants and encourages the librarian to write a grant for creating a literacy resource center at the library. (Blackstone)

❦ A neighborhood librarian obtains a grant from a national organization that enables a local literacy organization to set up a hotline, meeting space, and a coordinator for the program at the library. (Rudy Lozano)

❦ A local library holds an awards ceremony for community activists in which a local resident who started a group called "Fighters Against Diabetes" is honored, and now this person writes a regular column about the library in a newspaper with a citywide distribution. (Kelly)

❦ At a neighborhood library the "community file," which contains articles and personal testimonies about the community, is organized and maintained by a local volunteer. (Albany Park)

❦ A children's librarian realizes that many of the neighborhood children are not able to come to the library for storyhour and so decides to make regular visits to local synagogues, schools and hospitals to tell stories to children who would otherwise not be able to benefit from this activity. (Blackstone)

❦ A library makes use of local storytellers to tell stories in Korean to local children. (Albany Park)

❦ A librarian uses personal initiative to become the first in the district to conduct tours of the library in Spanish. (Rudy Lozano)

❦ A librarian starts a chess club in which he teaches anyone who wants to learn how to play. (Rudy Lozano)

People with Disabilities

❦ Local libraries have had great success in providing special materials for sight and hearing impaired members of the community. Now many of these libraries are beginning to expand their outreach programs to also provide materials and support for developmentally disabled residents of the community at all age levels.

Youth

- Through a program coordinated by the city, three teenagers who need jobs work for the summer at a severely understaffed local library. (Marshall Square)

- A children's librarian uses leftover money from a grant to buy books for preschoolers to hire local teenagers to design the learning program for these preschoolers. (Logan Square)

- Students enrolled in the literacy program at their local library are encouraged to become teachers for other students just coming into the program. (Stateway Gardens)

- A librarian compiles a mailing list of young people who come to the library so they can receive a newsletter about library activities and be invited to help form an advisory council. (North Pulaski)

Seniors

- Senior citizens at a local housing development who are ill call a neighborhood librarian for help, and this librarian arranges to have library assistants deliver groceries to the shut-ins. (Stateway Gardens)

- A librarian works with the president of the local historical society to collect oral histories from senior citizens to compile a book that will chronicle the history of the neighborhood. (Kelly)

- Senior citizens from a local quilting guild make a quilt depicting the library and the community, and this quilt is now on permanent display in the library's auditorium. (Beverly)

- A neighborhood librarian holds birthday and holiday dinners at the library for members of a seniors self-help program, and once a week this librarian distributes clothing that the seniors have collected from the community. (Stateway Gardens)

- A librarian arranges for health providers from a local eye clinic to come to the library to screen seniors for cataracts. (Stateway Gardens)

❧ A library sponsors an intergenerational program that pairs seniors with first grade students in which they meet once a week to read and discuss books suggested by the library staff. (Connecticut)

❧ A retired schoolteacher uses local volunteers as assistants in the art classes for neighborhood children which he teaches at the local library. (Scottsdale)

Artists

❧ A local artist takes advantage of the library's display case to exhibit her cross-stitching. (Scottsdale)

❧ A librarian arranges for the work of local Korean artists to be shown at suburban libraries in neighborhoods with large Korean populations. (Albany Park)

❧ A librarian invites a local Polish dance teacher to stage a performance with his students at the library. (Portage-Cragin)

❧ Two artists who are friends of a local librarian do face-painting with young people enrolled in a summer reading program at the library. (North Pulaski)

In each of these examples, we have seen how people in communities have come to recognize that their relationships with local libraries can help them to be more effective in their own activities. At the same time we have also seen how creative librarians are recognizing that lending books is only one of the many ways in which a library can contribute significantly to the well-being of the entire community. In every one of these instances, joint planning that makes the most effective use of contrasting strengths and resources has been able to find ways to make both parties twice as strong as when they operated in isolation. As more and more people and organizations become involved in these sorts of relationships, the local library can become a central facilitator for continuing community development that is organized and driven by the talents and energies of the widest possible range of community residents.

Chart Two on the following page shows a representative series of mutually beneficial relationships of the type that can be developed between a neighborhood library and its community partners.

Chart Three on the page 204 represents the complex network of possibilities that exist for a local library that has fully developed itself as an essential community asset.

Chart Two: Strengthening Partnerships

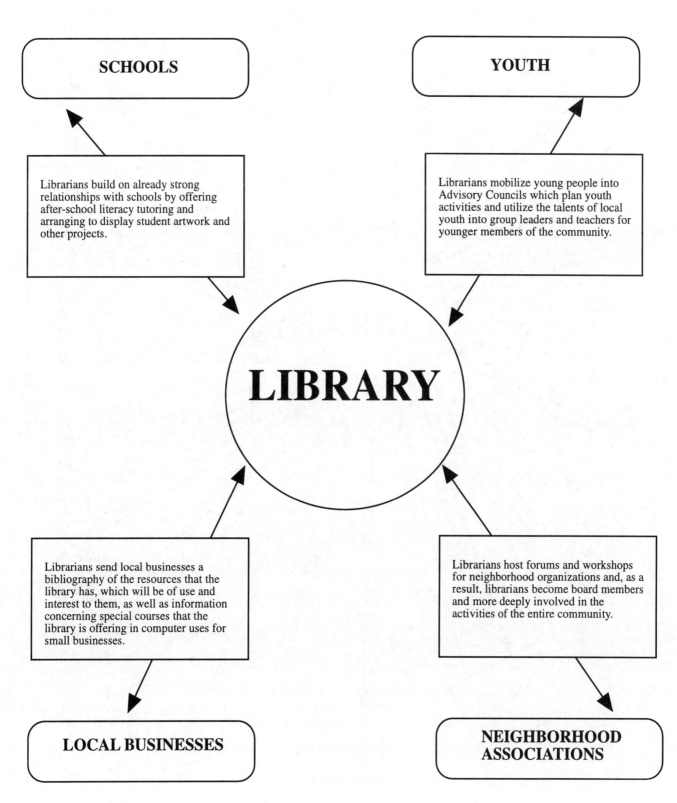

SCHOOLS

Librarians build on already strong relationships with schools by offering after-school literacy tutoring and arranging to display student artwork and other projects.

YOUTH

Librarians mobilize young people into Advisory Councils which plan youth activities and utilize the talents of local youth into group leaders and teachers for younger members of the community.

LIBRARY

Librarians send local businesses a bibliography of the resources that the library has, which will be of use and interest to them, as well as information concerning special courses that the library is offering in computer uses for small businesses.

Librarians host forums and workshops for neighborhood organizations and, as a result, librarians become board members and more deeply involved in the activities of the entire community.

LOCAL BUSINESSES

NEIGHBORHOOD ASSOCIATIONS

Chart 3: One on One Relationships

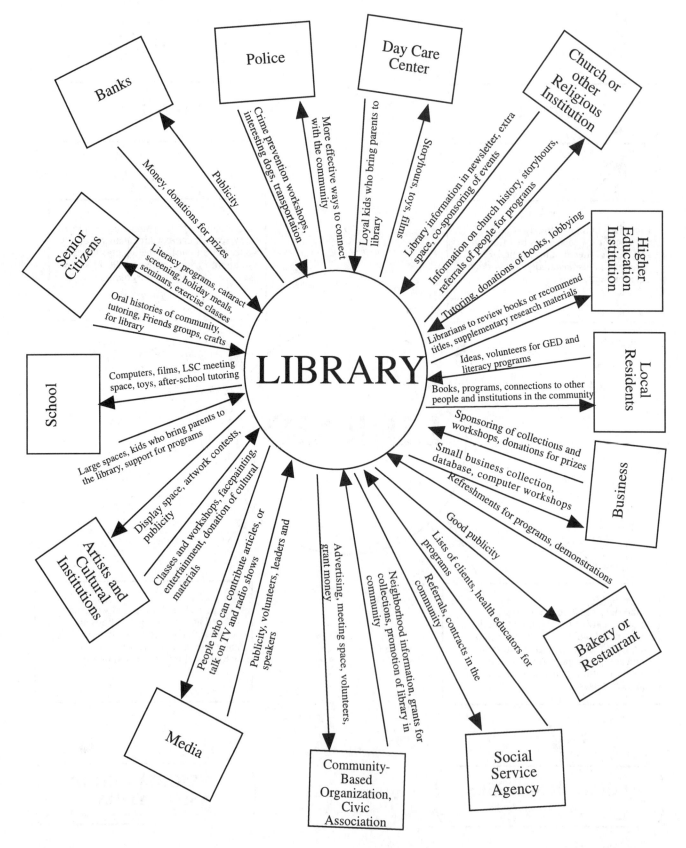

Building Bridges Between Libraries and Resources Outside the Community

Once a library has become enmeshed in a solid network of community relationships, that library can also be utilized as a connection to resources that exist outside the community. As an institution that is already connected to a larger system outside the neighborhood, each big city library receives its operating budget from a central library administration. But since libraries are funded according to the active support they receive from their communities, it is usually the libraries that have built strong community relationships that receive the most money. Thus through community support expressed in active partnerships, local libraries are in an excellent position to leverage financial resources for the local community.

Moreover, a community library can also attract outside resources on its own, independently from the system that supplies its basic operating budget. Foundations or public sector funding may support creative proposals from librarians who have learned to work closely with community residents.

- ❦ One librarian obtains money to house and provide a "hotline" service for a local literacy group.

- ❦ Another librarian writes a grant for "culture kits" to entertain and educate youngsters and, as a result, is able to acquire many unusual resources for the community, which serve to enrich and strengthen its ethnic characteristics.

In short, a fully mobilized local library can act as a powerful agent for attracting outside resources. When this happens, a strongly interconnected community is prepared to direct these newly available resources toward effective community-building strategies.

Sources and Contacts for the "Stories" in This Section

Aiken

Aiken, SC County Library
314 Chesterfield St. South
Aiken, SC 29801
(803) 642-2023 (Barbara J. Walker,
   Children's Librarian)

Albany

Albany Park Library
5150 N. Kimball Avenue
Chicago, IL 60625
(312) 744-1933 (Chahee Stanfield,
   Branch Head)

Austin

Austin Library
2121 W. 95th Street
Chicago, IL 60644
(312) 746-5038 (Donna Kanapes, Branch Head)

Beverly

Beverly Library
2121 W. 95th Street
Chicago, IL 60643
(312) 747-9673 (Debbie Shillow,
   Children's Librarian)

Blackstone

Blackstone Library
4904 S. Lake Park
Chicago, IL 60615
(312) 747-0511 (Cassandra Carr, Branch Head)

Kelly

Kelly Library
6151 S. Normal Blvd.
Chicago, IL 60621
(312) 747-8418 (Linda Greene, Branch Head)

Logan

Logan Square Library
3255 W. Altgeld
Chicago, IL 60647
(312) 744-5295 (Pamela Martin-Diaz,
   Children's Librarian)

Marshall

Marshall Square Library
2724 W. Cermak
Chicago, IL 60608
(312) 747-0061 (Julie Lockwood, Branch Head)

McKinley   McKinley Library
                        2021 W. 35th Street
                        Chicago, IL 60608
                        (312) 747-6082 (Betty Jane Leonard,
                            Branch Head)

North Austin   North Austin Library
                        5724 W. North Avenue
                        Chicago, IL 60639
                        (312) 746-4233 (Bruce Fox, Branch Head)

North Pulaski   North Pulaski Library
                        1330 N. Pulaski Road
                        Chicago, IL 60651
                        (312) 744-9573 (Nanette Freeman,
                            Children's Librarian)

Portage-Cragin   Portage-Cragin Library
                        5108 W. Belmont
                        Chicago, IL 60641
                        (312) 744-0152 (Carol Tarsitano, Branch Head)

Robert Taylor Homes   Robert Taylor Homes Library
                        5120 S. Federal Street
                        Chicago, IL 60609
                        (312) 747-2828 (Vernelle Madden, Branch Head)

Rogers Park   Rogers Park Library
                        6907 N. Clark Street
                        Chicago, IL 60626
                        (312) 744-0156 (Angie Spararo, Branch Head)

Rudy Lozano   Rudy Lozano Library
                        1805 S. Loomis
                        Chicago, IL 60608
                        (312) 733-4329 (Hector Hernandez,
                            Branch Head)

Scottsdale   Scottsdale Library
                        4101 W. 79th Street
                        Chicago, IL 60652
                        (312) 747-0193 (Bernadette Nowakowski,
                            Children's Librarian)

Stateway Gardens   Stateway Gardens Library
3618 S. State Street
Chicago, IL 60609
(312) 747-6872 (Leanna Newson, Branch Head)

Whitney Young   Whitney Young Library
7901 S. King Drive
Chicago, IL 60619
(312) 747-0039 (Mae Gregory, Branch Head)

Introduction—Schools and Community Renewal

Today, all over the U.S., creative educators are reconnecting their institutions with their local community, building new alliances which recognize that healthy schools and healthy communities reinforce each other. Why is this happening? A strong and lasting alliance of this kind must be based solidly on the recognition by both school officials and community development leaders that they share important values and interests. Both groups must understand first that healthy communities produce and support educational excellence, and second, that good schools are the best guarantee of a community's future. To our schools we have entrusted the keys to our communities' futures. On the shoulders of our community-based leaders we place the challenge to rebuild today while at the same time establishing for residents a stake in tomorrow.

All too often, the present-oriented community builders and the school-based trustees of the future operate independently, on completely separate tracks, in totally divorced words. The good work of community builders proceeds without involvement by young people or the schools. And the schools do not think very creatively about how they might connect young people to the future in concrete ways.

Instead, school leaders repeatedly call upon the local community leadership to join the schools in solving their fiscal and legislative crises. Many school people call this effort a "school-community partnership." Unfortunately, throughout the United States there are signs that the "partnership" is weakening. One of the reasons is that often it is not a partnership at all.

In fact, as schools have become more professionalized and centralized, they have tended to distance themselves from their local communities. The vital links between experience, work, and education have been weakened. As a result, public and private schools in many rural and urban communities have lost their power as valuable community resources. And many economically distressed towns, communities, and neighborhoods have begun to struggle toward economic revitalization without the valuable contributions of the local schools. It is interesting to note that concern about the schools' isolation is a major topic among human service providers as well.

Clearly, we need to create a new kind of partnership in which both schools and communities contribute directly to the strengthening and development of each other. These new partnerships must be able to provide a firm foundation for both educational renewal *and* community regeneration. To achieve this important goal, creative educators and innovative community builders must now begin to work together to discover new ways to mobilize the many and varied resources of local schools as essential components of on-going community development efforts. What this means is that each local school should be seen not only as an "educational institution" but also as a rich collection of specific resources which can be used for strengthening the social and economic fabric of the entire community.

A solid and lasting alliance of this kind must always be based on the recognition by *both* school officials and community development leaders that they share essential values, interests and goals. Both groups must come to understand that just as healthy communities produce and support continued educational excellence, at the same time local schools that have fully integrated their resources within the community will become the best and most certain guarantee for that community's increased future strength and prosperity.

Rediscovering Schools as Assets Within the Community

An initial list of a school's assets might begin with these nine important elements:

Facilities. Schools are places where community groups can meet. They also can serve as places that "incubate" community activities— from small businesses to neighborhood festivals to social service programs.

Materials and Equipment. Even resource-strapped, economically disadvantaged schools have at least some of the following resources which can be shared with and/or used in support of various local community groups:

- Computers
- Fax and xerox machines
- Audiovisual equipment
- Science equipment
- Athletic equipment
- Wood-working equipment
- "Shop" and car-repair equipment
- Printing equipment
- Dark room and other photographic equipment
- Books, videos and audiotapes
- Art materials
- Musical instruments
- Kitchen utensils
- Furniture

Purchasing Power. The materials, commodities, and services purchased by schools can be directed to initiate, suppot, or expand neighborhood enterprises, including those created by local young people.

Employment Practices. As a major employer in most neighborhoods and towns, the school's hiring practices can focus upon local residents.

Courses. Through existing classes or newly created evening courses, schools can provide education and training for residents or groups who seek to participate in the area's development efforts.

Teachers. In every neighborhood the teachers are a concentrated pool of highly trained and specialized adults with critical skills and essential knowledge that they can contribute to the efforts of local groups involved in development activities.

Financial Capacity. Schools have the local power to generate and receive special funds through bond issues and proposals to government agencies, corporations and foundations not usually accessible to community groups. This special capacity can be an important resource in a community development strategy.

A Focus for Adult Involvement. The local school is potentially a strong magnet for attracting the interests and commitments of parents and other adults in the community.

Young People. The students with ideas, energy, and idealism can become important actors through classes, projects and internships which involve them in the local community development process. These same young people are also important linkages to the other adult leadership in the community.

Finally, in addition to rediscovering that each local school is a rich mine of valuable resources, it is also important to recognize that a renewed focus on "locality" on the part of both education and economic development leaders presents a promising arena for the proper utilization of these resources. School reformers—whether they advocate "choice," or vouchers, or school-based management—are increasingly convinced that, while national resources and standards still continue to be important, it is really the culture, curriculum and commitment of the local school that are most crucial to genuine educational success. Similarly, effective community development efforts are now being seen as those which engage *local* energies and which carefully tailor innovative programs and approached to specific *local* conditions. In other words, we are beginning to learn that only local groups can fully catalyze the participation and continuing commitment of local people, and only these kinds of participation and continuing commitment can insure genuine success in education and community development efforts.

Mapping Community Assets as Potential Partners for Local Schools

Having mapped the enormous potential contributions that might be made by local schools, how do neighborhood leaders and educators go about mobilizing these resources for community building? A simple four-step process includes the following:

- ❦ First, make a thorough inventory of the resources of each local school.

- ❦ Next, compile an inventory of the key assets and resources of the community as these are represented by local individuals, associations, organizations, and other institutions. When this has been done, it will be discovered that these community assets fall into the following categories: (a) citizens' associations and not-for-profit organizations of all types; (b) publicly funded institutions such as hospitals, parks, libraries, and community colleges; (c) the private sector including small businesses, banks and local branches of larger corporations; and (d) local residents and special interest groups of "labelled people" such as "seniors," "youth," "welfare recipients," and "artists."

- ❦ Then, use the information that has been obtained from these inventories to build strong, concrete, mutually beneficial "partnerships" between local schools and the individuals, organizations and association that exist within the community.

- ❦ Finally, on the basis of these "partnerships" and the local school's active participation in the community building process, go on to build new relationships with resources that exist outside the immediate community.

Chart One on the next page illustrates the kinds of relationships that can exist between a local school and its community partners.

Building Productive Relationships Between Local Schools and the Community

When the assets of *both* the local school and the local community have been mapped, then educators and community leaders can begin to work together to develop a series of new partnerships that will connect the local school with the on-going process of building a stronger community.

Chart One: Potential Partners

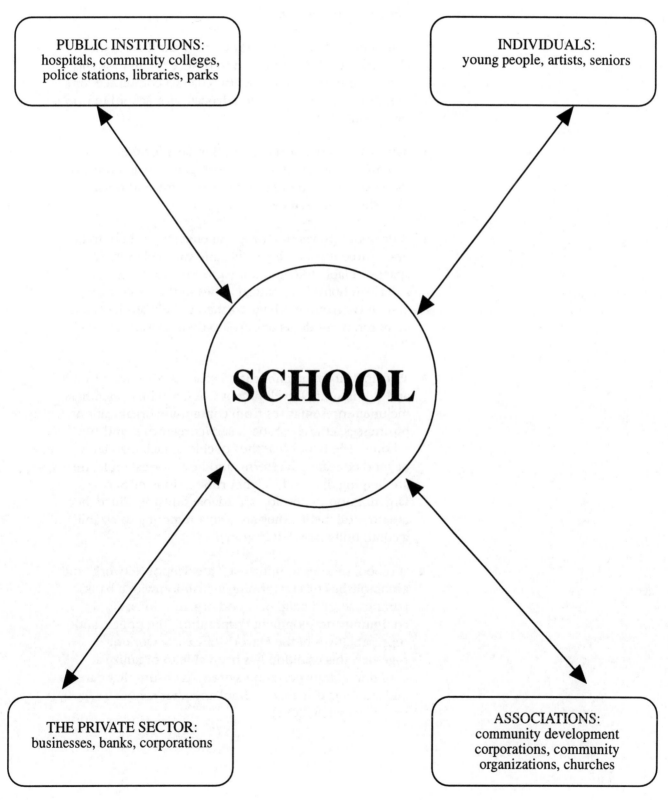

Let us now examine a few examples of this process in action as it has occurred in a variety of communities.

Local Schools and Community Associations

Citizens' Associations

❧ The principal of a school for teenage mothers is the chair for a coalition founded to reduce infant mortality in the community, and she also chairs a committee for a coalition that monitors and advocates for school reform. (Simpson)

❧ The same school hosts prevention fairs for the community in which the principal gets a wide variety of local agencies and organizations to come and present workshops and seminars. (Simpson)

❧ A drop-out prevention program enables a school to be open three nights every week, and this makes extra space available to community groups. Now the local alderman holds his political rallies in the auditorium, and an art group has been formed to help students and community residents to develop their artistic abilities. (Orr)

❧ Principals from neighborhood schools organize a Family and Community Development Council whose members include representatives from community organizations, businesses, churches, social service agencies, and schools. The issues that they decide to tackle go far beyond educational reform, and now, for example, they are helping the local Neighborhood Housing Services Organization to develop affordable housing. Since there are no local media, they are also attempting to establish a community newsletter. (Orr)

❧ A school decides to initiate a "Safe School Network" and accomplishes this by forming a coalition with a bank, parents, several neighborhood organizations, a community development corporation, the police, and representatives of the Mayor's office. By working together, this coalition has been able to organize a community transportation system to ensure that parents and students can get to school and after-school programs safely. (Orr)

❧ A group of twelve schools in one neighborhood decide to form a network in order to improve the capacity of their schools and to facilitate community groups to help themselves in a more effective manner. By combining their resources, this "network" has been able to improve the quality of education, to connect the community with the larger city and its institutions, and to share ideas about solving the problems of the community. (Orr)

Religious Institutions

❧ The Urban League connects churches with schools through an adopt-a-school program in which churches provide tutoring for neighborhood school children. As a result, the church gains an opportunity to become better connected to its neighborhood. (Chicago Urban League)

❧ A church forms a relationship with a local school through which students are allowed to use the church's youth center. (St. Sabina)

Cultural Organizations

❧ The Hispanic Club at an urban high school brings a sense of the importance of Latino culture to the community by hosting a Latino Cultural Week and organizing a food festival. (Boston)

Local Schools and Public Institutions

Parks

❧ A school obtains broad-based community support and lobbies the city to clean up the park across the street and to build new playground equipment. Now their students are able to play on the new equipment, and many of them go to the social center in the park for after-school activities. (Johnson)

❧ A school works together with the local park to offer a summer family sports program, and the school agrees to send flyers to other schools, churches and various organizations informing community residents of the types of sports activities that are available. (Orr)

Libraries

❧ The principal of a school works with a local library and other neighborhood organizations to create an anti-gang initiative in order to provide tighter security and special buses to ensure the safety of the students. After establishing this contact, the principal is invited to speak at the opening of the library's new computer facility. (Portage-Cragin)

Community Colleges

❧ A local community college participates in a consortium organized by a major university to encourage college attendance. Now, working together with community organizations and the parents and faculty of neighborhood schools, this community college has set up college clubs which provide enrichment programs including visits to colleges and which organize community members to act as mentors for students still in high school. (Olive-Harvey)

❧ Members of the faculty of a community college in a demographically changing neighborhood teach Spanish to the teachers of a local school. (Malcolm X)

Police

❧ Local police officers offer to provide student and teacher training in conflict resolution to four school districts in the community. Now, when a conflict arises in the school playground, designated students work with both parties in order to discover amicable solutions to the problem. As this program begins to become better established, students learn to ask for assistance before their differences of opinion escalate into conflict. (Phoenix)

Hospitals

❧ In cooperation with a local hospital, two high schools have developed school-based health clinics. One of these now has an infant and child development center (day care) and a leketek (play therapy) center, while the other has a WIC program and a counseling center.

Local Schools and the Private Sector

❧ A large corporation decides to honor four local students with outstanding attendance records by awarding them $500 scholarships to be used for higher education, and next year this corporation plans to give a special award to the student with the most impressive community involvement record. (Orr)

❧ A candy factory forms a partnership with a local elementary school in which employees take students on tours, provide uniforms for the school's basketball team, and sometimes make videos of special school events. (Johnson)

❧ The principal of a high school is on the board of a local business association where he cultivates partnerships with neighborhood businesses in order to facilitate relationships between students and future employers. (Orr)

❧ Students at an elementary school are matched with local businesses for summer internships which enable the businesses to tap into the skills of local youth and give the students a place to learn and earn some money outside of the school. (Prescott)

❧ In the 1990-91 school year, one school was able to spend $20,000 of its budget on hiring local people as tutors, teacher's aides and security personnel. It was also able to spend $2,000 on supplies obtained from local businesses. (Prescott)

Local Schools and Individuals Within the Community

Local Residents

❧ A school newsletter for the parents of students provides information to the community about the school's Women, Infants and Children (WIC) program, about where local women can get free mammograms, about housing developments in the neighborhood, and about special events of interest to the community. (Orr)

❧ A principal receives a special grant to establish "Project Better Day" in which twenty parents will be trained to be discussion leaders so that they can reach out to other neighborhood parents who are having difficulties with their families. (Johnson)

❧ A school establishes a parent center where community parents can meet and discuss issues of mutual concern. As a result, several parents have now been hired as staff for the school and for the clinics which are based at the school. (Orr)

❧ Through a newly developed "home-bound" program, students at a school for teenage mothers videotape post-natal classes to provide instruction for other teens who need to be taught in their homes. (Simpson)

❦ A children's literacy program at the same school teaches and encourages young mothers to read to their children. Since some of these teenage mothers have problems with reading, this program gives them an added incentive to become good readers. (Simpson)

❦ This same school has also started an infant boutique which provides useful products for the community and generates a cash-flow for the students who work there. The principal has recently received a special grant to buy infant care seats which will soon be sold along with infant clothing and other baby equipment. Now the students are designing and printing a brochure on car seat safety which will be marketed to schools and agencies in other inner-city neighborhoods. (Simpson)

❦ Students at a local school organize in order to set up recycling bins at their school so that students and community residents will be able to recycle paper and aluminum. Now a local recycling company has agreed to empty these dumpsters free of charge. (Peninsula)

❦ A man who is an FBI agent moves back to the community and now tutors students at his old school. (Johnson)

❦ Another resident of the same neighborhood who is a retired RTA bus driver now comes and picks up students once a week and drives them to the place where they get tutored. (Johnson)

People with Disabilities

❦ Students at a local elementary school perform skits and musical selections at a nearby home for the developmentally disabled. (Johnson)

❦ Through the "Special Friendship Club," local students work with mentally handicapped students to help to integrate them into community life. (National Youth)

Youth

❦ First graders at an elementary school ask community residents where they would like to have trees planted. Then, through a special grant that funds a "community facilitator" at the school, trees are bought, and students spend one day planting them at the desired places in the community. (Nobel)

❧ As a part of this same program, second graders conduct a voter registration drive, and fifth graders collect thousands of cans from the community which they crush using can crushers that they have designed and then deposit at a local recycling center. (Nobel)

❧ A local high school buys an abandoned house in the neighborhood so that it can be rehabilitated by students. (Orr)

❧ Students are recruited from two local high schools to participate in a community-based youth organization in which they will be paid and also receive credit at their schools for rehabilitating housing in their neighborhood. In the hope of obtaining these students as future workers, local businesses agree to pay for the house and the expenses involved in on-the-job training for the students in this project. (NW Side)

❧ A community-based development organization, three local high schools, and several non-profit service organizations form a youth enterprise network in order to facilitate the efforts of local schools to mobilize students to contribute to the development of their communities. As a result of this initiative, local schools set up a "desk-top" catering business which provides lunch for staff and people who work in the neighborhood. They are also able to establish a community resale shop where students get commissions for the clothing they collect from community residents. These students also get paid for working in the store. (Orr)

❧ Students at a vocational high school develop a student credit union using the skills that they have learned in courses taught by staff from a local community development credit union. Now anyone from the school or community can invest in this credit union, and the students operating it will talk to younger kids about the importance of saving and will teach incoming freshman how to continue to run the credit union effectively. (Flower)

❧ Students in North Carolina "map" their community in order to discover new business development opportunities and decide to open a "deli" for which a local CDC and school board share the start-up costs. Now fourteen students are employed at this deli, and plans are underway for the students to become owners by investing $500 each. (Rural)

Seniors

❦ A local high school hosts an annual brunch for senior citizens at which the student chorus and band present musical selections. (Orr)

❦ Students at a junior high school are paired with senior citizens at two local nursing homes. These students write letters to the seniors and meet with them on a regular basis. As a result of these relationships, the nursing home offers its space to the school for special events. (Piccolo)

Artists

❦ A city-wide organization that finds work for local artists provides an artist in residence for an elementary school where this artist spends six months making murals with the students over the walls of the school. (Johnson)

❦ A school decides to sponsor a community arts festival in which entries are accepted from students at the high school and all the elementary schools, as well as from community artists. (Orr)

All of these stories are specific examples of how "school/community partnerships" can be of equal benefit to *all* the parties that are involved. As local schools begin to discover and participate more fully in these kinds of successful relationships, new opportunities for further development and creative cooperation will constantly be revealed.

Chart Two on the next page shows how a local school can become connected with community-based partners.

Chart Three on the page following represents the complex network of partnerships that might exist for a local school that has fully developed itself as a dynamic community asset.

Chart Two: Strengthening Partnerships

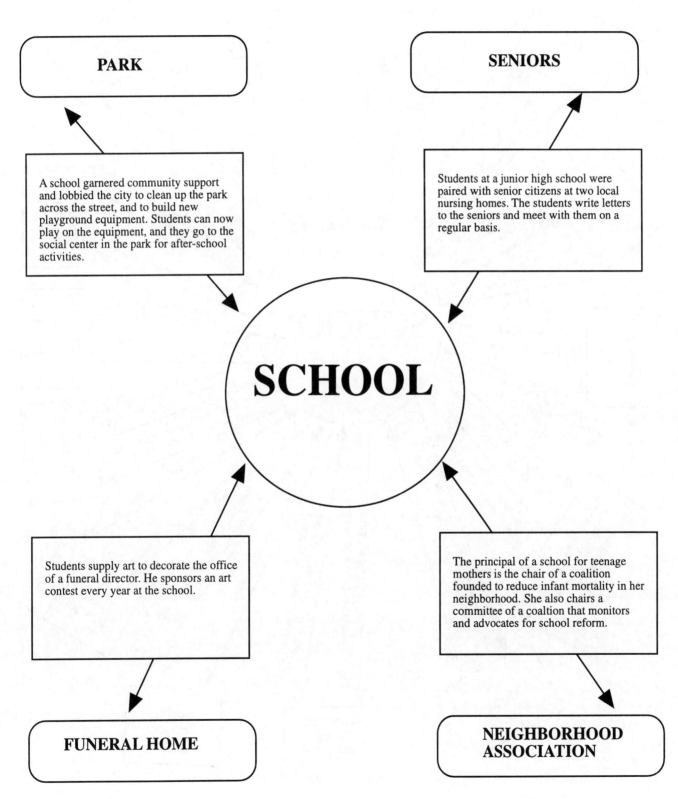

PARK

A school garnered community support and lobbied the city to clean up the park across the street, and to build new playground equipment. Students can now play on the equipment, and they go to the social center in the park for after-school activities.

SENIORS

Students at a junior high school were paired with senior citizens at two local nursing homes. The students write letters to the seniors and meet with them on a regular basis.

SCHOOL

Students supply art to decorate the office of a funeral director. He sponsors an art contest every year at the school.

The principal of a school for teenage mothers is the chair of a coalition founded to reduce infant mortality in her neighborhood. She also chairs a committee of a coaltion that monitors and advocates for school reform.

FUNERAL HOME

NEIGHBORHOOD ASSOCIATION

Chart Three: One on One Relationships

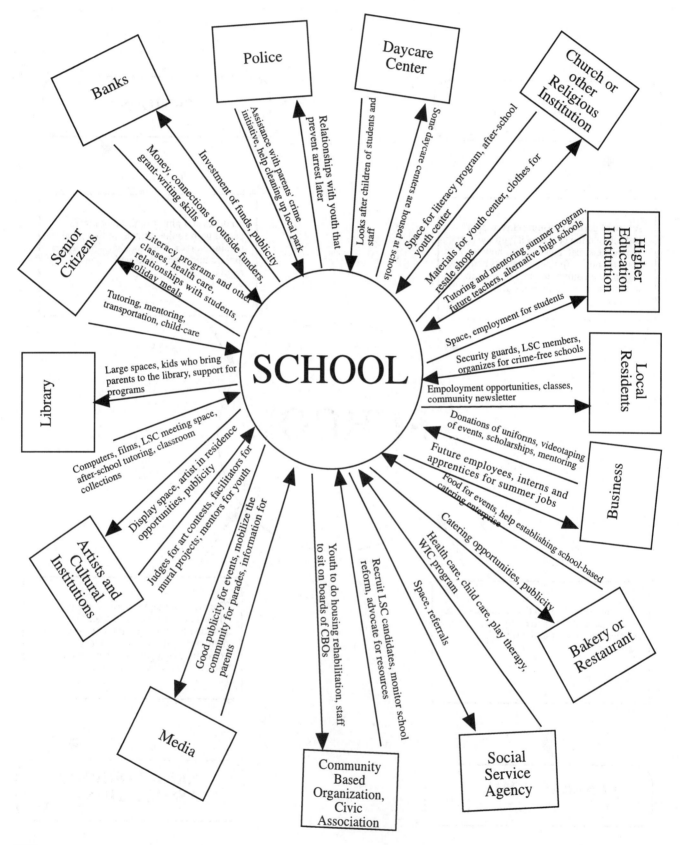

Building Bridges Between Local Schools and Resources Outside the Community

Schools are very visible and highly respected institutions in their communities, and they play a large role in the daily lives of many community residents. But they are also connected to a larger educational system that extends beyond the immediate community and to many different sources of outside support.

Here are a few examples of schools which have attracted significant outside resources to use in community-building projects:

❧ A school receives outside funding to establish a "Lighthouse Program" which will provide an alternative educational experience for high school dropouts. This new "Community Lighthouse Program" then extends educational services to the rest of the community developing a reading workshop for parents, ballet and sewing classes, and a family development institute among its many programs. (Orr)

❧ The principal of an elementary school attracts the support of the Amoco Foundation, and now employees of Amoco tutor students in math and science in the hope that these students will later be hired as employees. As a result of this program, Amoco also has donated playground equipment to the kindergarten classes and provides gifts and a party for the entire school at Christmas. (Johnson)

❧ In partnership with a large city-wide bank, a local high school is able to organize a network comprised of ten elementary and junior high schools in order to coordinate community development activities. As part of this effort, the bank provides connections with city organizations, businesses and institutions, as well as some funding and assistance in planning and development. (Orr)

❧ A school applies for and receives a special grant from the state department of conservation to establish a nature trail behind the school. Now teachers and students are actively involved in cleaning debris, pruning trees and brushes, planting new plants, and constructing a nature trail with specially constructed bird and squirrel houses. (Orr)

Sources and Contacts for the "Stories" in This Section

Boston

Boston Technical High School
55 New Dudley Street
Roxbury, MA 02120
(617) 445-4381 (Yolanda Pinto)

Flower

Flower Vocational High School
3545 W. Fulton Street
Chicago, IL 60624
(312) 534-6755 (Dorothy Williams, Principal)

Johnson

Johnson Elementary School
1420 S. Albany
Chicago, IL 60623
(312) 534-1830 (Mattie Tyson, Principal)

National Youth

National Youth Leadership Council
1910 W. Country Rd. B
Roseville, MN 55113
(612) 631-3672

Nobel

Nobel Elementary School
4127 W. Hirsch
Chicago, IL 60651
(312) 292-5365 (Mirna Hernandez, Principal)

NW Side

Northwest Side Community Development
  Corporation
Youth as Resources Project
5174 N. Hopkins Street
Milwaukee, WI 53209
(414) 332-3310 (Linda Stringl)

Orr

Orr Community Academy
730 N. Pulaski
Chicago, IL 60624
(312) 265-5000

Peninsula

Peninsula High School
14105 Purdy Drive NW
Gig Harbor, WA 98335
(206) 851-6131

Phoenix

City of Phoenix Police Department
620 W. Washington Street
Phoenix, AZ 85003 (Sergeant Frank
Drozanowski)

Piccolo   Piccolo Middle School
1040 N. Keeler
Chicago, IL 60651
(312) 292-5565 (Dr. Thomas Stewart, Principal)

Portage-Cragin   Portage-Cragin Library
5108 W. Belmont
Chicago, IL 60641
(312) 744-0152 (Carol Tarsitano, Branch Head)

Prescott   Prescott Elementary School
1632 W. Wrightwood
Chicago, IL 60614
(312) 532-5505 (Karen Carlson, Principal)

Simpson   Simpson School
1420 S. Paulina
Chicago, IL 60608
(312) 534-7811 (Doris Williams, Principal)

St. Sabina   St. Sabina Church
1210 W. 78th Place
Chicago, IL
(312) 483-4300 (Rev. Michael Pfleger)

Introduction—Community Colleges and Community Renewal

In the past two decades more and more people have attended classes at local community colleges in order to "keep up" with the current job market and to acquire new skills that will enhance their job security and improve their future possibilities. As a result, community colleges have continually grown larger and more complex in the total range of training and services which they offer to their communities.

But, although no one would question the ability of community colleges to provide for the "adult education" needs of their communities, what is often overlooked is the fact that each community college is actually a complex constellation of resources that can be mobilized to build better communities. Today, both community leaders and educators are building positive, new partnerships linking community colleges with other institutions and groups in their communities.

By connecting their own resources with those of the community, community colleges help to create a better, more secure future both for themselves and for their neighbors.

Rediscovering Community Colleges as Assets Within the Community

Community colleges differ from each other in many ways. Each offers a unique gathering of specific assets and opportunities. Yet *every* community college, whether large or small, urban or rural, offers certain sets of resources which can be mobilized effectively to assist in the on-going process of community renewal:

Personnel. In every community college, the members of the faculty and the administrative staff are a collection of highly trained and specialized adults whose skills and knowledge can make significant contributions to the efforts of local organizations involved in community development. For example, faculty members may be "experts" in practical matters such as computer utilization and "systems organization," and administrators may prove to be extremely helpful in organizing fund-raising and grant-writing activities.

Moreover, in addition to the many contributions that can be made by faculty and administrators, the local community college can also become the focal point for mobilizing the special talents and energy of students, their families and other "volunteers" from the local community. Very often the community college can respond directly to the expressed needs of the community by establishing new classes and special events.

Space and Facilities. No matter what their size or configuration, all community colleges have spaces that can be utilized effectively by community groups. Unlike most local schools and universities, community colleges tend to be most active in the late afternoon and evening. This means that space may be available during the morning and early afternoon at which times local schools and universities may be overcrowded and in need of additional space.

In addition to indoor space, many community colleges also have access to various kinds of outdoor space such as parking lots, sports facilities, and landscaped "park" areas. These outdoor spaces can often be put to constructive use by community leaders seeking to establish partnerships with their local community colleges.

In addition, some community colleges have health clinics and other social service resources that are open to all residents of the community.

Materials and Equipment. Community colleges vary greatly in terms of the specific materials and equipment that they have to share with residents of the community. Nevertheless, all community colleges have at least some of the following resources which might be utilized by various local community groups:

- Computers
- Fax and photocopying machines
- Audiovisual equipment
- Scientific equipment
- Athletic equipment
- Wood-working equipment
- "Shop" and car-repair equipment
- Printing equipment
- Darkroom and other photographic equipment
- Books, videos and audiotapes
- Art materials
- Musical instruments
- Kitchen utensils
- Furniture

Expertise. Most community colleges have learned to reach out to the community and to offer classes and workshops beyond the boundaries of the college itself. This means that essential training in a wide variety of practical skills can be offered to certain "marginalized" groups (such as "seniors," "welfare recipients," and people who are "disabled") who might otherwise be excluded from classes.

Economic Power. Community colleges are often able to provide jobs (as well as job training) for residents of the community. This means that many students are able to extend their education by working part-time for the community college where they are currently being trained.

In addition, community colleges that have formed partnerships with other local institutions are in an excellent position to find work for their students and graduates in these institutions, thus linking the community college with the community on yet another level.

Also, community colleges often have access to both public and private funds that are available for positive community-oriented projects. In support of activities and programs of this kind, staff and faculty of community colleges are frequently of great assistance in writing grant proposals.

The resources which have just been listed are only a few of the many that can be found in local community colleges. For these resources to become assets for the purpose of community building, however, community colleges need to be actively linked to the other major resource centers of the community.

Mapping Community Assets to Discover Potential Partners for Community Colleges

Now that we have identified at least some of the many resources that community colleges can offer to the process of community building, we must go on to examine the means by which neighborhood leaders can most effectively mobilize these resources and turn them into valuable assets for community building. This effort to connect the local community college with the process of community building involves the utilization of a four-step process.

- First, make a thorough inventory of the specific resources of each local community college.

- Next, compile an inventory of the key assets and resources of the community as these are represented by local individuals, associations, organizations, and other institutions. When this has been done, it will be discovered that these community assets fall into the following categories: (a) citizens' associations and not-for-profit organizations of all types; (b) publicly funded institutions such as hospitals, parks, libraries, and schools; (c) the private sector including small businesses, banks and local branches of larger corporations; and (4) local residents and special interest groups of "labelled people" such as "seniors," "youth," "welfare recipients," and "artists."

- Next, build strong reciprocal relationships between the assets of the community college on the one hand, and those of the local community on the other.

        ❦ Finally, build bridges based on the strengths of the community college to resources outside the community.

The chart on the next page illustrates the relationships that can exist between a local community college and its community partners.

Building Productive Relationships Between Community Colleges and the Community

When the assets of both the local community college and of the wider community have been mapped, then the staff and faculty of the community college can begin to work together with community leaders to develop a series of new partnerships that will connect the local community college with the process of building a stronger community.

Let us now examine a few examples of this process in action as it has occurred in a variety of communities.

Local Community Colleges and Community Associations

Citizens' Associations

❦ The president of a local community college establishes a Community Advisory Council in which a group of civic and neighborhood representatives meet every month to discuss how the community college might better serve the needs of the community. (Olive-Harvey)

❦ The development director at a local community college helps to write a grant for a coalition of community groups that has come together in order to improve education and training opportunities in the community. (Truman)

❦ A local community college provides the headquarters for a coalition of community organizations that have formed a united front to make sure that local school reform is effective. (Malcolm X)

❦ At this same community college the Director of Business Development participates in a coalition of community groups that have joined together to create an economic development action plan for three surrounding neighborhoods. (Malcolm X)

❦ A local community college establishes an "Inter-Agency Food Network" as part of its Community Resource Center in order to provide technical assistance to food pantries and emergency distribution programs. (Truman)

Chart One: Potential Partners

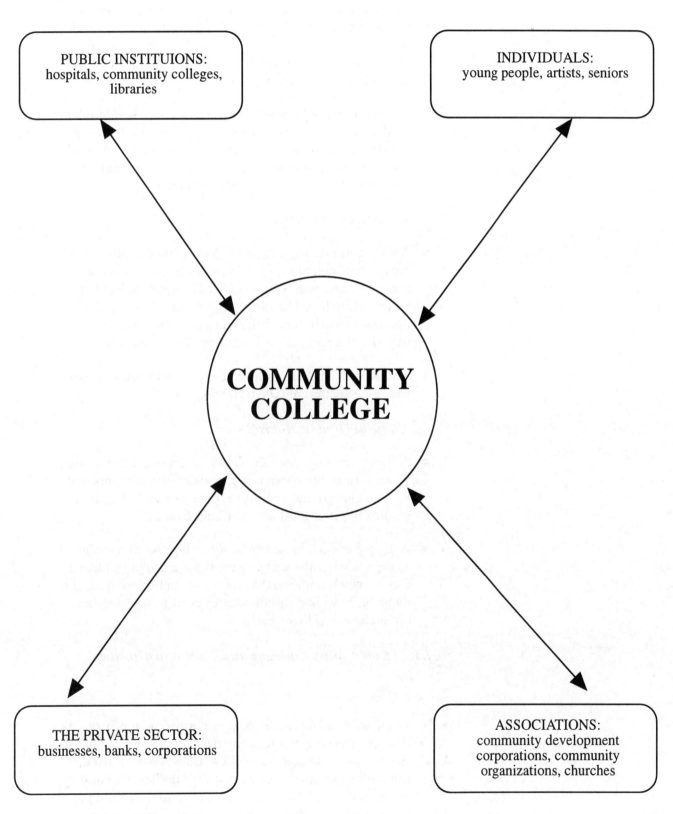

PUBLIC INSTITUIONS:
hospitals, community colleges,
libraries

INDIVIDUALS:
young people, artists, seniors

COMMUNITY COLLEGE

THE PRIVATE SECTOR:
businesses, banks, corporations

ASSOCIATIONS:
community development
corporations, community
organizations, churches

❦ Another community college actively encourages local organizations to use its space—a neighborhood swim club uses the college pool for training and competition; a local soccer club uses the soccer fields; a neighborhood elementary school has their graduation ceremony in the college's auditorium; the local chamber of commerce holds its meetings at the college; town hall meetings for the Congressional district are also held at the college. (Olive-Harvey)

❦ A community college gives office space to a community media workshop which is a non-profit group that assists community groups to gain access to the media. One of the directors of this workshop is a faculty member who also runs the college newspaper. (Malcolm X)

Religious Institutions

❦ A local community college works together with a coalition of neighborhood churches to co-sponsor a series of parenting reading classes that will be held at several churches. The idea of this initiative is to help parents to teach their children to read and also to improve the parents' own reading skills. (Malcolm X)

❦ Another community college co-sponsors a fashion show with a local church. (Olive-Harvey)

Cultural Organizations

❦ A community college hires a neighborhood artist to lead an art tour of the community in which the students will visit various art and sculpture museums as well as the studios of other local artists. (Long Island)

❦ A library and a local community college work together to organize booths and programs for a Korean Cultural Day in which traditional Korean storytelling, singing and dancing, as well as discussions of current social issues, are included. (Albany Park)

Local Community Colleges and Public Institutions

Parks

❦ In a park in a largely Latino neighborhood, a nearby city college uses park facilities to offer its program in English as a second language. After these classes have started, the park supervisor notices that the families who initially come to the park for classes now also are beginning to utilize the recreational programs which the park offers to the community. (Ekhert)

Libraries

❧ A local librarian works with the local community college to bring a self-employment training program to the library. (Austin)

❧ A librarian is able to set up an after-school tutoring program for the young people of the neighborhood by using students from the local university. (Blackstone)

❧ A neighborhood librarian helps the local community college develop a Korean Studies Program in response to the needs of the neighborhood. (Albany Park)

Schools

❧ A local community college participates in a consortium organized by a major university to encourage college attendance. Now, working together with community organizations and the parents and faculty of neighborhood schools, this community college has set up college clubs which provide enrichment programs including visits to colleges and which organize community members to act as mentors for students still in high school. (Olive-Harvey)

❧ Members of the faculty of a community college in a demographically changing neighborhood teach Spanish to the teachers of a local school. (Malcolm X)

❧ Students at a community college form a band which performs in parades and at local festivities in order not only to display their musical talents but also to give a "drug-free" message by talking to neighborhood youth and affirming the advantages of education and other positive alternatives. (Wright)

Police

❧ A local community college working together with community organizations and the district police department develops a "positive alternatives project" in which after-school classes are offered to help youth develop leadership abilities and higher self-esteem. (Wright)

❧ As a part of this same initiative, young people supervised by community college faculty now run a silkscreening business out of the police station. (Wright)

❦ Police officers go to local schools to recruit students for new classes being offered by the community college. (Wright)

Hospitals

❦ A community college forms a partnership with a local hospital to provide basic skills training for a group of women who will be hired immediately by the hospital upon completion of this training program. (Malcolm X)

Local Community Colleges and the Private Sector

❦ Neighborhood merchants and bankers have started to make donations to the local community college. For example, one merchant donated old cars for the auto repair class, and a bank donated money for a reception held at the college to honor local merchants. This process generates valuable publicity for both the giver and the receiver, and the representatives from the business or bank gets his/her picture in the local newspaper along with a representative from the college. (Olive-Harvey)

❦ Another community college teaches courses in Spanish, reading and math to customers and employees at a local Sears store. (Malcolm X)

❦ An art class held at a community college focuses on teaching students to make jewelry that can be sold to neighborhood jobbers. (Wright)

❦ This same community college has established a self-employment training program for women and minorities, and now many of the graduates of this program are starting their own businesses. (Wright)

Local Community Colleges and Individuals Within the Community

Local Residents

❦ Many community colleges host information fairs that are open to both students and the surrounding community. For example, one community college has chosen to sponsor career fairs, school fairs, community fairs, and art shows; and another community college holds a health fair as well as an annual arts fair. (Malcolm X, Olive-Harvey, etc.)

❧ A community college opens an information center in order to make materials relevant to the community available to students and residents. (Olive-Harvey)

❧ Two local community colleges work together on a project called "Partners in Learning" which is concerned with introducing new methods and materials for teachers and parents to help students with science and math. (Truman, Loyola)

❧ A community college produces a brochure on local architecture to record the history of the community. (Truman)

❧ A community college recruits neighborhood adults as tutors in reading for young people enrolled in the Saturday program that this college has initiated. (Wright)

❧ Two local community colleges work together to provide faculty assistance and space for community-based choirs composed of neighborhood residents as well as students of the two colleges. (Olive-Harvey, Malcolm X)

People with Disabilities

❧ Many community colleges have developed special programs to fit the specific needs of the disabled of the community. Some provide special "home study" programs for those who are confined to their residences. Special classes are frequently offered such as those in instruction in "signing" for those who are or who will be working with hearing impaired.

Welfare Recipients

❧ The management committee at a neighborhood housing project recruits students for job-training courses at a local community college. (Olive-Harvey)

❧ The same community college sponsors a series of sewing classes at another local housing project. (Olive-Harvey)

Youth

❧ A local community college works together with the mayor's office to create a "Youth Empowerment" program in which neighborhood youth are trained to lead classes for younger students that are held in a local park, churches and five schools throughout the summer. (Wright)

❧ The same community college adopts a local school so that students from this school can come to the college on Saturdays to use the computers, the gym, and other resources that their own school does not possess. (Wright)

❧ Many community colleges have partnerships with local schools in order to encourage the students of these schools to attend college. For example, a staff member at one community college goes to local schools to give advice on education and to conduct motivational workshops. (Olive-Harvey)

❧ Another community college initiated a program involving studying the community as "ecosystem" for local high school students in which these students investigate their community and collect samples representative of their community's ecology. (Truman)

Artists

❧ A local community college has established an "artist-in-residence" program in which the purpose is to enable the artist to work on his personal style for a year without having to worry about income and also for the artist to "humanize and demystify the world of art for the everyday individual." As a part of this program, the artist visits civic, arts and community groups as well as local schools giving lectures, workshops and demonstrations. He works out of a donated storefront in town and encourages the public to drop by and watch him work. (Central Florida)

❧ A community college hires a neighborhood artist to lead an art tour of the community in which the students will visit various art and sculpture museums as well as the studios of other local artists. (Long Island)

❧ A community college hosts a concert of performances by young music students enrolled in a Suzuki program. (Queensborough)

Seniors

❧ Two seniors are on the faculty at a local community college where one teaches the Lakota language and the other is an instructor in Ojibwe. (NAES)

All of these stories present specific examples of how mutually beneficial partnerships can be established between community colleges and community leaders who are active in the public, private and non-profit sectors of the community. Chart Two on the next page illustrates how a local community college can become connected with local partners.

Chart Three represents the complex network of actual partnerships that might exist for a local community college that has fully developed itself as a dynamic community asset.

Chart Two: Strengthening Partnerships

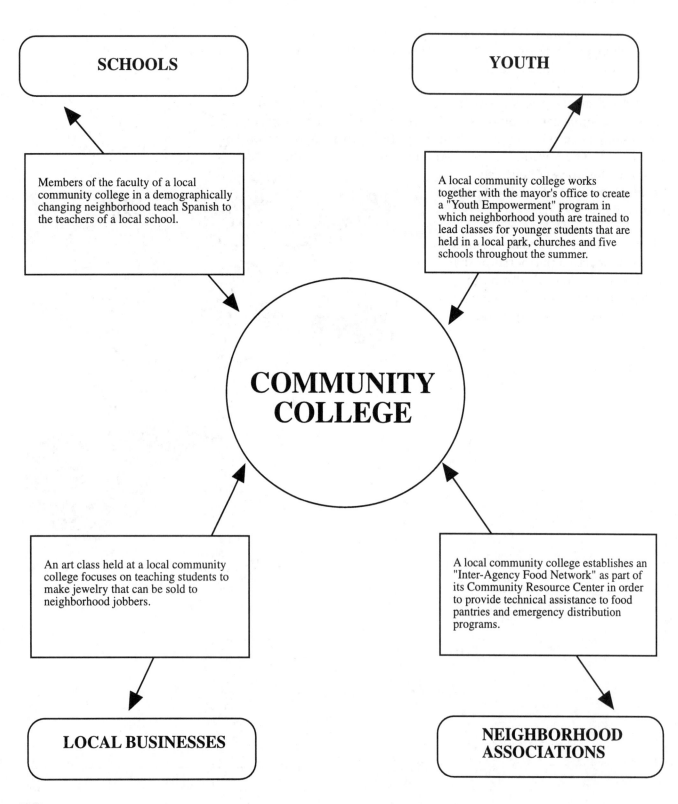

SCHOOLS

YOUTH

Members of the faculty of a local community college in a demographically changing neighborhood teach Spanish to the teachers of a local school.

A local community college works together with the mayor's office to create a "Youth Empowerment" program in which neighborhood youth are trained to lead classes for younger students that are held in a local park, churches and five schools throughout the summer.

COMMUNITY COLLEGE

An art class held at a local community college focuses on teaching students to make jewelry that can be sold to neighborhood jobbers.

A local community college establishes an "Inter-Agency Food Network" as part of its Community Resource Center in order to provide technical assistance to food pantries and emergency distribution programs.

LOCAL BUSINESSES

NEIGHBORHOOD ASSOCIATIONS

Chart Three: One on One Relationships

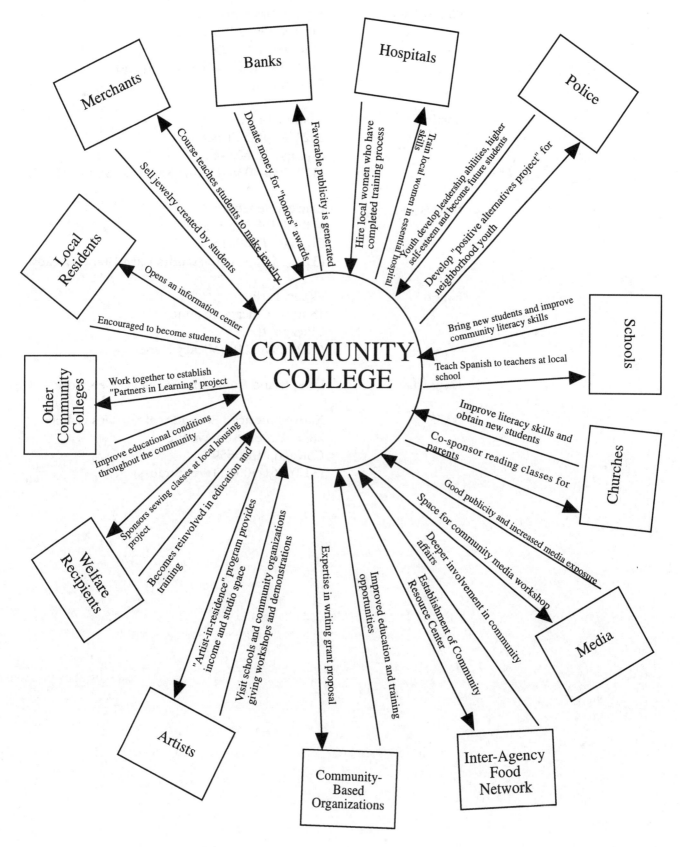

Sources and Contacts for the Stories in This Section

Albany Park   Albany Park Library
5150 N. Kimball Avenue
Chicago, IL 60625
(312) 744-1933 (Chahee Stanfield,
Branch Head)

Austin   Austin Library
2121 W. 95th Street
Chicago, IL 60644
(312) 746-5038 (Donna Kanapes, Branch Head)

Blackstone   Blackstone Library
4904 S. Lake Park
Chicago, IL 60615
(312) 747-0511 (Cassandra Carr, Branch Head)

Ekhert   Ekhert Park
1330 W. Chicago Avenue
Chicago, IL
(312) 294-4710 (Mickey Maher)

Long Island   Long Island Community College, New York

NAES   Native American Educational Services College
2838 W. Petersen Avenue
Chicago, IL 60659
(312) 761-5000 (Terry Strauss)

Introduction—Police and Community Renewal   **POLICE**

    ❦ An extensive education and activities program developed by
a neighborhood police station together with several local
community organizations has been able to provide youth in
the community with positive alternatives to joining gangs.

    ❦ A conflict mediation program introduced by the local police
department into neighborhood schools trains teachers and
youth to respond to threatening situations in nonviolent
ways that will not cause further escalation of the social
tension.

What do these two stories have in common? Each illustrates a commitment by local police leadership to playing an active, positive role in the
continuing process of building stronger local communities. Too often
in the past, particularly in distressed city neighborhoods, the local
police department has been viewed as a "quasi-military," even alien
institution by the residents of the community. But promising new
approaches are beginning to re-open the possibilities for new forms of
productive police/community partnerships.

Here are just a few of the many ways in which communities have been
able to utilize their local police departments in creative ways that
strengthen the community as a whole:

    ❦ Police officers participate in local community meetings where
threats to community safety are identified and new strategies
developed; then these officers work in cooperation with community leaders to address those problems, calling in appropriate
agencies and institutions where and when they are needed.

    ❦ Police officers organize diverse community residents and organi-
zations to find solutions to continuing neighborhood problems.
One officer, for example, conducts a survey of the neighborhood
and organizes members of the community to find a solution to
the proliferation of local gang activities. As a result, a local police
officer is able to mobilize local residents to clean up a vacant lot
that has been used for loitering, to organize neighborhood
businesses to provide better lighting and to cease sales of drug-
related equipment, and to inspire the entire community to
become involved in an annual neighborhood pride day.

    ❦ Local police departments are discovering how productive it is to
build mutually beneficial relationships with public housing and
other city agencies, schools, churches, professional sports teams,
community colleges, universities, social service agencies, parks,
restaurants, businesses, landlords, and nonprofit advocacy
groups. For example, at a public housing site in North Carolina,
community police officers opened a storefront policing opera-

241

tion with the assistance of the public housing authority. As a result of this more intimate contact with local residents, a far greater level of trust and confidence was established between the community and the local police department.

Rediscovering the Police as Assets Within the Community

Local police departments are filled with untapped resources which can be mobilized effectively for the purpose of community building. The beginning of an inventory of these specific assets would include:

Personnel . Police officers are the primary assets of local police departments. Some of the skills and capacities which they bring to the challenge of community-building include:

❧ their technical training in fields such as computers and communications, vehicle operation and repair, self-defense, and investigation and research;

❧ their networks of connections, and in some cases, knowledge of the community;

❧ their skills in such areas as leadership development and conflict resolution.

Space and Facilities. Police stations can serve as settings for community meetings and educational activities. For example, some stations are particularly well-adapted for community meetings because they are fully accessible to disabled residents.

Economic Power. Police leaders may be able to hire local residents to perform some of the assignments that would otherwise keep officers at the station. Moreover, since local police stations in large cities are part of larger departments, funds from downtown may be available for special education and community relations projects. Some police departments have even gone so far as to invest part of their pension funds in specific community development efforts.

Thus, when we begin to view local police officers as having capacities beyond their ability to respond to crimes we can begin to use their other skills and assets to help build a safer and stronger community.

Mapping Community Assets to Discover Potential Partners for the Police

Just as local police departments are full of underutilized assets, so too are local community-based organizations and institutions. Building relationships between local police, on the one hand, and neighborhood organizations and institutions on the other, is the path toward a safe community. The process we are discussing involves four basic steps:

❧ Community leaders make an "asset list" of all the specific resources that are found within the local police department.

❧ A similar asset inventory is then made in the surrounding community, which includes all the resources of the community's various organizations, associations and institutions. This inventory should include:

> ❧ Citizens associations such as block clubs, business associations, neighborhood coalitions, and church groups.
> ❧ Public institutions such as schools, libraries, parks, and community colleges.
> ❧ Representatives of the private sector such as local businesses, restaurants, banks, and branches of larger corporations.
> ❧ Groups of more or less "marginalized" individuals such as "youth," "senior citizens," "public housing residents," and people with disabilities.

❧ At this point, concrete and mutually beneficial "partnerships" can be established between the local police and a wide range of community-centered resources.

❧ Next, beyond these local relationships, police can now use their greater visibility and power to construct new bridges to outside resources which will enhance the capacity of local communities.

Chart One on the next page shows the relationship of the local police to potential partners that exist within the community in each of the four categories listed above.

Building Productive Relationships Between the Police and the Community

It is clear that each local police department is full of assets and resources that can be utilized within the community to create greater strength and coherence. Creating a series of partnerships with local community groups will benefit both the police and the neighborhood.

Neighborhood associations that have been organized directly around community safety issues are obvious choices as potential partners for local police department. But it should be remembered that these are only the most logical places for this process to start. A more complete list of potential partners would include the following:

Chart One: Potential Partners

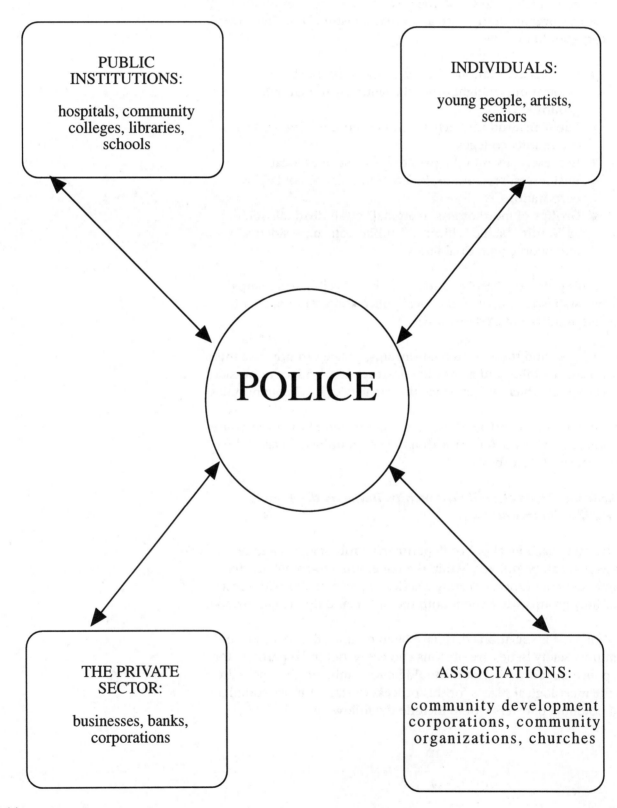

Local Police and Community Associations

Citizens Associations

❦ A citizens forum prioritizes problems in the community and identifies the issues that should be addressed by the local police department. (Louisville)

❦ A community group (composed primarily but not exclusively of members of the local chamber of commerce) volunteers to identify viable targets in the community for police attention. (Seattle)

❦ A neighborhood liaison officer is assigned to attend all neighborhood association meetings in order to become more knowledgeable about major incidents in the community and to provide reports about continuing local problems and concerns. (Portland)

❦ Police officers attend meetings of a local crime reduction project in order to better cooperate on confronting issues and developing appropriate strategies. (Seattle)

❦ A neighborhood association distributes a newsletter to 5000 members, which contains up-to-date information about community safety supplied by the local police department. (Chicago)

❦ A local police station has created a "victim advocacy program" in which a police department representative gives upcoming court information to a neighborhood association so that a group of concerned citizens from this group may attend the court in support of the crime victim. (Chicago)

❦ Police officers work together with leaders from minority advocacy groups to establish contingency planning in the event of racially motivated violence and go out to the scene together with representatives of this group in order to develop appropriate strategies. (Waterloo)

❦ A local police department, in cooperation with local minority leadership, is attempting, with the aid of a federal community block grant, to purchase a tavern and convert it into a drop-in and referral service in which police officers would be available so that local residents would not have to leave the neighborhood in order to file a complaint. (Waterloo)

❦ Neighborhood associations are asked by local police to cooperate in a park watch program and, as part of this program, members of these associations clean up graffiti and establish new levels of contact with local youth. (Chicago)

❧ A neighborhood association recruits its members to participate in a citizen patrol created in cooperation with the local police department. (Portland)

❧ Police officers gather information about deteriorated buildings and pass this information along to the appropriate city agencies for follow-up. Then a cleanup effort is initiated, which uses offenders referred by the court system for community service as laborers on this project. (Los Angeles)

❧ A task force comprised of block clubs, neighborhood associations, and the local police department cooperate in sponsoring an antidrug rally. (Chicago)

❧ Community organizations raise money at a neighborhood festival to outfit the local police department with bicycles for a new bike-patrol program. (Chicago)

Religious Institutions

❧ In response to a continuing series of neighborhood problems, crime prevention officers from the local police department sponsor community- safety meetings in local churches, and neighborhood associations agree to publicize these meetings by mobilizing "phone trees." (Chicago)

Cultural Organizations

❧ Local police create a hotline focusing on break-ins and theft, and this hotline is publicized by a local African-American broadcasting coalition. (Youngstown/NNFPC)

Local Police and Public Institutions

Parks

❧ In cooperation with the Parks Department, the local police guild organizes a recreation program for the children of the community in which police officers serve as volunteers. (Seattle)

Libraries

❧ A representative from the local police precinct comes to the library to give workshops on crime prevention. (Whitney Young)

❧ A farewell luncheon held just before a local library closed for renovation became a real community event when members of the police department, a hospital director, members of the senior center, and a representative of Volunteers for Housing were among the guests who were able to attend. (Kelly)

Community Colleges and Universities

❧ A junior college and a district police station work together to offer education for local young people. The content focuses not only on traditional subject matter but also on issues of self-esteem and self-worth. (Chicago)

❧ A local police department recruits students of social work from a local university and assigns one student to work with a volunteer uniformed officer as a counseling team which is dispatched to calls such as family fights, attempted suicides, neighborhood disputes, etc. (Multnomah County/NNFPC)

❧ Police Neighborhood Resource (PNRC) officers, university fraternity members, and individuals from the community establish a basketball league for 10-12 year olds, and the local university agrees to provide space for their games to be played. (Greensboro)

Schools

❧ An officer from the local police department functions as a School Resource Officer in the community school district where his function is not only to provide security but also to investigate reports of child abuse or neglect. (Phoenix)

❧ Police officers as members of the Community Relations Bureau provide teacher and student training in conflict resolution at four local school districts. (Phoenix)

❧ The Drug Abuse Resistance Education (DARE) program, which focuses on building self-esteem and devising strategies for preventing potential drug use, is taught to fifth-graders by local police at 35 community schools. (Chicago)

❧ A police department develops an incentive program in cooperation with neighborhood associations in which bicycles are offered to "at risk" children who show improvement in school work and behavior. (Madison)

❧ A local police department works with a community school to take "at risk" students who have shown improvement on escorted trips to professional basketball games; the team donates the tickets, the police provide the escort and encouragement, and the schools are responsible for developing the incentive program. (Aurora)

Hospitals

❦ Local police officers work with community health inspectors to identify clear health violations and to provide security during these inspections. (Minneapolis)

Local Police and the Private Sector

❦ Two local police officers work with local businesses, private sanitation companies and neighborhood associations to develop a comprehensive response to gang activities and organize a neighborhood clean-up campaign. This effort is so successful that it culminates in a neighborhood pride day in which local businesses offer jobs to community residents. (San Diego)

❦ The local police department links the court system with private and public institutions willing to provide work for misdemeanor offenders so these offenders can be given opportunities to participate in community service as an alternative to incarceration. (Chicago)

❦ A foot patrol officer coordinates donations from local businessmen to finance a neighborhood clean-up program. As a part of this program, the officer arranges for men who frequent a community day center to clean the area in front of neighborhood stores in exchange for bus tokens and meals in local restaurants. (Aurora)

❦ Local businesses contribute office space in order to establish neighborhood storefront police stations, and, once this is done, neighborhood associations agree to pay for on-going utilities costs. (Portland)

❦ A police department requests the telephone company to cut off incoming telephone service to pay phones in the neighborhood where there has been recurrent drug trafficking. (Chicago)

❦ With local police acting as liaisons, a neighborhood sets up a telephone hotline to receive information concerning community crime issues, and a local newspaper agrees to provide free advertising about the service. (Seattle)

❧ Local media institutions—e.g., newspapers, radio stations, church bulletins—participate in a coordinated campaign to highlight community problems which have been identified by a citizens' project committee in cooperation with the local police precinct. (Louisville)

❧ A grocery chain provides Thanksgiving turkeys for distribution by police officers among elderly and blind neighborhood residents. (Greensboro)

❧ Police Neighborhood Resource officers accompany 190 children from a local housing project to Ringling Brothers Circus. (Greensboro)

❧ Local police in cooperation with neighborhood businesses and a private benefactor initiates a program which gives under-privileged children the opportunity to attend Chicago Cubs ball games and to visit Brookfield Zoo. (Evanston)

❧ Funded by a major private foundation, local teenagers are hired by police officers to patrol at recreational facilities and at a center for senior citizens during the summer months.

❧ Neighborhood police officers solicit donations from the Salvation Army to provide for a needy resident in a local housing project who had recently had surgery. (Greensboro)

❧ The neighborhood Police Activities League works with local businesses to establish a program in which youth are exposed to various job opportunities and meaningful work experiences during the summer. In cooperation with this program, churches provide classroom space, and local businesses donate materials. (Phoenix)

❧ Local businesses and neighborhood associations provide bicycles for bike patrol officers in their business district. (Portland)

Local Police and Individuals Within the Community

Local Residents

❧ Police specialists train local landlords to screen potential renters who might be involved in criminal activity and to upgrade their facilities in order to make their properties more crime proof and safer for local residents. (Portland)

❧ A police department cooperates with social service agencies by referring individuals to them who under prior police policy would have been arrested. (Waterloo)

❧ Local police work as mediators during landlord-tenant disputes in order to prevent minor grievances from turning into more serious offenses. (Oakland/NNFPC)

❧ Volunteers are trained in police-community relations, interviewing techniques, referrals, record keeping, and the use of local and citywide social service directories, and then these volunteers are placed in neighborhood police precincts to perform some of these non-essential police functions and to serve as first contact persons to the community. (New York City/NNFPC)

❧ A team composed of a local police officer and a paid civilian community organizer are assigned to each district in the city in order to educate citizens about community safety matters. Working as a team, the community organizer's primary responsibility is to educate and build relationships with local citizens' groups while the police officer's primary responsibility is to coordinate community action. (Minneapolis)

People with Disabilities

❧ Police officers on a special mental health crisis intervention team receive training from a local mental health clinic so that they can identify mental illnesses and appropriate medications. (Waterloo)

Welfare Recipients

❧ Policing "mini-stations" are establiushed in local public housing areas so that officers can tutor children after school. (Savannah)

❧ A local housing authority agrees to provide space in one of its developments for the opening of a neighborhood resource center sponsored by the local police department. (Greensboro)

❧ Police officers organize a series of athletic competitions between teams from local housing developments. (Savannah)

❧ Local police set up an "adopt-a-family" program which links wealthier families to lower income families so that everyone can be provided with gifts and meals during the holiday season. (Chicago)

Youth

- A police department solicits donations within the department in order to enable local children to attend summer camp day programs. (Evanston)

- Local police initiate a safe trick or treat program for neighborhood children during Halloween in which community businesses distribute candy to the children. (Aurora)

- Police officers organize dramatic performances by local children during Halloween which incorporate messages about community safety and drug education. (Savannah)

- Local police working with the Boy Scouts of America establish a Law Enforcement Explorer Program in which young people are exposed to the possibility of a career in policing while actively cleaning up graffiti, working with the local park systems planting trees, and assisting at picnics for senior citizens. (Chicago)

- The Enrichment Role Model Program pairs a local police officer with children from low and moderate income families targeted by local churches and boys and girls clubs. Group and individual activities involved in this program include visits to the state legislature, colleges, planetariums, sports events, etc. (Greensboro)

- A district police department cooperates with the local park system in forming a football league for neighborhood youth. (Chicago)

- A one week camp is established in order to improve relationships between troubled youth and the local police. This camp features all kinds of activities among which are included classes on drug abuse and community issues. (Louisiana/NNFPC)

- A bike patrol program is established in specific neighborhoods where back alleyways provide fast escape routes for burglars. This program not only diminishes crime in the neighborhood but also builds better relationships between kids and the police when these kids begin to ride their bikes along with the officers. (Baltimore/NNFPC)

- A local youth club assigns teenage workers to a community anti-graffiti program coordinated by volunteers from the local police district. (Seattle)

Artists

❧ In many communities local police departments have worked with neighborhood artists to create crime prevention posters and to organize the painting of murals on walls and fences formerly covered with gang grafitti.

Seniors

❧ A local police department recruits and trains four senior citizens to visit other seniors in order to provide them with crime prevention and safety information. (Cottage Grove/NNFPC)

❧ A local crime prevention officer collects pallets and wood from neighborhood lumberyards in order to re-build doors for senior citizens who had recently been burglarized. Neighborhood youth agree to assist in the construction of these doors under the tutelage of retired carpenters who reside in the community. (Chicago)

❧ Over two thousand senior citizens are recruited and trained by a community police department to look for, describe and report local problems. As a result, many of the major thoroughfares leading into the city are now posted with signs which read: "Warning: This city is protected by Senior Power Neighborhood Watch." (Mansfield/NNFPC)

Thus we have seen how local police departments have been able to enter into a series of "partnerships" with other organizations, institutions and groups of individuals in order to make their community a stronger, safer place in which to live.

Chart Two on the next page shows a representative series of mutually beneficial relationships between local police and their community partners.

Chart Three on the page following Chart Two represents the complex network of possibilities that exist when local police have fully developed their community partnerships.

Chart Two: Strengthening Partnerships

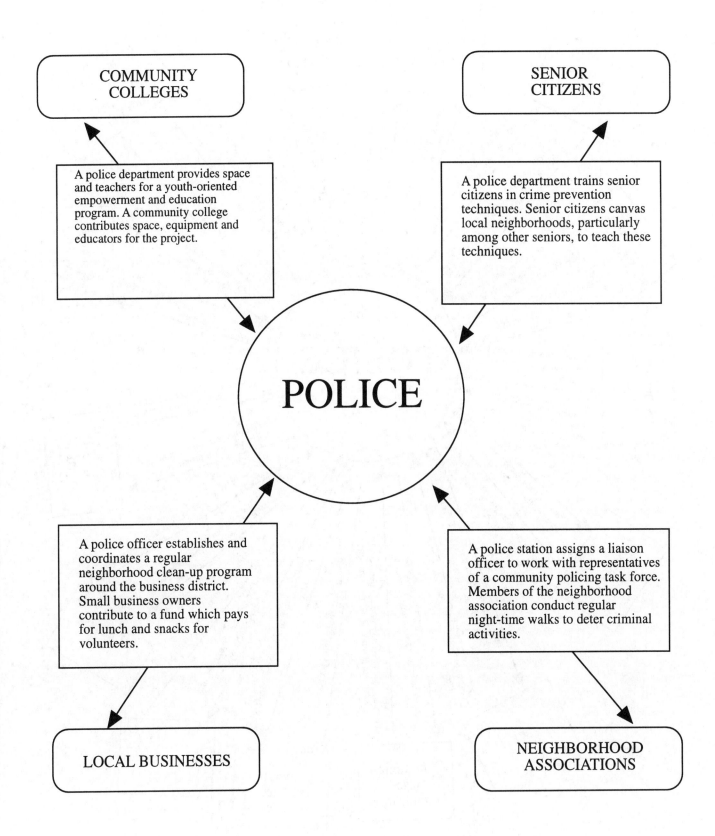

Chart Three: One-on-One Relationships

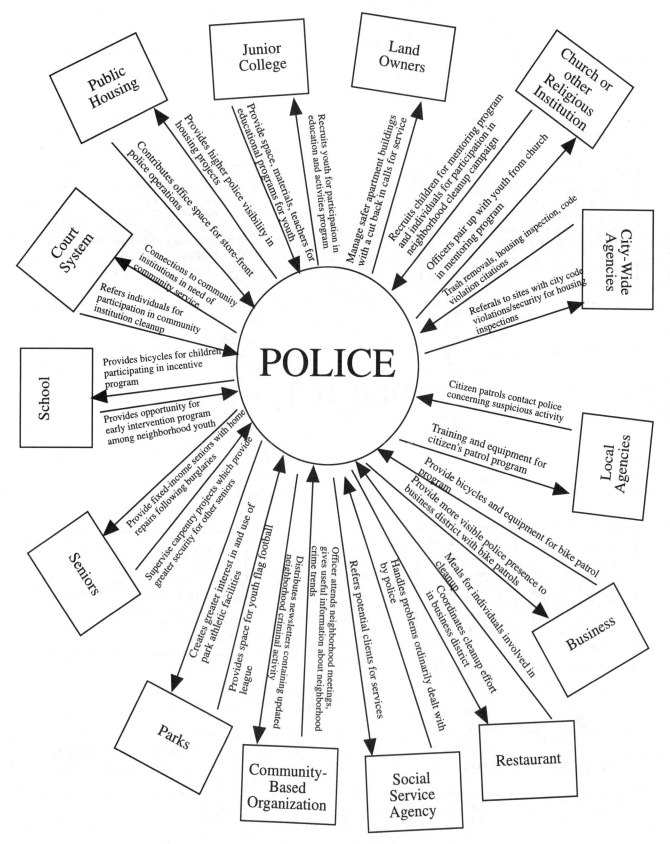

Building Bridges Between the Local Police and Resources Outside the Community

Once strong and viable relationships have been built within the community, a local police department can begin to turn toward leveraging outside resources. This may mean re-defining a pre-existing relationship with city-wide agencies and police department headquarters, and it may also mean developing new relationships where no prior contact had ever existed. For example, a creative police station may find that police department headquarters will be willing to help expand their community partnership programs. Moreover, other city state-wide agencies may also be convinced that they can take a more effective approach to solving community problems by supporting programs already initiated by local police departments. Furthermore, local police can help community groups attract new sources of funding from public and private sources because of the credibility and legitimacy which they bring to a local project.

Sources and Contacts for the "Stories" in This Section

Aurora	Aurora, Colorado Police Department 15001 East Alameda Drive Aurora, CO 80012 (303) 341-8597 (Captain Ron Sloan)
Chicago	15th District Police Station 5327 W. Chicago Avenue Chicago, IL 60651 (312) 746-8300 (Commander LeRoy O'Shield)
Evanston	Evanston Police Department 1454 Elmwood Avenue Evanston, IL 60201 (708) 866-5062 (Sergeant Bob Heytow)
Greensboro	Greensboro Police Department 300 W. Washington Street Greensboro, NC 27402 (919) 373-2236 (Mildred H. Powell, Community Relations Director)
Houston	Houston Police Department Crime Prevention Through Environmental Design (712) 247-4823 (Phymeon Jackson)
Kelly	Kelly Library 6151 S. Normal Blvd. Chicago, IL 60621 (312) 747-8418 (Linda Greene, Branch Head)
Louisville	Louisville 4th District Police 3419 Bohne Avenue Louisville, KY 40211 (502) 588-2478 (Captain David Robinson)
Madison	Madison Police Department City-County Building 211 S. Carroll Street Madison, WI 53703 (608) 266-4897 (Stephanie Bradley Peterson)
Minneapolis	Minneapolis Police Department Community Crime Prevention 217 South Third Street Minneapolis, MN 55401

NNFPC   National Neighborhood Foot Patrol Center
                School of Criminal Justice
                Michigan State University
                560 Baker Hall
                East Lansing, MI 48824-1118
                (800) 892-9051
                (from: *Community Policing Programs: A Twenty Year
                Review* available from Michigan State University)

Phoenix   City of Phoenix Police Department
                620 W. Washington Street
                Phoenix, AZ 85003-2187
                (602) 262-7331 (Sergeant Frank Drozanowski)

Portland   Portland Bureau of Police
                Community Policing Division
                1111 S.W. Second Avenue, Room 1552
                Portland, OR 97204
                (503) 796-3126 (Arlene Martinez)

San Diego   San Diego Police Department
                Southeastern Division
                7222 Skyline Drive
                San Diego, CA 92114

Savannah   Savannah Police Department
                Savannah, GA
                (912) 651-6690 (Major Reynolds)

Seattle   Crime Prevention Unit
                610 Third Avenue
                Seattle, WA 98104

Waterloo   Waterloo Police Department
                715 Mulberry Street
                Waterloo, IA 50703
                (319) 291-4353 (Sergeant Paul H. Fitzgerald)

Whitney Young   Whitney Young Library
                7901 S. King Drive
                Chicago, IL 60619
                (312) 747-0039 (Mae Gregory, Branch Head)

Introduction—Hospitals and Community Renewal

Traditionally we think of hospitals exclusively as institutions that provide medical treatment for sick people in the community. This passive, "response to emergency" role seems to be especially true in lower-income communities.

Yet today many innovative hospitals are demonstrating a new understanding of their roles in communities. This new understanding recognizes the relationship between healthy individuals and healthy communities, and stresses a variety of creative prevention strategies. As one hospital director put the point:

> "You really can't expect health care to be effective in the long term in a community that has severe housing problems. If people don't have good housing, which supports and nurtures their health, then we in the hospital will be forced to respond by providing very expensive care that will be futile in the face of growing health problems."

In other words, hospitals are now recognizing that supporting community development builds healthy communities and contributes to their own institutional well-being.

Rediscovering Hospitals as Assets Within the Community

The resources that hospitals possess to catalyze community development are many and varied. They include, for example, the following:

Personnel

The personnel of a hospital are its greatest assets. Although hospital staff are usually busy people with many responsibilities, they need not be "married" to the hospital entirely in terms of their traditional roles and functions. As a matter of fact, many innovative hospitals are encouraging their staff to play an active part in the life of the surrounding community. As the president of a large urban hospital recently said:

> "This institution is 2,500 people, not 532 beds. This puts a focus on the talent and caring of the hospital's employees. It takes down the walls and allows our people to be in many places in our neighborhood. Wherever our people are, the hospital is."

Examples of staff involvement include membership on community boards, volunteering for local projects, providing technical assistance in areas such as child care and prevention, and many more.

Space and Facilities

Of the many resources that a hospital possesses, perhaps the most obvious is its space. This space can become a vital resource to many community groups or smaller institutions. Some hospitals are now actively encouraging the community to find ways to use their walls, conference rooms, auditoriums, kitchens, cafeterias, gyms, etc. For example, one hospital has a gym which is used by a local school for after-school sports and for physical education classes throughout the day. Another employed a community artist to paint its interior walls and allocated an old unused kitchen as his studio while he was engaged in this process.

Materials and Equipment

A listing of the various material assets available in most hospitals would include such resources as:

- photocopy machines
- fax machines
- computers
- audiovisual equipment
- kitchen utensils
- ambulances
- medical equipment (available for use outside the hospital)

Expertise

Hospital personnel with wide professional skills and experience can reach out to the community in many ways.

Economic Power

Hospitals control significant budgets. Committed hospital leadership can direct some of those resources toward building the local economy. For example, hospitals can hire local residents, purchase goods and services locally, even invest in local credit institutions. And they can certainly help local community builders secure financial support for their work.

Mapping Community Assets as Potential Partners for Local Hospitals

Once the community-building assets of local hospitals have been discovered, it becomes possible to link these assets with appropriate partners currently active within their community. "Mapping" the assets of the local neighborhoods will uncover four sets of potential community partners:

❦ Community organizations and associations of various kinds.

❦ Publicly funded institutions such as schools, parks, and the police.

❦ The private sector which includes local businesses and also branches of larger corporations.

❦ Individuals and groups of "labeled" people such as "youth," "seniors," "artists," and others with special interests, abilities and capacities.

The specific nature of these groups will always vary from community to community and, as a result, the resources of each local hospital will be mobilized in ways that are uniquely appropriate to its own community setting.

Chart One on the next page illustrates the relationships that can be built between a local hospital and its community partners.

Building Productive Relationships Between Hospitals and the Community

When the assets of both the local hospital and the neighborhood within which that hospital is located have been "mapped," then hospital personnel can begin to work with other community leaders to build a stronger and healthier community. Following are examples of the mutually beneficial relationships which are being developed between hospitals and their community partners.

Hospitals and Community Associations

Citizens Associations

❦ A local hospital learns to develop close relationships with a wide variety of community groups. For example, one hospital often uses staff volunteers to do photocopying and envelope-stuffing when certain neighborhood organizations need to do a mailing. When a local music school needed a printer, hospital leaders donated an old model they were no longer using. As a result of actions of this sort, when the hospital was applying for additional funding for new high-tech equipment, various community organizations wrote letters to the funding agency in support of the hospital's request. (Lutheran)

Chart One: Potential Partners

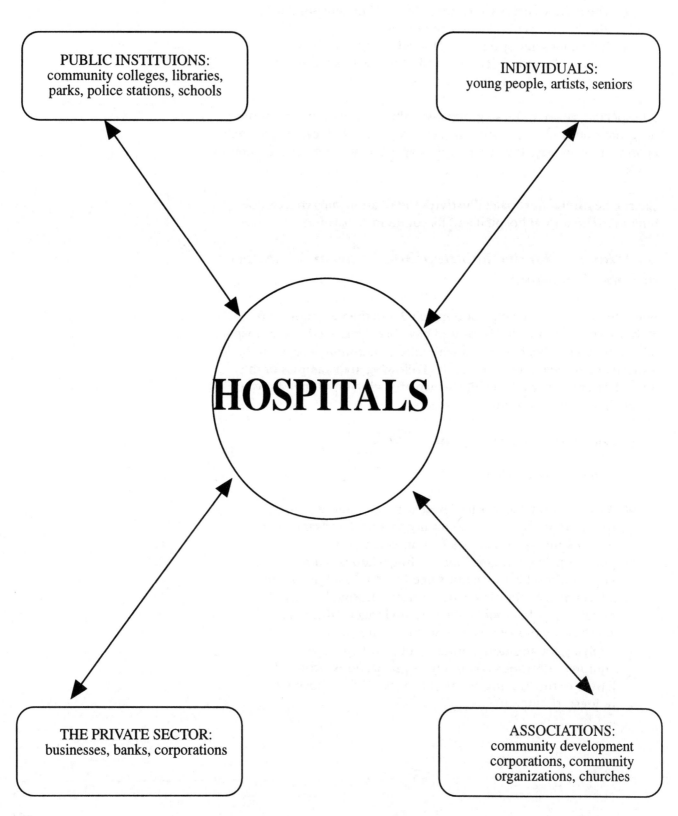

❦ A hospital forms a partnership with an alternative school for high school dropouts, the local police department, and a social service agency in order to provide programs which prevent the institutionalization of troubled youth. (Mt. Sinai)

❦ A hospital works with a local health clinic to provide special services that are more culturally sensitive to the neighborhood's Asian population. (Lutheran)

❦ A Community Development Corporation and a local hospital develop a plan in which they offer neighborhood residents a 50% discount on all "wellness" programs they offer to the community. (Riverside)

❦ A hospital creates a community development corporation to spearhead economic development efforts in the neighborhood. This CDC has a board that is made up of community members as well as hospital staff, and in its first five years of operation, this CDC negotiates $4.5 million in mortgages and contributes $350,000 in equity to cover the rehabilitation costs for 300 units of housing for low- to moderate-income families. (Montefiore)

❦ Another hospital forms a partnership with two local development corporations to invest $3-million to subsidize 100 new homes in the surrounding community, and 15 of these new homes are built on land donated by this hospital. (Mt. Sinai)

❦ A local hospital facilitates the formation of a coalition of 40 neighborhood groups in order to focus effectively on the rehabilitation of existing buildings. The president of this hospital then serves as the first president of this new community development corporation which re-develops 700 abandoned housing units, thereby stabilizing the neighborhood's housing market. (Lutheran)

❦ A hospital facilitates tenant organizing around issues of child care, security and beautification in a local housing development by sponsoring workshops on various aspects of tenant management and by providing the headquarters for the local housing authority's citywide tenant patrol. This hospital also underwrites and facilitates grant proposals for the tenants organization, provides administrative assistance and even donates money for certain special projects. (Mt. Sinai)

Religious Institutions

❧ Hospital staff volunteer to participate in the chaplaincy program administering pastoral care to patients. (Mt. Sinai)

❧ Another hospital sponsors community meetings with ministers from churches of various faiths to discuss issues of relevance to themselves and the community and to collaborate on solutions by sharing their resources. (Lutheran)

❧ A hospital organizes a consortium of local churches to create three resale boutiques which will be run by the women's board of the hospital, the proceeds of which will be divided among the churches. (Mt. Sinai)

❧ A hospital forms a network of community barbershops and churches to conduct blood pressure screenings for young men in the neighborhood. (Mt. Sinai)

❧ A hospital sponsors an awards ceremony for a local association of Hispanic ministers who are receiving special certificates from the hospital for completing training that enables them to be HIV counselors. (Lutheran)

❧ In a neighborhood experiencing a large influx of Cambodian immigrants, medical staff at the local hospital become aware of the need for a Buddhist temple in the community. The Cambodians are referred to a development corporation affiliated with the hospital which helps them form a nonprofit organization and negotiate financing for a location in which a temple could be established. (Montefiore)

Cultural Organizations

❧ A local hospital sponsors a Chinese health fair in which local volunteers provide translations of relevant information, doctors donate prizes, and students from a local school perform. (Arcadia)

Hospitals and Public Institutions

Libraries

❧ A children's librarian in a rural area makes regular visits to the waiting room at the County Health Department in order to do a reading program with the children who are there waiting to be seen. (Aiken)

Community Colleges and Universities

❧ A nurse from a local hospital recruits students from health occupation classes at a number of local vocational schools for a "career day" in order to increase these students' awareness of careers in nursing. (Veterans Affairs)

Schools

❧ A hospital has a gym that is now being utilized by local schools and churches for physical education classes and after-school sports events. (Nazareth)

❧ Another hospital has developed a community sex education program for 4th-8th graders at seven local schools. At one of these schools, where there are 500 kids enrolled in the program, there has been a dramatic reduction in pregnancies. (Mt. Sinai)

❧ A hospital extends its medical services to a school by adopting it through the Board of Education, and now this hospital provides medical examinations for all the eighth graders involved in athletic programs. (St. Elizabeth's)

❧ Employees from a hospital tutor seventh and eighth graders at a local school. (Mt. Sinai)

Police

❧ A hospital develops a partnership with the local police department to get referrals for its rape counseling program and its child abuse clinic. Hospital employees now volunteer once a month in the emergency room in order to provide counseling for victims of rape. (Mt. Sinai)

Hospitals and the Private Sector

❧ A local hospital always makes a concerted effort to support local businesses when buying supplies. This means that two neighborhood printers are utilized regularly by the public relations department. Freelance photographers hired for special events are residents of the neighborhood. Employees use a local car service rather than public transportation when they need to leave the community for meetings. The catering department uses a food distribution company located across the street from the hospital whenever the need arises. (Lutheran)

❦ A CDC that is an affiliate of a hospital works in partnership with the local merchants association to develop a security network linking 40 participating stores to a computerized surveillance system that began with its hub at the hospital. The same CDC assists local merchants with grant proposals, newsletters and the advertising of special events. (Montefiore)

❦ Another hospital forms a partnership with a large manufacturing company and an association of community residents to rehabilitate existing housing in the neighborhood. This partnership is controlled by a governing board of community members, and at the present time over $55 million has been reinvested in the community and 3100 people have been assisted with housing rehabilitation. (Mt. Sinai)

❦ A hospital forms a partnership with a chain of department stores to open neighborhood health clinics in two of its branches. The same hospital already runs many other health centers including three in high schools and two at public housing developments. (Mt. Sinai)

❦ A hospital develops relationships with local factories and businesses to provide referrals for their Employee Assistance program, a substance abuse recovery program. (St. Elizabeth's)

❦ A hospital creates a neighborhood development corporation which has rehabilitated 900 housing units and brought $155 million in various investments to the neighborhood. (Riverside)

❦ A local hospital wins a $20,000 award from a private foundation for being "the one nonprofit doing the most to improve the quality of life" in the city. The hospital then uses this money to give $1,000 grants to local homeowners and businesses for facade improvements. (Mt. Sinai)

Hospitals and Individuals Within the Community

Local Residents

❦ When making hiring decisions, a hospital always gives preference to local candidates over outsiders of equal merit. (Lutheran)

❦ Seventy-five percent of another hospital's employees are from its own neighborhood. (Mt. Sinai)

❧ A local hospital provides adult basic education, high school equivalency and ESL classes, as well as cooking and sewing classes and consumer awareness programs for community residents as well as its own employees. (Lutheran)

❧ Another hospital establishes a community-owned bookstore and a food cooperative that has targeted contracts at community vendors. This hospital has now created a CDC which is working on a mixed-income housing development for families with working parents. (Drew)

❧ People who are enrolled in a hospital's methadone program initiate an AIDS volunteer organization in which volunteers from the neighborhood provide companionship, run errands, pay bills, and intercede with landlords on behalf of people with AIDS. (Montefiore)

People with Disabilities

❧ A local hospital finds suitable and interesting work for a developmentally disabled adult in their mailroom. Now this disabled person is the hospital's official "mailman" and delivers mail that has been specially color-coded for him to deliver to the proper destinations. (Logan Square)

Youth

❧ A hospital builds a community nursery school for preschoolers that is located across the road from the hospital. (Southeastern)

❧ A hospital forms a partnership with the city so that local youth can be employed for the summer and, in many cases, these entry-level jobs lead to permanent positions. For example, the current assistant director of security originally started as a temporary youth worker. (Lutheran)

❧ A local hospital, in partnership with the CDC that it founded and supports, sponsors summer programs for neighborhood youth in which they have painted the local subway station, done landscaping in the neighborhood, and painted equipment in a nearby playground. Most recently, some of these young people painted a mural at the hospital depicting the history of the community and the hospital's role in it. Among its many other initiatives, this CDC has also helped a local dance company obtain a grant to restore an abandoned movie house, and it has created a park for residents of a building that they had rehabilitated. (Montefiore)

Seniors

❧ When a church asks for a hospital's help in building housing for the elderly, a staff member from the hospital sets up a nonprofit corporation with community members and hospital personnel on the board. The hospital then donates $50,000 to get this new corporation off the ground and hires a consultant to steer their grant proposal through HUD. (Southeastern)

❧ A hospital turns its former building into rent-subsidized apartments for local senior citizens. (Lutheran)

❧ A hospital lobbies HUD to add call buttons and "community space" to a senior citizens building in order to help these seniors stay out of nursing homes and hospitals. (Riverside)

Artists

❧ A hospital employee who is on the board of the neighborhood arts council photocopies fliers for a community arts fair and circulates these fliers to all other employees of the hospital. (Lutheran)

❧ A local artist spends a sabbatical as "artist in residence" at a community hospital where he uses an old kitchen as his studio and employs other local artists to paint murals and graphics and to put on performances at the hospital. He stimulates patients and staff to make art themselves, "negating the feeling that art has been imposed on them." (Senior)

In each of these examples, we have seen how local hospitals have been able to connect with other institutions, organizations or individuals within their community in order to establish a series of mutually beneficial partnerships. Successful relationships of this kind benefit *both* the local hospital and the community because in these instances each of the partners magnifies the resources and, therefore, the effectiveness of the other.

Chart Two on the next page shows how a local hospital can become connected with its community partners.

Chart Three on the page following represents the complex network of partnerships that might exist for a local hospital that has fully developed itself as a dynamic community asset.

Chart Two: Strengthening Partnerships

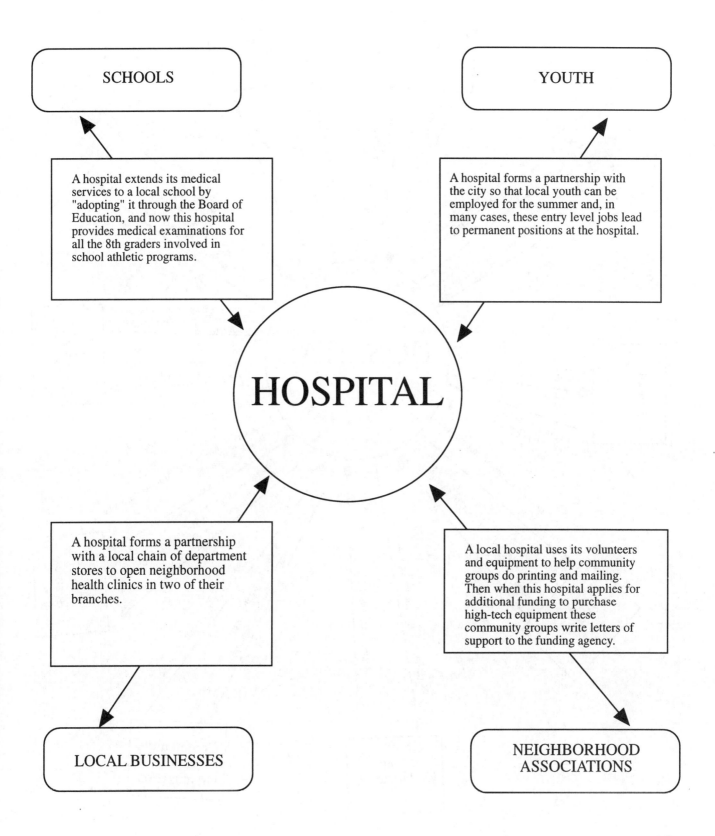

SCHOOLS

A hospital extends its medical services to a local school by "adopting" it through the Board of Education, and now this hospital provides medical examinations for all the 8th graders involved in school athletic programs.

YOUTH

A hospital forms a partnership with the city so that local youth can be employed for the summer and, in many cases, these entry level jobs lead to permanent positions at the hospital.

HOSPITAL

A hospital forms a partnership with a local chain of department stores to open neighborhood health clinics in two of their branches.

A local hospital uses its volunteers and equipment to help community groups do printing and mailing. Then when this hospital applies for additional funding to purchase high-tech equipment these community groups write letters of support to the funding agency.

LOCAL BUSINESSES

NEIGHBORHOOD ASSOCIATIONS

Chart Three: One-on-One Relationships

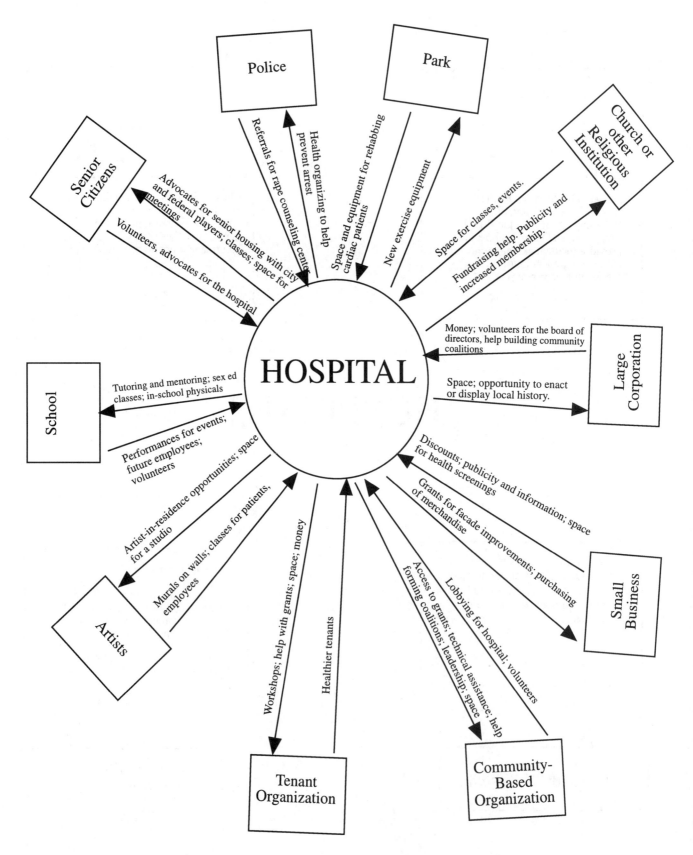

Building Bridges Between Hospitals and Resources Outside the Community

Once a local hospital has established a solid series of community partnerships, it can then begin to involve itself in advocacy work which will connect people in the neighborhood with resources that are available outside the immediate community. The unique role that hospitals can play as advocates is made clear by the president of a hospital in Brooklyn, New York:

"Other community groups formed, and Lutheran's role changed to that of bridge between them and local politicians. We were important as a technical support group. The intelligence of our staff, as accountants, architects, as spokesmen, was put at the community's disposal. We helped the neighborhood organize politically so that it was in a position to bargain for government resources on its own. We haven't got any money of our own, but we're smart and ambitious and we can be a catalyst."

Other examples of successful community-building advocacy work by local hospitals include the following:

❧ The director of the local hospital foundation meets with state and federal officials in Washington on behalf of neighborhood residents who are lobbying for a highway to come through their community. (Riverside)

❧ A hospital advocates for federal funds that are funneled through the city and then loaned to community groups to be given back for neighborhood projects. When the community pays back the loans to the city, this money will then be reinvested in the hospital's neighborhood. (Riverside)

❧ A hospital organizes a task force to negotiate with the city to raze buildings and to create new sidewalks, curbs, lights and landscaped medians. (Mt. Sinai)

❧ The same hospital organizes a coalition of hospitals in its area to protest proposed health care budget cuts. As a part of this effort, the board of trustees and other staff members travel to the state capitol to hold meetings with key legislators, and they produce a packet of information to illuminate the issues for people in their community who then organize a massive letter-writing campaign in response. (Mt. Sinai)

Sources and Contacts for the "Stories" in This Section

Aiken	Aiken, SC County Library 314 Chesterfield Street South Aiken, SC 29801 (803) 642-2023 (Barbara J. Walker, Children's Librarian)
Arcadia	Arcadia Methodist Hospital 300 Huntington Drive Arcadia, CA 91007 (818) 445-4441 (Nancy Baillie, Director of Volunteer Services)
Drew	Martin Luther King-Drew Medical Center 1521 E. 120th Street Los Angeles, CA 90059 (213) 563-4974 (Lewis King, Dean of Medicine)
Logan Square	Logan Square Neighborhood Association 3321 W. Wrightwood Chicago, IL 60647 (312) 384-4370 (Rosita De La Rosa)
Lutheran	Lutheran Medical Center 150 55th Street Brooklyn, NY 11220 (718) 630-7000 (Mary Theresa McKenna, Assistant Director of Community Relations)
Montefiore	Montefiore Medical Center 111 E. 210th Street Bronx, NY 10467 (212) 920-4011 (Fred Yaeger, Press Manager)
Mt. Sinai	Mount Sinai Hospital 15th and California Chicago, IL 60608 (312) 650-6489 (Diane Dubey, Director of Public Affairs)
Nazareth	St. Mary of Nazareth Hospital 2233 W. Division Chicago, IL 60622 (312) 770-2227 (Victor Villalobos, Community Relations Specialist)

Riverside

Riverside Hospital
Toledo, OH 43604
(419) 729-6000 (Hugh Grefe, Executive Director
of Riverside)

Senior

Peter Senior
Department of Architecture & Landscape
Manchester Polytechnic
Manchester, NH
M15 6HA

Southeastern

Greater Southeastern Community Hospital
1310 Southern Ave. SE
Washington, DC 20032
(202) 574-6077 (Claudia Thorne, Director of
Program Development)

St. Elizabeth's

St. Elizabeth's Hospital
1431 N. Claremont
Chicago, IL 60622
(312) 633-5865 (Josie Vargas, Director of
Community Health Education)

Veterans Affairs

Veterans Affairs Medical Center
1055 Clermont
Denver, CO 80220
(303) 399-8020 (Patricia Grant, Assistant Chief
of Nursing Services and Education)

At the very center of the community building challenge is the effort to revitalize the community's economic life. As employers, particularly in manufacturing, have either moved their operations, cut back on jobs, or shut down plants entirely, more and more communities have suffered the consequences. It is by now painfully obvious that many localities—from city neighborhoods to smaller towns and rural communities—have been virtually unplugged from the mainstream economy, and that a major commitment to economic reconstruction is necessary.

In communities across the U.S., that commitment has been made by local residents. Community economic development organizations have proliferated, and have grown in sophistication as they have begun to master challenges such as housing rehabilitation and construction, enterprise development, and other local economic revitalization strategies.

This guide will not even attempt to summarize the many creative approaches to economic development which are now part of the community economic development arsenal. Interested community leaders should consult one of the many excellent technical assistance providers, or contact networks such as the National Congress for Community Economic Development (NCCED, 2025 Eye Street NW, Washington, DC, 20006, (202) 659-8411) in Washington, D.C., for state-of-the-art guidance to successful community development practice. Another very useful guide is "Working Neighborhoods: Taking Charge of Your Local Economy," (Center for Neighborhood Technology, 2125 W. North Avenue, Chicago, IL 60647, $5.)

Instead, this guide will summarize three creative but less visible paths which local leaders have been constructing, each of which can contribute significantly to rebuilding the economies of neighborhoods. Each of these paths is built by using mostly local materials, neighborhood assets which simply need to be rediscovered and fully mobilized. Each of these paths poses a different set of challenges to the creative community builder.

   ❧ The first asks: How might community builders recognize and capture the full economic development potential of all of our local institutions and organizations?

   ❧ The second asks: How can community builders capture local savings and expand the availability of vital capital and credit for community building purposes?

   ❧ The third asks: How can local development leaders maximize the creative uses of all of the physical assets of the community?

Together, these three challenges remind the community builder that even in the most devastated neighborhoods, some of the materials needed to construct a path toward economic well-being are still present, and can be mobilized for development purposes. Each of the next three sections will explore one of these challenges in more depth.

Thus, the first part of this chapter will lift up the potential for economic development of "non-economic" institutions in the community. The premise of this exploration is simple: in economically devastated communities where expectations of help from the outside are extremely low, the community builder must locate and mobilize *every* possible resource in the community—including those of an economic character. However, in many neighborhoods, many or most for-profit businesses have closed or moved away. Nonetheless, there remain many institutions such as schools, parks, libraries, hospitals, and human service agencies which seldom act strategically as major economic forces in the community. This first segment, then, will explore ways in which the underutilized economic power of local public and not-for-profit institutions can be harnessed for development purposes.

The second part of this chapter highlights the vast potential of two different kinds of *locally controlled lending institutions*—the community development credit union and the community development loan fund. These two vehicles represent examples of creative local responses to the absence of vital capital and credit in communities where disinvestment has been the rule. Obviously, CDCU's and CDLF's should not be regarded as the only viable approaches to rebuilding locally controlled economy, but as useful tools with many significant lessons to teach.

Finally, the third part of this chapter lifts up the important development potential represented by a community's *physical assets*—its land and buildings, infrastructure, transportation, etc. Particular attention is paid to ways in which community builders have begun to turn physical liabilities—vacant land and buildings, waste materials, etc.—into assets for community development purposes.

Again, this chapter is not meant to provide an exhaustive overview of local economic development strategies. Rather, the probes into the economic uses of non-economic institutions, examples of local lending vehicles and the development potential of local physical assets are all intended to stretch the imagination of community builders, and to underline the idea that no local assets can be overlooked if our desperate communities are to be economically regenerated.

Institutions are usually organized around a central function. The police department exists to build community safety. Hospitals are built to provide health services. Libraries contribute to the overall literacy of a community. Schools educate children. Parks provide recreation opportunities. And churches contribute to the spiritual well-being of a community. Through the course of this guide, we have tried to show that these services to the community can be expanded and enhanced by building relationships with partners in the community.

But there is another step that can contribute to the building of local communities. Each institution is also a player in the economy. But too often these institutions fail to see their potential positive impact on the **local** economy.

The church, the school, the police department, the library, the park, the human service agency, the hospital: each is an institution with the capacity to be a primary player in the local economy. A church, for example, can spend its money within the neighborhood. Likewise, a hospital or any other institution can expend its dollars in the local economy in a variety of ways. "Non-economic institutions" have the potential to be key players in building stronger, healthier economies depending on how they use their money.

What, then, are the ways in which non-economic institutions can get involved in the local economy? How great an impact can these institutions, used to thinking and acting without regard to their economic impact, have on the local economy?

- ❦ A library can purchase some or all of its supplies from local vendors, perhaps focusing on businesses owned by persons of color or women or worker cooperatives.

- ❦ A hospital can mandate preferential hiring of neighborhood residents.

- ❦ A school can create new businesses, operated by students participating in an entrepreneurship training program, which serve teachers, students and local community residents.

- ❦ A church can establish a foundation through which investment or grants are made in neighborhood-based projects.

- ❦ A police department can invest some of its pension fund in local community development efforts.

These examples demonstrate some of the ways local institutions can build the local economy. In general, there are eight basic methods for local institutions to invest in building their community:

- ❦ Local purchasing

- ❦ Hiring locally

- ❦ Developing new business

- ❦ Developing human resources

- ❦ Freeing potentially productive economic space

- ❦ Local investment strategies

- ❦ Mobilizing external resources

- ❦ Creating alternative credit institutions

We will explore each of these strategies, which are depicted in the chart on the next page, in the sections which follow.

Local Purchasing: Patronizing Local Vendors and Businesses

Each one of our "non-economic" institutions has some of the same essential economic powers as local residents—only much greater. One such power lies in the ability to make decisions about purchasing. Just as a city resident may decide to drive to a suburban mall to shop for his or her family, an institution can order supplies, materials and equipment from outside the neighborhood, city, state or country. Local residents may, however, decide to patronize local businesses just as institutions may decide to turn their economic assets back into the community.

Most low-income neighborhoods experience a net outflow of economic resources. Institutions can become primary players in helping to close that loop.

- ❦ In Chicago, the Board of Education has granted local schools control over their own budgets for supplies and textbooks. Schools can purchase goods and some services from local suppliers if those vendors are approved by the Board of Education. The leverage granted to local schools, which came about largely due to grassroots pressure, enables schools to make purchasing decisions that benefit the local economy. In a modest first year of local purchasing, one school spent over $20,000 in the local neighborhood. (Prescott)

Investing in Neighborhood Economies:
The role of local institutions

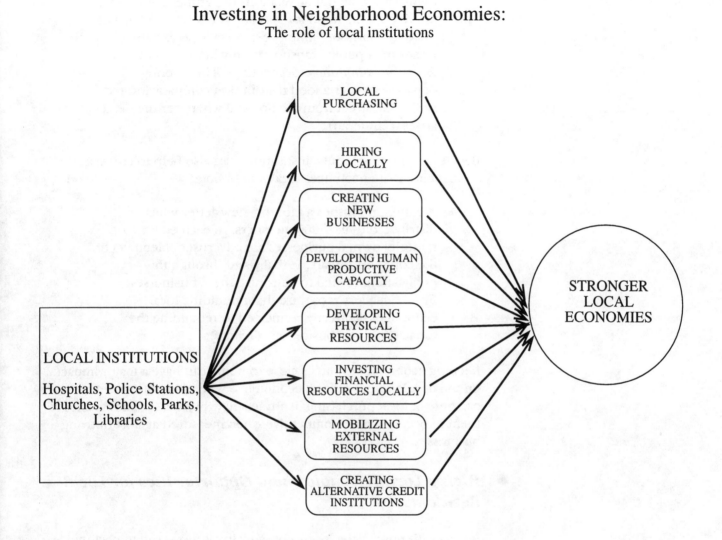

❦ A local hospital always makes a concerted effort to support local businesses when buying supplies. This means that two neighborhood printers are utilized regularly by the public relations department. Freelance photographers hired for special events are residents of the neighborhood. Employees use a local car service rather than public transportation when they need to leave the community for meetings. The catering department uses a food distribution company located across the street from the hospital whenever the need arises. (Lutheran)

Besides purchasing locally, institutions can also help to create an atmosphere that encourages local purchasing:

❦ A church publishes a monthly newsletter which is distributed to its 4,000 members. In each edition local minority-owned businesses are advertised. Members of the congregation are, verbally and through this publication, invited to patronize these businesses. Church leaders recognize that rebuilding local economies is directly connected to rebuilding the capacity of local businesses. (Trinity)

Keeping economic resources close to home can have a major impact on the development of local economies. When institutions set an example of local purchasing, it attracts new businesses and enables them to become more competitive when measured against outlying businesses.

Hiring Locally: Employment Opportunities for Local Residents

Just as with purchasing, non-economic institutions can impact the capacity of the local economy to create jobs for local residents both directly and indirectly. The following examples show how two hospitals and two churches go about making jobs over which they have control available to local residents:

❦ Whenever making hiring decisions a nonprofit hospital gives preference to local candidates over outsiders of equal merit. (Lutheran)

❦ Seventy-five percent of another hospital's employees are from its own neighborhood. (Mt. Sinai)

❦ One congregation contracts with city agencies and local businesses to provide labor support through its Manpower program. (Christian)

❧ Another congregation always hires out to local contractors when construction or repair projects are undertaken. (UCRP)

There are other indirect ways of achieving the same goals in cases when an institution may not have the capacity to hire significant numbers of local residents.

❧ A parish establishes a working relationship with area businesses by providing meeting space for the local business association. The church presents its own agenda to the association by advocating for a local business code of ethics. The church takes the relationship one step further by advocating for fair local hiring practices—even advocating for a minimum of 50% local hiring. (St. Sabina)

❧ A community college builds relationships with local businesses and institutions in order to funnel its own students directly into internships or jobs upon graduation in its community. The college forms a partnership with a hospital, for example, to provide skills training for a group of women who would be hired immediately by the hospital upon completion of training. (Malcolm X)

❧ Two local police officers work with local businesses, private sanitation companies and neighborhood associations to develop a comprehensive response to gang activities and organize a neighborhood clean-up campaign. This effort is so successful that it culminates in a neighborhood pride day in which local businesses offer jobs to community residents. (San Diego)

This is just the beginning of a look at the many ways in which local institutions can directly or indirectly enhance the capacity of the local economy to provide jobs for local residents. When residents live and work in the same neighborhood, the benefits are many: transportation costs are practically eliminated; workers have a far greater stake in the success of local businesses as well as the neighborhood as a whole; and awareness of the issues and needs of the neighborhood is heightened.

Creating New Businesses: Keeping Economic Activity Locally Focused

In some neighborhoods, the prevailing institutions and businesses are resistant to an emphasis on building the local economy. They may be more interested in extracting resources from the community without returning economic opportunities. Owners of local businesses, large and small, may not even live in the immediate neighborhood. Therefore, a neighborhood institution or organization may attempt to build its own businesses, thereby guaranteeing local hiring and utilization of local resources. Local institutions creating new businesses can provide new jobs in the local economy, supplement the funding of programs of an institution, and bring economic activity under local control.

- ❧ A coalition of congregations came together to build and rehab housing in low-income neighborhoods. A spinoff corporation of one of the congregations organizes and staffs the project. (Bethel)

- ❧ A hospital organizes a consortium of local churches to create three resale boutiques which will be run by the women's board of the hospital, the proceeds of which will be divided among the churches. (Mt. Sinai)

- ❧ Another coalition of congregations developed a housing corporation to build a 130-unit complex with an emphasis on creating community space where diversity could thrive. (Fourth)

- ❧ A local high school enters into a partnership with a community development corporation and several nonprofit technical assistance organizations. The resulting network enables students to create school-based enterprises. Students at the school currently operate a catering business for staff and individuals working in close proximity to the school. Students also operate a resale shop which is open to the student body and the community. (Orr)

- ❧ A hospital establishes a food cooperative and a community development corporation that has targeted community-based vendors for contracts. The development corporation has established a bookstore as a community business. (Drew)

When a local institution helps to create a business, it is often the most marginalized residents who are then drawn back into the productive side of the local economy. While some see senior citizens, youth, the disabled and welfare recipients as drains on the local economy, institutions that recognize their economic potential can enhance the productive capacity of formerly marginalized residents.

- ❧ Youth participating in an entrepreneurship curriculum have run a successful deli after having completed a survey of the economic potential of such a venture. The school provided the framework for the process. (Rural)

❧ A church developed its own recycling and construction businesses, creating many new employment opportunities. (Bethel)

❧ A school has started an infant boutique which provides useful products for the community and generates a cash-flow for the students who work there. Now the students are designing and printing a brochure on car seat safety which will be marketed to schools and agencies in other inner-city neighborhoods. (Simpson)

Developing Human Resource Potential: Unleashing the Energies of Local Residents

We have looked at purchasing and hiring locally. Both are direct and immediate solutions to enhancing local economies. We have also looked at the possibility of creating new businesses.

There are also longer-range policies and practices which local institutions might implement. Creative approaches which both involve local residents in economic activity and which at the same time build their skills and capacities are particularly important. This capacity-building activity is, in fact, a solid investment in the future of the community.

Here are a few examples of how local institutions are building the local economy by investing in human resources:

❧ A school's vocational education project develops a curriculum based on the understanding that "vocational programs should provide broad, long-term skills which enable students to exercise more control over their lives and participate actively in running their communities' institutions." The project emphasizes active problem-solving skills needed to run an enterprise instead of tracking certain students into traditional, passive training programs.

❧ The principal of a high school is on the board of a local business association where he cultivates partnerships with neighborhood businesses in order to facilitate relationships between students and future employers. (Orr)

❧ The Director of Business Development at a community college participates in a coalition of community groups that have joined together to create a multi-year economic development action plan for three adjacent neighborhoods. (Malcolm X)

❦ Students at an elementary school are matched with local businesses for summer internships which enable the businesses to tap into the skills of local youth and give the students a place to learn and earn some money outside of the school. (Prescott)

❦ A hospital decides to purchase a tract of abandoned property in a deteriorated section of a neighborhood. The hospital uses the land to expand its own services, while sending a signal to the community that it is there to stay. The hospital becomes a primary anchor institution in the neighborhood around which the local economy is able to revitalize itself. (Mt. Sinai)

Expanding the Economic Base: Freeing Institutional Space and Physical Resources for Community-Based Ventures

Each institution has building space, materials and equipment which can be utilized in neighborhoods to begin community enterprises. Any one of these institutions might simply provide space for the start-up of cottage industries or help to advertise local enterprises.

For example, churches and schools have opened spaces for day care centers and health clinics; parks and social service agencies have hosted artisans and crafts-makers whose products then become marketable; community newspapers and other communications vehicles are produced in local schools, churches or community colleges. Here are a couple of other examples of creative uses of church space.

❦ A church invited a children's nursery school to become a tenant in the building. The expanded children's program helps the church to meet its bills, provides jobs and an oppotunity for church members to participate on the board. (UCRP)

❦ As a part of a community college's initiative, young people supervised by college faculty now run a silkscreening business out of the local police station. (Wright)

❦ A local librarian develops the resources for a "tool-lending library," and two neighborhood residents start an informal business using the tools they have borrowed. (Austin)

❦ A hospital turns its former building into rent-subsidized apartments for local senior citizens. (Lutheran)

❦ Students at a local school organize in order to set up recycling bins at their school so that students and community residents will be able to recycle paper and aluminum. Now a local recycling company has agreed to empty these dumpsters free of charge. (Peninsula)

❦ A community development corporation created from a neighborhood church worked with another congregation to turn its rectory into transitional housing for 20 families. The parish leases the old rectory for $1 per year. (Bethel)

❦ An art class held at a community college focuses on teaching students to make jewelry that can be sold to neighborhood jobbers. (Wright)

❦ This same community college has established a self-employment training program for women and minorities, and now many of the graduates of this program are starting their own businesses. (Wright)

Local Investment Strategies: Keeping Investment at the Neighborhood Level

One of the most powerful resources available to any institution is its financial capacity. This capacity can come in many different forms, including:
   ❦ endowments
   ❦ savings or investment portfolios
   ❦ special collections or fund-raising drives
   ❦ discretionary funds
   ❦ pension funds

Traditionally, these financial resources have been invested in "safe" funds outside of the local economy. These funds, if returned to local neighborhoods, have the potential of financing a wide range of sustainable economic development projects.

Some of the creative vehicles through which these resources can be invested include:

   ❦ direct contributions
   ❦ foundations
   ❦ community development loan funds
   ❦ credit unions
   ❦ community development credit unions

If local institutions invested even a fraction of their investment portfolios, millions of dollars would suddenly be available to local economies. Here are some of the concrete examples of local investment happening in communities across the country.

❦ A church joins with seven community groups to form a community development credit union in order to invest in community-based projects. (Bethel)

❦ A school provides the space, resources and training for students to open a youth credit union. Youth learn basic financial skills and the value of investments at the same time. (Flower)

❦ A hospital helps to establish a community development corporation whose focus is housing, and subsequently invests $50,000 in the project. (Southeastern)

Clearly more resources are available for investment in local efforts. Furthermore, a direct financial investment by an institution usually means that it has a direct stake in the success of the program, and will work to see that it thrives.

Economic Bridge Building: Local Institutions Serving as Conduits for Outside Resources

We have looked at some of the ways in which non-economic institutions can contribute to the economic life of local communities. All of these have focused on the resources available *within* neighborhoods. However, many institutions have numerous contacts outside of neighborhoods. Most are part of larger institutional bodies that have access to far greater resources. Individual schools belong to school systems. Police stations belong to police departments. Neighborhood libraries belong to citywide library systems. Churches are members of regional and national denominational institutions. And all of these institutions have access to other significant regional and national institutions and organizations. What are the implications of these relationships?

City churches have been able to cultivate relationships with wealthier suburban congregations. These suburban congregations have in turn supported the initiatives of city congregations. In North Carolina, for example, a statewide credit union helped city and suburban congregations establish a common pool of resources which was used to renovate church buildings and expand church space for community-based development projects such as child care. (Self-Help)

The linkages that local institutions already have can pave the way for valuable resources flowing into the neighborhood:

❦ The Board of Pensions of a national church body creates the first social investment pool capitalized by church pension funds. The plan gives pastors and other church members a choice in allocating pension monies. Two of the five options are considered to be socially responsible. (ELCA)

❧ A hospital advocates for federal funds that are funneled through the city and then loaned to community groups to be given back for neighborhood projects. When the community pays back the loans to the city, this money will then be reinvested in the hospital's neighborhood. (Riverside)

❧ Several church denominations invest pension funds in a revolving loan fund in New England which then makes low-interest loans available for community-based housing projects. $700,000 is initially placed in the loan fund which has grown by more than ten-fold. (Institute)

❧ Another local hospital facilitates the formation of a coalition of 40 neighborhood groups in order to focus effectively on the rehabilitation of existing buildings. The president of this hospital then serves as the first president of this new community development corporation which re-develops 700 abandoned housing units, thereby stabilizing the neighborhood's housing market. (Lutheran)

❧ A school attracts the support of a major private foundation that arranges to provide mentors and tutors and donates playground equipment to the school. The private foundation hopes through the partnership to strengthen the children's math and science skills so they can be hired in the future. (Johnson)

❧ A local hospital wins a $20,000 award from a private foundation for being "the one nonprofit doing the most to improve the quality of life" in the city. The hospital then uses this money to give $1,000 grants to local homeowners and businesses for facade improvements. (Mt. Sinai)

❧ This same hospital forms a partnership with a large manufacturing company and an association of community residents to rehabilitate existing housing in the neighborhood. This partnership is controlled by a governing board of community members, and at the present time over $55 million has been reinvested in the community and 3100 people have been assisted with housing rehabilitation. (Mt. Sinai)

❧ Another hospital creates a neighborhood development corporation which has rehabilitated 900 housing units and brought $155 million in various investments to the neighborhood. (Riverside)

❧ Still another hospital creates a community development corporation to spearhead economic development efforts in the neighborhood. This CDC has a board that is made up of community members as well as hospital staff, and in its first five years of operation, this CDC negotiates $4.5 million in mortgages and contributes $350,000 in equity to cover the rehabilitation costs for 300 units of housing for low- to moderate-income families. (Montefiore)

❧ A local community development corporation, built from a neighborhood church, works with individuals from outside of the community who can provide expertise. One working relationship utilizes the skills and experiences of a suburban home builder who specializes in energy-efficient homes. (Bethel)

❧ In partnership with a large city-wide bank, a local high school is able to organize a network comprised of ten elementary and junior high schools in order to coordinate community development activities. As part of this effort, the bank provides connections with city organizations, businesses and institutions, as well as some funding and assistance in planning and development. (Orr)

It is clear, then, that local institutions often have the capacity and status to attract resources from outside the neighborhood. Well-established institutions with a good track record are most likely to be able to assist local initiatives in accessing support. In addition to building bridges to foundations, state and federal agencies, or other sources, local institutions are connected to their own governing bodies which may be in a position to invest in the neighborhood economy.

Commitment to Community: Ongoing Support of Economic Activity

The key to building sustainable local economies is in developing a strong resource base—both human and physical—which is appropriate for that particular community. Sporadic infusions of capital, relief financing and dependence on external sources of expertise and aid cannot, in the long run, guarantee a thriving local economy. Many neighborhoods have experienced such neglect and economic devastation that short-term financing of special projects and programs will not go very far in helping to rebuild the local economy. In some instances the human and physical infrastructure has to be rebuilt brick by brick.

By investing in the local economy, institutions demonstrate a commitment to the economic health and well-being of the neighborhood. But it is not simply a benign display of support. If an institution makes a commitment to invest locally, it will want local economic initiatives to succeed. Indeed, it will be in the self-interest of the institution, both directly and indirectly, for the local economy to flourish. The ongoing support of local economic activity by institutions that possess power and status, is essential to the rebuilding of the community.

Credible institutions lending their name to a project or actively participating in the project can attract new resources into a neighborhood. It is a sign of the institution's commitment to the local community, an important indication that **this** community is here to stay.

Contacts for Stories in This Section

Austin   Austin Library
2121 W. 95th Street
Chicago, IL 60644
(312) 746-5038 (Donna Kanapes, Branch Head)

Bethel   Mary Nelson, President
Bethel New Life, Inc.
367 N. Karlov
Chicago, IL 60624
(312) 826-5540

Christian   Christian Family Center Church
Rev. Tony E. Pierce
1800 W. Bradley Avenue
Peoria, IL 60606
(309) 673-2600

Drew   Martin Luther King-Drew Medical Center
1521 E. 120th Street
Los Angeles, CA 90059
(213) 563-4974 (Lewis King, Dean of Medicine)

ELCA   Evangelical Lutheran Church in America
8765 W. Higgins Road
Chicago, IL 60631

Flower   Flower Vocational High School
3545 W. Fulton Street
Chicago, IL 60624
(312) 534-6755 (Dorothy Williams, Principal)

Fourth   Fourth Presbyterian
Rev. Ted Miller
126 E. Chestnut
Chicago, IL 60611
(312) 787-4570

Institute   Institute for Community Economics
Revolving Loan Fund
Sister Louise Foisy
151 Montague City Road
Greenfield, MA 01301
(413) 774-7956

Johnson	Johnson Elementary School 1420 S. Albany Chicago, IL 60623 (312) 534-1830 (Mattie Tyson, Principal)
Lutheran	Lutheran Medical Center 150 55th Street Brooklyn, NY 11220 (718) 630-7000 (Mary Theresa McKenna, Assistant Director of Community Relations)
Malcolm X	Malcolm X College 1900 W. Van Buren Chicago, IL 60612
Montefiore	Montefiore Medical Center 111 E. 210th Street Bronx, NY 10467 (212) 920-4011 (Fred Yaeger, Press Manager)
Mt. Sinai	Mount Sinai Hospital 15th and California Chicago, IL 60608 (312) 650-6489 (Diane Dubey, Director of Public Affairs)
Orr	Orr High School 730 N. Pulaski Road Chicago, IL 60624
Peninsula	Peninsula High School 14105 Purdy Drive NW Harbor, WA 98335 (206) 851-6131
Prescott	Prescott School 1632 W. Wrightwood Chicago, IL 60614
Riverside	Riverside Hospital Toledo, OH 43604 (419) 729-6000 (Hugh Grefe, Executive Director of Riverside)
San Diego	San Diego Police Department Southeastern Division 7222 Skyline Drive San Diego, CA 92114

Self Help	Self Help Credit Union Laura Benedict P.O. Box 3619 Durham, NC 27702 (919) 683-3016
Simpson	Simpson Alternative School 1321 S. Paulina Chicago, IL 60608
Southeastern	Greater Southeastern Community Hospital 1310 Southern Avenue SE Washington, DC 20032 (202) 574-6077 (Claudia Thorne, Director of Program Development)
Trinity	Trinity United Church of Christ Rev. Jeremiah Wright 532 West 95th Chicago, IL 60628 (312) 962-5650
Truman	Truman College 1145 W. Wilson Avenue Chicago, IL 60640
UCRP	United Church of Rogers Park Rev. Kerm Krueger Ashland & Morse Avenues Chicago, IL 60626 (312) 761-2500
Wright	Wright College 3400 N. Austin Avenue Chicago, IL 60634

Introduction

A basic problem for many low-income communities today is the lack of access to credit. Dozens of neighborhoods have been redlined by major financial institutions and then simply abandoned when overhead costs became too great to provide for the savings needs of individuals on limited incomes.

What did this mean for local communities? Where lending had once been available to rehab housing, and to finance small business start-up and expansion, housing purchases, medical payments, major consumer purchases and travel, a vacuum came into being. Without necessary credit, housing stock deteriorated rapidly, no new small businesses developed, no business expansion occurred and no new investment in the community took place. Communities were simply left to their own devices without the necessary access to capital. This is what "disinvestment" means.

A neighborhood may have many of the component parts necessary to engage in a strong community rebuilding effort. But a lack of access to capital and credit will have a debilitating effect on every effort to rebuild. This guide has shown how "non-economic" institutions can act as bridge builders to outside resources in order to make substantial funding available. However, even these efforts do not guarantee that resources will be sufficient or accessible. The infusion of capital through short-term relief aid or time-specific grants may provide a temporary boost to the local economy, but it is in no way a replacement for either the generation of capital and credit from within the community, or for attracting capital from outside the community.

Astute community builders, responding to the growing local credit vacuum which has characterized neighborhood life over the last 20 years, have constructed a vital new industry which injects desperately needed loans into local economies.

Referred to collectively as "Community Development Financial Institutions," these locally accountable lending structures come in a range of shapes and sizes. They include community development banks (e.g., South Shore Bank in Chicago); micro-loan funds (e.g., the Women's Self-Employment Project, also in Chicago); community development loan funds; and community development credit unions. 1993 estimates of the scope of these community development financial institutions place their total number at about 450, managing a total of about $700 million in assets. (See *The Neighborhood Works,* August-September, 1993, for a good summary of CDFIs.)

Two forms of CDFIs, the community development banks and the micro-loan funds, have received considerable attention in the last few years. Both are valuable strategies for community building, and deserve thorough exploration. For materials relating the ground-breaking experience of South Shore Bank, one of four community development banks currently operating, contact Shorebank Corporation, 7054 S. Jeffrey Blvd., Chicago, IL 60649, (312) 288-1000.

One source of good materials on micro-loan funds, as well as the other forms of CDFIs, is the Coalition of Community Development Financial Institutions, 213 W. Ferry Road, Yardly, PA 19067, (215) 736-1644.

This guide will introduce the two other major forms of Community Development Financial Institutions in somewhat fuller fashion. Community Development Credit Unions (CDCUs) and Community Development Loan Funds (CDLUs) are both important tools for generating local access to credit, and both can be built on the existing asset base of the community—the savings of individuals, as well as the assets and connections of local associations and institutions.

Community Development Credit Unions are very local, community-based institutions whose specific mission involves lending in low-income communities. CDCUs must attract most of their capital from the local community, and do all of their lending within set community boundaries. Community Development Loan Funds, on the other hand, can attract capital from a much wider set of investors, and often loan in many different low-income communities.

CDCUs and CDLUs, then, are two community-based institutions that effectively combine the resources of local community residents and local institutions with resources from outside the community.

This guide will now introduce each of these approaches a bit more fully. We will **not** emphasize the technical details involved with founding and operating either a CDCU or a CDLU. Rather, we want to underscore the usefulness and versatility of these vehicles by summarizing a few of the thousands of creative loans made by each, stories of investments which contribute to rebuilding communities.

For much more extensive, excellent materials and technical assistance dealing with Community Development Credit Unions, contact:

National Federation of Community Development
   Credit Unions
120 Wall Street, 10th Floor
New York, NY 10005
(212) 809-1850

For more on Community Development Loan Funds, contact:

National Association of Community Development
    Loan Funds
924 Cherry Street
Philadelphia, PA 19107-2405
(215) 923-4754

Community Development Credit Unions (CDCUs)

Community Development Credit Unions differ from traditional financial institutions in that they intentionally and primarily seek to make lending available for the development of low-income communities. CDCUs have made lending available to individuals normally shut out of the financial market for the start-up or expansion of businesses, the purchase or remodeling of homes, or for education. Lending is also made for consumer purchases, hospitalization or travel.

Besides loans to individuals, which enhance the quality of life in low-income communities, CDCUs have developed innovative loan programs and made loans to community-based organizations and coalitions to enhance their development work in the community. In one neighborhood, a community-based organization identifies homes in need of weatherization. Upon identifying the homes, the CBO refers the owners to the local CDCU for the lending sufficient to complete the weatherization project. The CDCU benefits from the loan fees it collects from home owners. Home owners benefit from the savings on energy costs. And the CBO further develops its contacts and image in the community.

Many existing CDCUs were established independently during the civil rights era and as part of federally sponsored community action programs. Churches formed coalitions to build CDCUs in order that some form of credit would be made available in local neighborhoods. Groups of community activists got together to form CDCUs. And dozens of community-based organizations and neighborhood associations combined resources to found a CDCU. In every case, a cooperative effort was needed to start a democratically-controlled local financial institution that could and would respond to the particular credit and banking needs of low-income communities.

CDCUs: Well-Suited to Local Economies

The CDCU is particularly well-suited to lending in low-income communities. Although the exact number of CDCUs is not known, hundreds of CDCUs around the country are currently making an impact in local neighborhoods through a variety of lending and savings programs and initiatives.

❧ **Providing basic banking services.** CDCUs have, for some communities, replaced the bank as the primary financial institution. CDCUs provide basic savings and checking account services for members used to relying on credit exchanges for the bulk of their banking needs. Savings and reinvestment in the local community is thereby enhanced.

❧ **Flexibility.** CDCUs are able to make and structure loans to fit the resources of individuals without lengthy credit histories or ability to repay a loan over a short period of time.

❧ **Small loans.** CDCUs make loans that fit the capacity of consumers or entrepreneurs. A typical CDCU loan may be as low as $500 and go as high as $10,000 or more where business and mortgage lending is taking place. In most cases, traditional lending sources will not make credit available at these lower levels.

❧ **Loans to women and minorities.** Recognizing that women and minorities have had limited access to credit markets, many CDCUs have established loan programs that lend exclusively to these groups.

❧ **Providing second chances.** An individual who has defaulted on a first loan is often shut out of the credit market or forced to pay exorbitant interest rates. A CDCU generally takes social factors and extenuating circumstances into consideration when reviewing a loan application. In many cases, a loan will be made and structured carefully to avoid a second default.

❧ **Utilizing resources of middle-income individuals.** CDCUs are able to take advantage of the mixed income structure of many neighborhoods. Deposits of middle-income individuals and families can be used for lending among low-income individuals.

❧ **Immediate reinvestment in the community.** CDCUs are chartered with the immediate community in mind. In addition to each shareholder having a stake in the CDCU (enhancing local participation and control of local resources) all lending takes place within the immediate community. Residents are thereby empowered to assert control over their own resources.

The real advantage of CDCUs is not just that they contribute to the overall economic development of local communities, but that they provide a vehicle for marginalized individuals to re-enter the mainstream economy. Women, persons of color, welfare recipients, youth and the working poor have most often been excluded from the economy. CDCUs are local assets that institutionalize the process of building access to the local economy.

Where Does the Capital Come From?

CDCUs are permitted to receive up to 20% of their deposits from sources outside the community. (Many CDCUs have, however, successfully applied for a waiver and receive in excess of 20% of deposits from outside of their geographic boundaries.) Since CDCU membership must be comprised of at least 51% who are living at or below 70% of the annual median income for the region, the infusion of outside investment enables many CDCUs to provide lending in areas that ordinarily might be closed to them. Outside deposits come from five major sources: religious institutions, foundations, banks, public institutions and socially conscious individual investors.

Religious Institutions

In North Carolina, a CDCU has established a program through which churches, large and small, pool their resources in order that smaller congregations in the pool can gain access to necessary funding at below market interest rates. Besides using the funding to carry out major rehab projects on their buildings, churches also expand the capacity of their mission by developing underutilized space. In some churches, day care centers are being built. The day care centers meet a real need in the community and provide employment opportunities. Without the partnership of larger, wealthier congregations outside of the community, however, a church with access to fewer resources would not be able to exercise as much economic power in the community. (Self-Help)

Foundations

A grant from a major foundation enabled the National Federation of Community Development Credit Unions to establish coalitions of CDCUs in four major cities. Through the grant, 24 CDCUs received funded deposits averaging $50,000. From these deposits a total of 120 community development loans were made, which amounted to a grand total of $640,000 in lending. The majority of the lending was in housing and small business development (working capital and inventory). When a foundation makes an investment in a CDCU, it enables local decision-making to take place by those who generally have excellent contacts in the community and an implicit understanding of the forces at work in the neighborhood. (National)

Banks

CDCUs argue that not only are they providing lending in communities that banks have left behind, they are also laying the groundwork for banks to return once it has been proven that low-income communities are creditworthy. As one CDCU administrator puts it: "We are developing future customers for the banks." That being the case, it behooves banks to invest in the development and growth of CDCUs.

In Philadelphia, a banking institution was convinced that it was in its self-interest to donate the building it vacated to the CDCU, particularly in light of the Community Reinvestment Act. A large building may bear too many liabilities for a CDCU to accept, but the Philadelphia CDCU was able to extract greater concessions, which made it a worthwhile venture. The bank agreed to pay for all the utilities for the first three years while the CDCU built up its ability to pay operational expenses. Other banks have simply made substantial investments in CDCUs. (Southwest)

State and Federal Agencies

In North Carolina, the Black Congressional Caucus of the state legislature enabled a grant of $1 million to be made to a coalition of CDCUs in order to support business lending among minorities. The grant was provided to a coalition which had as members 10 of the 13 CDCUs across the state. The coalition itself provides training and technical resources to its member organizations so that more effective lending can take place. (Self-Help)

In New York, a state development corporation deposits funds at a CDCU in Ithaca at a three percent rate of interest. The CDCU is able, in turn, to make loans available to women and minority business enterprises at seven percent. The differential in interest rates allows the CDCU to build its asset base while enabling local residents to develop or expand entrepreneurial ventures with funding well below market interest rates. Unfortunately, some CDCUs have been forced to turn down major investments because the point differential on interest rates was so minimal. However, in many cases, major funding from public agencies enables CDCUs to expand their mission in local communities. (Alternatives)

Individuals

As individuals become more aware of the wide rage of opportunities for socially responsible investing, CDCUs represent a viable option for investing in the development of low-income communities. In Dallas, a Texas congressional representative and the state attorney general have each invested $25,000 in a CDCU. Other smaller investments are made by individuals who do not need the highest rate of return on their deposits. Nonetheless, many CDCUs are able to pay dividends on their share draft deposits which in many cases match the rate offered through a passbook savings account. (Common Ground)

Creative Individual Loans

- ❧ A CDCU in Chicago made a $1,000 loan to a hospital janitor that enabled him to buy industrial supplies. Upon purchasing the supplies, he was able to begin contracting cleaning jobs during the evening. Eventually, he had enough contacts and jobs so that he could start his own business on a full-time basis. The CDCU was perhaps the only institution that would make a loan to an individual under these circumstances. (Northside)

- ❧ When the poor are able to afford the purchase of a car, it is more often than not a used car. Financing of used cars, particularly when purchased from a dealer, often exceeds the financing rates for new cars. CDCUs in Chicago have made loans available to low-income individuals and families to purchase used cars. They also make loans available for repairs on used cars. (Woodstock)

- ❧ A CDCU made a loan to an Hispanic woman after she came to a community presentation on financial alternatives. She was unaware of the existence of credit unions and subsequently became a member. The credit union loaned her a sufficient amount to begin her own printing business. (Woodstock)

- ❧ A CDCU in Chicago loaned a blind African-American man enough money to purchase a Braille typewriter and a photocopier. The loan, which was less than $1,000 but unattainable to him through traditional financial services, enabled the man to start up a business out of his home. (Woodstock)

- ❧ A Philadelphia low-income credit union made a loan to an individual for the purchase of clothing in New York City. He in turn sold the clothing by walking the neighborhood streets and projects. The initial $1,000 loan enabled him to make enough to continue sales on a part-time basis in addition to his regular full-time job. (Southwest)

- ❧ A Philadelphia CDCU made a housing rehab loan to a woman who subsequently opened a halfway house for schizophrenic people recently deinstitutionalized or who would have been better off in a community setting.

The woman was in delinquent status on her initial loan from the CDCU and was about to be foreclosed on her first halfway house. However, upon investigation, the CDCU discovered that her son had begun to exhibit signs of schizophrenia, almost causing her to experience a nervous breakdown. Following the initial stages of trauma, the woman was able to begin to catch up on her delinquent loan and make application for the second rehab loan. (Southwest)

❦ A long-time member of a Philadelphia CDCU fell on hard times when her husband left her and left all the bills with her. She declared bankruptcy on all her debts save her CU loan. Making small incremental payments on the loan, she was finally able to get back on her feet. She remarried, became a pastor, opened a store front church with ministries to youth and homeless and eventually, with the help of a loan from the CDCU, purchased a building she had been leasing. (Southwest)

❦ A jazz musician wanted to purchase a computer for his home. He had an uneven source of income—music production and lessons. Nonetheless, the CDCU made the loan to him, recognizing his good credit record and the amount of research he had done before making application for the loan. (Southwest)

❦ A CDCU on the Lower East Side of New York City made a loan, in cooperation with three other New York CDCUs, to a cooperative tenants group. With the loan the cooperative was able to buy out the original purchase loan of an apartment complex, rehab the building and convert it into a tenant-owned and managed building. (Lower East Side)

❦ A woman who had defaulted on her student loan was given no opportunity by the local bank to reestablish credit. The CDCU, however, recognizing her commitment to repay the student loan and reestablish herself as a good risk, provided a loan to her. With the loan, the woman was able to establish a good credit rating. (Lower East Side)

❦ A Chicago CDCU made a travel loan to a neighborhood artisan's co-op so a staff member could travel to Brazil and purchase items for resale at the shop. (Northside)

❦ The same CDCU made a loan to a minority business to purchase a floor-waxing machine, just as the business was starting out. The purchase enabled the company to secure a number of new contracts. (Northside)

❧ A CDCU made a loan to a mom and pop candy maker which enabled the owners to purchase a piece of equipment needed to produce fine chocolates. The candy makers won a contract with the Trump Plaza to provide 75,000 pieces of candy to the hotel. Typically, mom and pop companies cannot get major loans from traditional banking services because their financial records are not sufficient. CDCUs have the flexibility to provide these types of loans. (Brooklyn)

❧ A CDCU made a loan to a bed-and-breakfast which enabled it to purchase a restaurant which allowed the B&B to expand its own services. The loan came under a special investment of the Urban Development Corporation through which loans are made available to minorities running or developing small businesses. (Brooklyn)

❧ A pastor who was able to lease a gas station, which was badly needed in the community, received a $2,000 loan from a CDCU to purchase his first allotment of gas. The loan was made after he got the community to pitch in $1,000 as a sign of good faith and commitment to the station. Following the start-up of the station, the CDCU made a second loan which enabled him to purchase a car inspection and car wash equipment. The pastor returned a third time to his CDCU for a loan to purchase a carburetor testing device. The CDCU would have been unable to make all three loans at one time, but by setting up staged lending, it enabled the pastor to fully equip his gas station. (Common Ground)

❧ A young woman received ownership of a nine-unit apartment building when her father died. The building needed a new roof, staircase and east wall. It was also 18 years in arrears on property tax payments. In order to qualify for a federal housing preservation program, she needed to pay off the back taxes. A CDCU provided the loan which enabled her to pay off the taxes. The building now provides seven units of housing for lower income people and two units of middle-income housing. (Union)

❧ A CDCU made a first-time loan to a nonprofit recycling operation in order that it could purchase a truck and materials. The recycler returned for grants several more times and was finally able to compete for a major city recycling contract. Currently the recycling center has revenues of $1 million and employs 23 individuals. (Self Help)

- A CDCU made a $750 loan to a welfare mother for the purchase of new furniture for her home. With the loan she was able to begin a day care center in her home. She is currently billing more than $60,000 annually in day care services. The CDCU made the loan when no other financial institution would listen to her. (Vermont)

- A Vancouver Credit Union made a loan of $1,800 available to a local residents' association. With the loan, the association was able to pay the first three month's rent on a store front, which was then opened as a seniors store, administered and operated by and for seniors. (Vancouver)

- A CDCU in North Carolina encourages its small business lenders to bring a certain level of savings into a lending relationship. A used car dealer was encouraged to set aside a certain amount of savings and a certain amount from each sale of a used car. Through the partnership, the used car dealer was able to open his business, ensure financial solvency over time, and achieve a net worth of $75,000. The CDCU also benefited from the partnership as its own investment base grew. (St. Luke's)

- A CDCU made available a loan to a foreigner working at a major university. The secondary market would not approve his application because he did not have a green card. Alternatives Federal Credit Union approved his application because he had a solid application and they were confident that he would soon have his green card. (Alternatives)

- A couple filed for bankruptcy on their business after a lengthy illness of the husband and the wife's resignation to care for him and their child. After they recovered from bankruptcy, the secondary market refused the loan. Noting that the circumstances that led to bankruptcy in the first place were beyond their control, and taking into consideration the wife's well-paying job, the housing loan was granted. (Alternatives)

Beyond Individual Loans: More Creative Loan Programs

- A CDCU in New York City developed a prototypical loan for tenant-owned cooperative buildings. The co-ops, in "high risk" neighborhoods, were often not able to get fire and liability insurance. Under a master insurance plan developed by the CDCU, the co-ops were able to buy fire and liability insurance under a power of attorney scheme, which allowed for the policy to be cancelled if it was not paid in full. The CDCU provided the funding for the payment on the policy. (Self Help Works)

- The New York State Development Corporation deposited funds at a New York City CDCU at a very low interest rate. The CDCU in turn made loans available to women and minorities at a slightly higher rate. The loan fund has enabled several minority and women's businesses to get off the ground including a mail order catalog company and a greeting card production company. The loans are available for between $1,000 and $7,000 for terms of up to 60 months at a low interest rate. (Alternatives)

- A branch office of a CDCU in North Carolina is establishing a church-based loan pool. Churches in a particular region from the same denomination provide capital for a loan pool that will be used by other churches for necessary capital improvements or community outreach. One of the goals is to create more day care space in underutilized church space through the loan pool. (Self Help)

- A branch office of a statewide CDCU is prepared to make commercial start-up loans of less than $10,000 available to public housing residents. Traditional funding sources do not make commercial loans of less than $10,000 available. (Self Help)

- A CDCU created a "Rhodes Scholar" Program through which a local nonprofit organization deposits $25 into a child's account following the receipt of good grades. Local businesses back up the program with their own contributions. Most of the children and the parents have added to their credit union savings accounts. (Vermont)

❧ Dreams for Dollars is the name of a credit union for youth. The credit union is completely administered and staffed by youth. Staff from the "adult" credit union serve as consultants to the process. (Alternatives)

❧ Ten banks and a CDCU combined to form a loan pool for minority business lending. An entrepreneur who has been turned down for loans on two occasions is referred to the program and receives entrepreneurial training, specifically addressing the reasons for which the loan was rejected. The applicant, following training, then receives a loan from one of the ten banks, given on a rotating basis. The risk to the bank is low since the loans are low level and given on a rotating basis and the business owner gets immediate access to mainstream lending if successful in the program. (Self Help)

❧ A California CDCU has lending available at 3% interest for persons interested in starting up day-care operations. (Santa Cruz)

❧ Alternatives Federal Credit Union allows individuals to refinance new car purchases at a more favorable new car loan rate within 30 days of original purchase. (Alternatives)

❧ A CDCU has entered into a partnership with a local community organization. The CBO identifies families and individuals who need weatherization and energy efficiency work done and the credit union provides the loan. (Northside)

❧ A Dallas CDCU has structured its loans to ensure repayment and make repayments easier to lenders. Monthly payments on loans are tied to an individual's pay day. Problem loans are thus caught earlier on in the process and can be restructured or dealt with accordingly. (Common Ground)

❧ A Dallas CDCU has made "risky" loans to individuals starting up day-care centers. In order to reduce risk the sponsoring CDC has placed a compensating balance in the account of the CDCU. (Common Ground)

Community Development Credit Union Contacts

Alternatives
Alternative Credit Union
Bill Myers
301 W. State St.
Ithaca, NY 14850
(607) 273-4611

Brooklyn
Brooklyn Ecumenical Group
Elizabeth Shoy
541 Atlantic Avenue
Brooklyn, NY 11217
(718) 858-8803

Common Ground
Common Ground Community FCU
John Fullinwider
5405 East Grand
Dallax, TX 72223
(214) 631-3628

Lower East
Lower East Side Credit Union
Linda Levy
37 Avenue B
New York, NY 10009
(212) 529-8197

Northside
Northside Community Credit Union
Elaine Graham
4554 N. Broadway, Suite 240
Chicago, IL 60640
(312) 728-0424

St. Luke
St. Luke Credit Union
Ruffin Gill
P.O. Box 548
Windsor, NC 27983
(919) 794-3242

Santa Cruz
Santa Cruz Community Credit Union
Jeff Wells
P.O. Box 1877
Santa Cruz, CA 95061-1877
(408) 425-7708

Self Help
Self Help Credit Union
Laura Benedict
P.O. Box 3619
Durham, NC 27702
(919) 683-3016

Self Help Works	Self Help Works Mark Farrell 40 Prince Street, 2nd Floor New York, NY 10012 (212) 226-4119
Southwest	Southwest Germantown Associated Federal CU Terry Trudeau 5521 Germantown Avenue Philadelphia, PA 19144 (215) 843-4151
Union	Union Settlement of East Harlem Lillian Bent 237 E. 104th Street New York, NY 10029 (212) 360-8800
Vermont	Vermont Development Credit Union Lisa Kilborn 64 North Street Burlington, VT 05401 (802) 865-3404
Vancouver	Vancouver City Community Foundation Robyn Allan 515 W. 10th Avenue Vancouver, BC V5Z 4A8 CANADA

Other Important Contacts

National	National Federation of Community Development Credit Unions, Inc. Clifford Rosenthal 59 John Street, 8th Floor New York, NY 10038 (212) 513-7191
	Professor John Ibister Professor of Economics Merrill College University of California/Santa Cruz Santa Cruz, CA
Woodstock	Woodstock Institute Kathryn Tholin 407 S. Dearborn, Suite 550 Chicago, IL 60605 (312) 427-8070

Community Development Loan Funds

Community Development Loan Funds (CDLFs) exist to provide credit to groups and initiatives normally shut out of the traditional funding market. Because they can attract a broader range of investors that the Community Development Credit Unions, CDLFs often take on larger loans.

In general, a Community Development Loan Fund has three purposes:

❧ assist those who need capital the most;

❧ engage those who have access to capital by providing solid investment opportunities;

❧ provide an example to traditional lending institutions so they might broaden their lending base (CDLFs often make up only one piece of the total lending package or make an initial loan which allows a group to acquire additional funding).

Why are CDLFs effective agents in low-income communities? CDLFs traditionally have close ties to the community; they understand a variety of models of community economic development; they have low overhead costs; they provide both loan capital and technical assistance needed to carry out the loan; and they have a steadfast commitment to the projects for which the loans were made available (banks often have a low level of personal commitment). These examples of CDLF lending illustrate their capacity to impact local economies.

*Community Development Loan Funds: Creative Lending Stories**

❧ A CDLF made a loan available to a community land trust. The land trust was incorporated to purchase properties and hold them in trust in perpetuity to insure that a constant housing stock is available for low-income residents. The Land Trust owns the land beneath a property and the individual or family owns the house and reserves the right to purchase the home at a price to keep it affordable if a family moves out. The CDLF made a loan of $40,000 available to the land trust to purchase deposits and to acquire and renovate its first property. The loan was made as the land trust was just getting started so it was ineligible for ordinary financing. (Capital)

❦ A revolving loan fund makes small loans available to low- and moderate- income residents in New York. Loans are used to improve housing conditions. The loans are small, at below-market rates of interest and are amortized over longer periods of time. One loan of $500 was given at 6% and amortized over two years (affordable monthly payments of approximately $25 per month). (Catskill)

❦ A CDLF is a coalition of church and community groups working together to promote community-based economic development. The CDLF made a $7,000 loan available to a crafts cooperative organized in response to the needs of women in West Virginia. These women often live in isolated communities and had little access to jobs or transportation. With the capital loan, the organization, called Wellspring, was able to begin a marketing operation through a retail shop and wholesale catalog. The one-of-a-kind crafts of the women are then sold throughout the state. (Appalachian)

❦ A $20,000 loan from a CDLF enabled a Community Economic Development Corporation in Dallas to purchase 40 lot sites for houses that would have been demolished by a major corporation. With the help of the start-up loan, the CEDC has been able to acquire, renovate and lease 50 housing units to families earning less than $12,000 per year. (Institute)

❦ A CDLF was created by Koinonia Partners, an intentional community. The Fund makes loans available to low-income families with no-interest mortgages. Families with incomes between $400 and $1,000 per month are eligible to purchase homes with $700 downpayments and $100 monthly mortgage payments. (Koinonia)

❦ A CDLF makes loans available to microenterprises on reservations, ranging from arts and crafts producers to firewood vendors and small contractors. In general, the Fund provides technical assistance and loan capital of up to $10,000 to resident members of the Oglala Sioux tribe. The Fund received its start-up from a couple of major grants and receives investment from socially responsible corporations, churches, foundations and individuals. (Lakota)

❧ A CDLF made its first loan to a group of 13 families living in a mobile home park. The loan enabled the families, all of whom owned their homes, to purchase the land. The other prospective buyer was a corporation interested in developing condos. The condos would have been priced out of the buying range of the park dwellers. (New Hampshire)

❧ A CDLF has provided 130 loans to dozens of cooperatives in midwesternstates. The loans are intended to promote the development of cooperative enterprises. One of its best loans was a $40,000 loan to a Madison cooperative grocer amortized over a five-year schedule. The loan was part of a package which enabled the co-op, an anchor business in the neighborhood, to complete a major expansion project. The cooperative failed to get an expansion purposes loan from traditional funding sources. The CDLF subsequently worked with the cooperative on refining the terms and conditions of the expansion. (Northcountry)

*These sample stories are reported in the *Directory of Members and Associates* (1989 edition) of the National Association of Community Development Loan Funds.

Community Development Loan Fund Contacts

Appalachian

Human/Economic Appalachian
    Development Community Loan
    Fund
Miriam Ellard
P.O. Box 504
Berea, KY 40403
(606) 986-1651

Capital

Capital District Community Loan
    Fund
Susan Kenney
33 Clinton Avenue
Albany, NY 12207
(518) 436-8586

Catskill

Catskill Mountain Housing Devel-
    opment Corporation Revolving
    Loan Fund
Judy Rundberg
P.O. Box 473
Catskill, NY 12414
(518) 943-6700

Institute

Institute for Community Econom-
    ics Revolving Loan Fund
Sister Louise Foisy
151 Montague City Road
Greenfield, MA 01301
(413) 774-7956

Koinonia

Koinonia Fund for Humanity
George Theuer
Route 2
Americus, GA 31709-9986
(912) 924-0391

Lakota

The Lakota Fund
Gerald Sherman
P.O. Box 340
Kyle, SD 57752
(605) 455-2500

New Hampshire

New Hampshire Community
    Loan Fund
Julie Eades
Box 666
Concord, NH 03301
(603) 224-6669

Northcountry

Northcountry Cooperative
    Development Fund
Karla Miller
2129-A Riverside Avenue
Minneapolis, MN 55454
(612) 371-0325

Other Important Contacts

National Association of Commu-
    nity Development Loan
    Funds
924 Cherry Street
Philadelphia, PA 19107-2405
(215) 923-4754

Introduction—Turning Local Liabilities into Community Building Material

Until now we have been thinking in terms of resources within the community which already exist as assets. Individuals, associations and institutions represent a wide array of resources that can be enhanced and more fully utilized within communities. Local economies can be strengthened both by mobilizing the economic potential of non-economic institutions and by building Community Development Financial Institutions.

But there is one other group of potential assets which is available to every community. The physical structures, land transportation system and other infrastructure—all of these physical assets are important for community-building.

In this final section of our community economy exploration, we will concentrate on those physical assets which are less obvious. In fact, we will focus on physical **liabilities**: vacant and abandoned spaces and buildings, and waste. We focus on these liabilities because they are, at the same time, potential assets. Many creative community groups have taken these "liabilities" and transformed them into assets. They have taken an abandoned building and transformed it into an arts center. They have literally taken trash out of the community land fill and transformed it into cash, valuable commodities, even art.

We will turn our attention first to the ways in which communities have reclaimed vacant and abandoned spaces and buildings, and then to creative uses of waste.

Reclaiming Vacant and Abandoned Space

Introduction

Communities in cities across the United States are littered with abandoned buildings, vacant lots and underutilized space. In Chicago alone, some 92,000 lots sit vacant, 10,000 properties stand vacant or abandoned, and many buildings and properties are underutilized. A community leader from one neighborhood estimates that one-half of the total property in the neighborhood is comprised of vacant lots. Valuable space in our cities rapidly deteriorates, creates hazards and contributes to the overall disintegration of a community. At the same time, individuals and families search in vain for affordable housing, small business entrepreneurs look for an environment that will attract customers, artists dream about community arts centers, and community groups think about ways to make their neighborhoods more livable, more whole.

In their present condition, vacant lots, abandoned buildings and underutilized space are liabilities. Multifamily apartment complexes standing in a state of utter disrepair become a gathering point for drug dealing, prostitution, violent crime, theft and desolation. Vacant warehouses and factories are easy marks for vandalism and gang activities. Vacant lots become catch-alls for abandoned vehicles, broken glass, trash and unsightly vegetation. All of the abandoned and vacant properties contribute to the visual and spiritual disintegration of a neighborhood.

But unused and underutilized property is more than just a neighborhood hazard. Owners of many of these properties have not made required property tax payments in years. It is a financial drain on city and subsequently local resources. The city then finds itself in a dual fix. It must pay millions of dollars to secure abandoned properties and clear vacant lots, while simultaneously losing millions of dollars in financial revenues in the form of property taxes. In addition, the mere presence of abandoned and deteriorating properties keeps potential investment in the community at bay.

Abandoned and vacant properties have always been thought of as liabilities: they are unsafe, they absorb precious resources and they inhibit economic and residential development. What would happen if communities began to perceive those same properties as potential assets? A vacant lot filled with junk does have the potential of becoming a community garden. A vacant school becomes a combined-use living and learning center. An abandoned industrial site becomes a small business incubator. And an abandoned warehouse becomes a theatre, complete with retail, rehearsal and workshop space. The possibilities go on and on. Some of these possibilities are illustrated by the graphic on the next page, "From Abandoned and Vacant Space to Community Resources: Turning Liabilities into Assets."

The process by which communities can transform vacant and abandoned space into valuable assets involves four basic steps:

- Make an inventory of vacant and abandoned space.

- Acquire the space, using a variety of approaches, often with the help of partners.

- Initiate and develop an appropriate project.

- Maintain a viable, ongoing project.

We will look at each of these steps in a bit more detail.

**From Abandoned and Vacant Space to Community
Resources: Turning Liabilities into Assets**

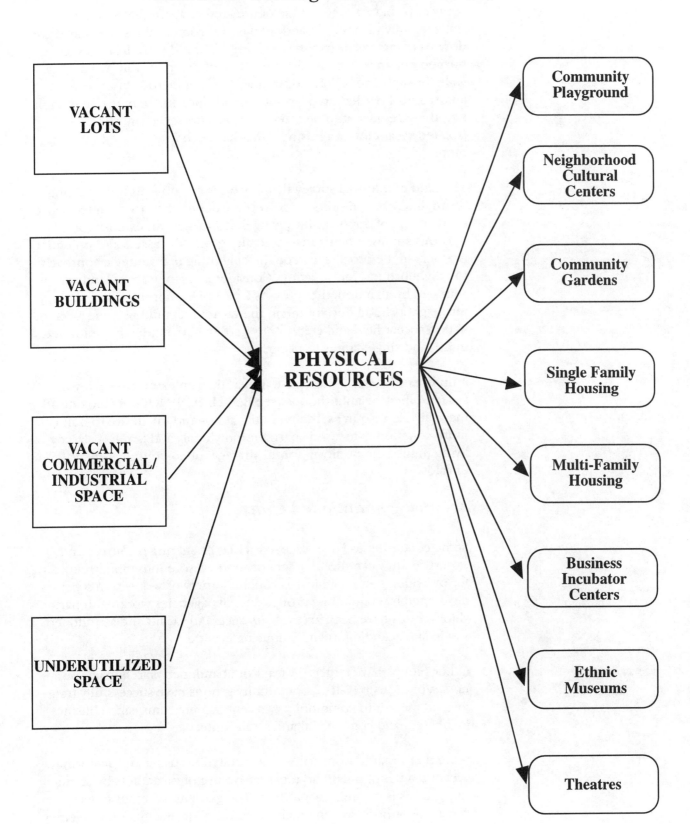

Identifying Abandoned and Vacant Space

Many of us have a vague sense of the kind of space that is under-utilized, fully vacant or abandoned in our communities. We may drive down a commercial strip in which every second store front is vacant, burned out and/or in an advanced state of deterioration. We may also walk through a residential district and find numerous homes and apartments boarded up or in such an advanced state of disintegration that they are only fit to be razed. We may, however, only find an isolated vacant lot or a business that has been for sale for a year or more.

The kind of informal survey that any of us can do simply by walking through our neighborhood, however, can only give us a limited sense of the range of opportunities lying in dormancy. An extensive and rigorous survey, when considered along with the assets and potential partners in the process, can be the beginning of a strategic approach to neighborhood rejuvenation. Consider a vacant tract of land surrounded by abandoned homes. As a part of a comprehensive strategy for neighborhood development, the vacant lot could become a combination soccer field and community garden surrounded by renovated multi- and single-family housing.

A number of communities have undertaken an extensive survey of space in their neighborhoods (see Bethel, DSNI, IOP). By looking at the available resources, the potential assets and the desire to build more community-focused space for individuals and families already living in the community, a sound strategy for community renewal unfolds.

Acquiring Abandoned Space

Some communities have discovered that by sharing resources and expertise, they can turn a neighborhood eyesore into modern housing for individuals and families. Through a variety of acquisition schemes developed by community groups and city agencies working in partnership, groups have been able to gain access to vacant and abandoned single-family and multifamily housing facilities.

Other groups have targeted vacant or abandoned warehouses, businesses or industrial sites. Community groups have successfully transformed these into community arts centers, museums, small business incubators and commercial and retail centers.

Still other organizations have concentrated on using and acquiring vacant land. A popular and inexpensive use of vacant lots by community groups is community gardens. The gardens, whether flower, vegetable or both, are an ideal way to bring diverse peoples together over a common project. Both long and short-term leasing arrangements have augmented outright purchases for community groups.

The Roles of Partners in Acquiring and Developing Space

Community groups engaged in the process of converting abandoned space into livable, usable space, understand that they may not be able to do it alone. Churches may band together to develop a neighborhood strategy of community reuse of space. Block clubs may cooperate in converting vacant lots into community gardens and parks. And organizations may combine resources to build structures that enhance community. That is only the beginning, however.

Small community groups often need the assistance of policy advocacy groups in accessing city-owned or abandoned properties. Groups may not have the clout or the experience to succeed in attaining property alone, but working together with citywide groups that engage in policy advocacy and education and offer technical assistance in leveraging property, they can. Once the property has been acquired, however, the emphasis shifts to providing the skills necessary, through workshops and consultations, for developing and sustaining creative community-based projects.

A network of housing rehabilitation advocates in Chicago is one such entity that helps neighborhood groups acquire and develop multifamily dwellings into affordable housing for families. The network helps groups locate financing alternatives for their acquired properties. (Chicago Rehab) The graphic on the next page illustrates the range of partnerships which can help neighborhood groups acquire and develop space.

Developing Community Assets

Community builders are turning vacant and abandoned space into affordable housing, vibrant commercial space, cultural centers, and parks and gardens.

The renovation or redevelopment of affordable housing can, of course, have a carry-over effect on the rest of the community. New homeowners attract new businesses which attract new cultural centers and projects. Particularly when the parties involved in the construction of homes are committed to providing affordable housing, the danger of gentrification pushing long-time residents out of the neighborhood is diminished.

A number of community groups have, after gaining access to abandoned or vacant properties, developed several blocks of affordable housing for families and seniors through the establishment of a revolving loan fund or other financial vehicles. Many of these groups have asked the families themselves to become involved in the physical construction or rehabilitation of the properties. *Sweat equity* gives

Neighborhood Groups Creating New Community-Centered Space: Who are the Partners?

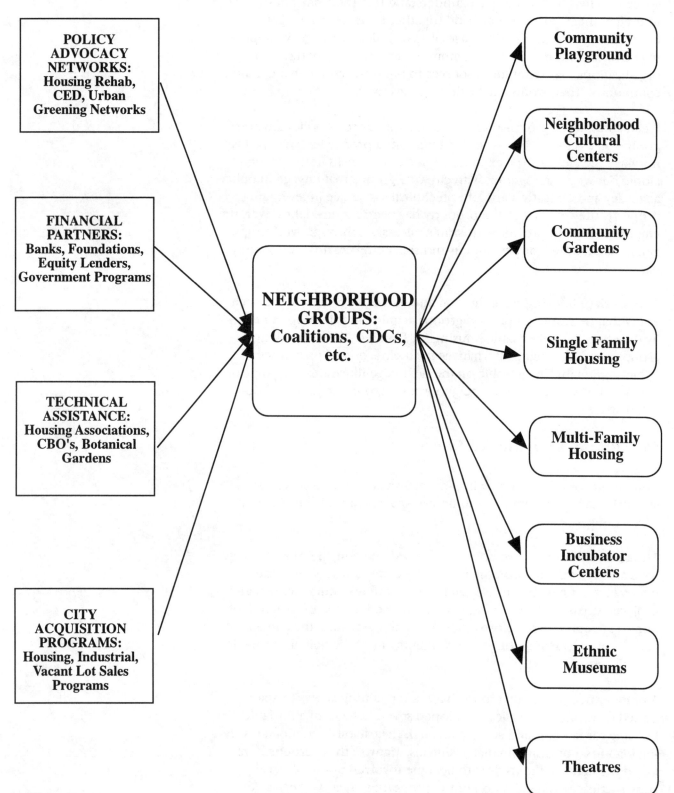

new homeowners a sense of participation and ownership in the community redevelopment process—even when that participation is localized in one home. They understand that all the parts make up the whole of community development.

Other groups have recognized that abandoned business and retail centers along the commercial strip of any neighborhood are a hindrance to reinvestment in the community. These groups have, however, discovered ways to utilize the resources available within the community to give the re-investment process a kick start. Available industrial space becomes a major recycling facility. (Bethel) An old, abandoned auto repair building now houses a business incubator. (Neighborhood)

Still other groups have discovered that building a cultural or arts center can have a dramatic impact on the economic and cultural vitality of a neighborhood, particularly when those centers reflect the ethnic and cultural heritage of the neighborhood. A museum, for example, can have a tremendous effect on the rest of the local business community.

Finally, community groups understand that a vacant lot can signal danger to community residents. Individuals often hang out amid debris and abandoned automobiles. Residents are often afraid to pass near the site. However, in many cases, neighborhood groups have turned these liabilities into assets as well, into parks and community gardens. The stories which begin below will illustrate all of these creative approaches.

Sustaining Vital Community Projects

The work has been done. The abandoned and vacant properties have been acquired, financed and built. Community has been enhanced. Now how do community groups go about sustaining these important projects over the long haul? Many community groups have built income-generating programs into their projects to keep them viable. Some examples:

- A CDC purchased a vacant school house with the intention of opening an elementary school after needed renovations. Recognizing, however, that it could never sustain its much smaller school financially, it converted the second floor of the building into 24 units of affordable housing. Many of the residents send their children downstairs to the school. (Bethel)

    ❧ A CDC purchased a vacant and severely deteriorated apartment complex. Over a two-year period it had renovated the building into 20 units of long-term transitional housing for homeless families. In the basement, the corporation houses a lunch and catering restaurant which simultaneously provides training for the homeless and unemployed. (CFLS)

Conclusion

Community builders have shown that it is possible, through sharing talents and resources, to turn neighborhood liabilities into community assets. The key is in partnerships—at each step of the way. If a group receives an abandoned house through a donation, it can benefit from partnerships with local groups or a citywide advocacy and technical assistance network which can assist in renovating the building. Another group may successfully acquire an abandoned industrial site and have the financing in order to complete the renovation on the project. A partnership with a community economic development network can assist the group in housing appropriate businesses at the site.

A successful renovation project or community garden project can be the first building block for renewal in the residential, economic, cultural and spiritual life of the community. In many cases, the process of renewing deteriorating community space involves a number of steps: identifying potential space, acquiring abandoned, vacant or underutilized space, developing the space with the assistance of rehab or greening networks and financial partners, and finally sustaining the project. Each step of the way can be made simpler by engaging in the process with viable partners within the community.

The stories which follow illustrate the wide variety of options open to community builders who look at liabilities and see potential assets.

Vacant Space Stories

Commercial, Industrial, Artistic Space

    ❧ A CDC purchased an old school building from the Chicago Board of Education, renovated it, and reopened an elementary school on the ground floor and 26 units of affordable housing on the upper floors. (Bethel)

    ❧ A CDC purchased a warehouse facility which had stood idle for 1-1/2 years and, after light renovation, opened a materials recovery facility which will employ 25 individuals. The facility is a middle station between initial collection and redevelopment of recyclable materials. (Bethel)

❧ A neighborhood council worked out an agreement with a religious order and the city park system. The park purchased a vacant mansion and leased it to the Council for a community arts and arts education center. The Council has done the majority of the renovation on the property. (North Lakeside)

❧ A neighborhood organization purchased an old auto parts warehouse and turned it into a center for business incubation. Thirteen local businesses—construction, light manufacturing, service—in the incubation phase share technical support and equipment at the center. Businesses that graduate are encouraged to continue to do business in the neighborhood. (Neighborhood)

❧ A neighborhood organization purchased a vacant warehouse and renovated the building. It now rents 22 spaces to local artists who utilize the space for offices, workshops, studios and galleries, and retail space. (Neighborhood)

❧ A Swedish gentleman purchased an old hardware store. He turned the building into a cultural center and museum, which contributed mightily to the revitalization of the commercial district of a neighborhood. (Swedish)

❧ A CDC in cooperation with a local theatre, hopes to gain access to a building left vacant by a newspaper publisher two years ago. The groups hope to purchase the building or receive it through a charitable contribution and create business space for five community-based organizations and redevelop the old warehouse space into a theatre. The organizations involved in the acquisition plan to share some space in the building for common purposes (i.e., conference rooms). (Howard)

❧ A local community and artists' advocate convinced a property owner with underutilized space to renovate the rooms into artist studios, gallery space and living quarters. The result was the creation of an artists' colony within 15 neighboring buildings. (Poughkeepsie)

❧ An arts foundation acquired a warehouse from a manufacturer of storm windows. The former warehouse now houses a theatre, workshop space, an art gallery, dressing rooms and storage space. The theatre produces dramas created by African or African-American playwrights. (ETA)

❧ A CDC became the primary equity partner with a private developer in a joint venture. The joint venture purchased from the original owner a 600,000 square foot industrial complex and redeveloped it into a multitenant industrial facility. (GNPDC)

❧ A CDC purchased a 20,000 square-foot industrial site from the original owner, invited an anchor tenant—a life skills training center—and redeveloped a commercial use site. (GNPDC)

❧ With the assistance of a special city commercial district designation program, which allowed the city to purchase blighted property and resell it to a development corporation, a CDC developed the property and was successful in attracting a major supermarket chain to locate at the site. The project stimulated additional development efforts in the immediate surrounding areas. (LADCOR)

Housing

❧ A church acquired tax delinquent properties and, with its own housing development staff, renovated the buildings and re-offered them to the community as affordable housing. (Lawndale)

❧ A nonprofit community-based organization held land for the benefit of the community and for individuals from within the community. The trust acquired land through purchase or donation and held the land in perpetuity. The land was removed from the speculative market and preserved for low-income homeowners at affordable rates. (South Atlanta)

❧ A housing corporation helped families move into abandoned buildings purchased from the HUD foreclosure list. Families participate with 60 hours of sweat equity and a three-year lease-to-purchase option. (ACORN)

❧ A housing corporation coordinated a group of squatters to take residence in abandoned buildings. The action, which was intended to effect policy change, actually was instrumental in getting the buildings turned over to the squatting families. (ACORN)

❦ A church in Peoria received a donation of two vacant houses. It initiated a revolving loan fund and eventually opened its own construction business which used community residents and minimum security prisoners as workers. The local community college provided training and oversight in construction. (Christian)

❦ A Washington human services agency purchased a 20-unit apartment building which was falling to pieces. With multilayered financing, volunteer support from a coalition of urban and suburban churches and donated materials, the complex was completely renovated into long-term transitional housing for homeless families. The basement of the complex is a restaurant which acts as an income-generating source and as a training ground for the unemployed. (CFLS)

❦ A youth construction project in New York provided training for youth to renovate city-owned abandoned buildings. The renovated units were then made available to young adults who cannot live with their families or who have been homeless. (Youth in Action)

Gardens

❦ A vacant lot owned by the city was leased at no charge to a group of Hmong families for gardening. The vegetables provide the families with produce from July through December. (Hmong)

❦ A recycling center is prepared to implement four plans utilizing vacant space in a neighborhood in Chicago. **Community gardens**—Utilizing composted soil and wood chips, the center is prepared to supply vacant lots with good soil for the start-up of a community garden project. **Family truck farming**—Through this program, the city would transfer ownership of vacant space in exchange for productive re-use. A family would be given ownership of a one-acre site and then collectively farm the site. Crops would be harvested and sold at a neighborhood vegetable market. **Community play lots**—Some lots could be cleared and seeded to provide space for community play lots or playing fields. Finally, some lots could be converted into **nursery salvage operations.** An example: the Center recently received 100 trees @ $500 value. The trees had been improperly balled and were therefore no longer marketable. A salvage operation could take those trees, replant and cultivate them over a year, and then resell the trees the following year. (Resource)

❧ Fourteen families in a Chicago neighborhood have garden plots on what used to be a vacant lot with cars and debris creating a local eyesore. The garden, leased from the city through a neighborhood association for $1 per year, has built a bridge between the diverse ethnic communities. (East Village)

❧ A group of local organizations in a Chicago neighborhood oversees an open space park which has developed at the site of a vacant lot. The lot was created after three neighborhood high rises were razed in order to create less dense living conditions and more open space. The park features space for concerts, family reunions, ball games and plots for gardening. (Howard)

❧ A block club gained access to a vacant lot with the assistance of a "greening" advocacy group and a local politician. The club created a community garden with 15 lots and space for children to play. The harvest that is gathered is then distributed throughout the community. (Grenshaw)

❧ A community garden project uses water conservation and soil preservation strategies in its community garden project. A 55-gallon drum serves as a water catchment device and an in-built pond serves as a drainage area. Of the produce harvested, 50% goes to the hungry through an interfaith coalition and 50% to the gardeners—neighbors, volunteers, schools, churches, small businesses. (SEED)

❧ A neighborhood association creates garden plots from vacant lots and encourages neighborhood residents to take responsibility for their own properties and adjacent lots. The lots are city-owned. The group gains access to the lots through the citywide "adopt-a-lot" program. (Slum Busters)

❧ A city-wide program in New York City, funded by Federal and state community block grants, has helped 600 community groups gain interim access to city-owned properties between demolition and redevelopment status. The community gardens produce $1 million in produce each year and have facilitated new neighborhood leadership and organization, as well as new connections between groups, institutions and a variety of people. (Green Guerillas)

❧ A community gardening network works in cooperation with public schools to develop community gardens and a curriculum package on horticulture. (Green Thumb)

❧ The Center for Alternative Sentencing and Employment Service Programs provides the opportunity for those in an alternative sentencing program to work with community groups starting a garden—particularly senior citizens who can garden but cannot build. In cooperation with the Green Thumb project, the Service Program links individuals to community groups to build raised beds, put in fences, etc. In many instances, long-term relationships are established through this function. (Green Thumb)

❧ A nonprofit member organization of 350 active members collects and redistributes plants and foliage to community gardening groups. It also provides technical assistance, workshops, horticultural and agricultural expertise, and organizing strategies. (Green Guerillas)

Vacant Space Contacts

Acorn

ACORN
Chris Brown
410 S. Michigan Avenue, 4th Floor Annex
Chicago, IL 60605
(312) 939-7488

Bethel

Bethel New Life
Kate Lane
347 N. Karlov
Chicago, IL 60624
(312) 826-5540

Chicago Rehab

Chicago Rehab Network
53 W. Jackson Blvd.
Chicago, IL 60604
(312) 663-3936

CFLS

Community Family Life Services
Rev. Thomas J. Knoll
305 "E" Street, NW
Washington, DC 20001
(202) 347-0511

Christian

Christian Family Center Church
Rev. Tony Pierce
1800 W. Bradley Avenue
Peoria, IL 60606
(309) 673-2600

Commons

Chicago Commons Association
Donald Duster
915 N. Wolcott
Chicago, IL 60622
(312) 342-5330

Community Land

Community Land Use Network
Barbara Shaw
343 S. Dearborn, Suite 910
Chicago, IL 60604
(312) 285-6606
(312) 939-7171

DSNI   Dudley Street Neighborhood Initiative
365 Dudley Street
Roxbury, MA 02119
(617) 442-9670

East Village   East Village Association
Marjorie Isaacson
P.O. Box 476622
Chicago, IL 60647
(312) 384-6088

ETA   ETA Theatre Creative Arts Foundation
Adena Brown
7558 S. Chicago Avenue
Chicago, IL 60619
(312) 752-3955

Greater North   Greater North Pulaski Development Corporation
Dan Immergluck
4054 W. North Avenue
Chicago, IL 60639-5220
(312) 384-7074

Greater Southwest   Greater Southwest Development Corporation
Harry Meyer
6249 S. Western Avenue
Chicago, IL 60636
(312) 436-1000

Green Guerillas   Green Guerillas
Barbara Earnest
625 Broadway
New York, NY 10012-2611
(212) 674-8124

Green Thumb   Green Thumb
Jean Weissman
49 Chambers Street
New York, NY 10007
(212) 233-2927

Hmong   Wong Vong
Hmong Gardening Project
5801 N. Pulaski
Chicago, IL 60646
(312) 462-7566

Howard

Howard Area Community Center
Sister Cecilia
7468 N. Paulina
Chicago, IL 60626
(312) 262-6622

Institute

Institute for Community Economics
   (Revolving Loan Fund)
Sister Louise Foisy
151 Montague City Road
Greenfield, MA 01301
(413) 774-7956

IOP

Interfaith Organizing Project of Greater Chicago
1617 W. Washington
Chicago, IL 60612
(312) 243-3328

Lawndale

Lawndale Christian Development Corporation
David Doig
3848 W. Ogden
Chicago, IL 60623
(312) 762-6389

Ladcor

Lawrence Avenue Development Corporation
Joel Bookman
4745 N. Kedzie Avenue
Chicago, IL 60625
(312) 478-0202

Neighborhood

Neighborhood Institute (Artist Center)
Deborah Merchant
1750 E. 71st Street
Chicago, IL 60649
(312) 288-3068

Neighborhood Institute (Business Center)
Olivia Grady
1750 E. 71st Street
Chicago, IL 60649
(312) 933-0200

North Lakeside

North Lakeside Cultural Center
Kathy Gemperle
6219 Sheridan Road
Chicago, IL 60660
(312) 561-0893

Open Lands   Open Lands Project
                              Kathy Dickhut
                              220 S. State Street
                              Chicago, IL 60604-2103
                              (312) 427-4256

Pride   People's Reinvestment and Development Effort
                              Mike Rohrback
                              342 S. Laramie
                              Chicago, IL 60644
                              (312) 379-4412

Resource   The Resource Center
                              Mike Dunn
                              222 E. 135th Place
                              Chicago, IL 60627
                              (312) 821-1351

Seed   Sustaining Earth Through Environmental Design
                              Jacqueline Batisse
                              221 W. 13th Street
                              Houston, TX 77008
                              (713) 866-5203
                              (713) 520-4669

South Atlanta   South Atlanta Land Trust
                              1523 Jonesboro Road, SE
                              Atlanta, GA 30315
                              (404) 525-2683

Southeast   Southeast Chicago Development Commission
                              Ed Stone
                              9204 S. Commercial Avenue
                              Chicago, IL 60617
                              (312) 731-8755

Swedish   Swedish-American Cultural Center
                              Kurt Matthiason
                              5236 N. Clark
                              Chicago, IL 60640
                              (312) 334-9619

Urban Homesteading Urban Homesteading Assistance Board
                              Theresa Kilbane
                              40 Prince Street, 2nd Floor
                              New York, NY 10012
                              (212) 226-4119

Urban Land

Urban Land Foundation
625 Indiana Avenue NW, Suite 400
Washington, DC 20004-2930
(202) 624-7130

Youth in Action

Youth in Action
1280 Fifth Avenue
New York, NY 10029
(212) 860-8170

A new guide to capturing capital budget dollars
for community building purposes adds another
potential community economic development
strategy. This new guide is called *Paving the
Way for Community Change.* It is available from
the Neighborhood Capital Budget Group, 343 S.
Dearborn Street, Suite 910, Chicago, IL 60604.
Phone: 312.939.7198.

Capturing Precious Community Resources: Waste and Energy

Harnessing the Benefits of Waste Resources

Traditional approaches to dealing with the stream of solid waste generated by business, industry and private homes are no longer practical. Many municipalities have recognized this simple fact and have implemented long-term goals to reduce the flow of solid waste. Some cities are hoping to divert as much as 50% of the solid waste stream through recycling measures. (Seattle, Washington, already exceeds this goal.)

How has solid waste been handled in the past and how might it be handled more efficiently in the future? Until the past several years, most cities simply collected the vast majority of their solid waste and transported it to city or surrounding country landfills. However, as landfills began to reach capacity and tipping fees began to rise, many cities began to search for alternative solutions to the solid waste problem. Some cities built incinerator facilities which seemed to solve the problem of waste disposal. However, although incinerators can generate a new source of energy through the burning process, the toxins released into the environment and the relatively high proportion of ash generated in the burning create yet another waste disposal problem.

Using these two approaches—incineration and dumping—communities were still locked into a paradigm that identified waste resources as a *liability*. It is clear, however, based on a large number of community-based projects and activities that exist today, that community waste can become a substantial *asset* for local neighborhoods. Waste products are not only valuable resources, but they represent an opportunity for neighborhood residents to connect and focus on rebuilding communities. As one community activist put it: "There is no social stratification when people bring their waste resources to our facilities. The homeless man brings the same stuff as the executive or lawyer. Our collection center becomes a real social happening."

Identifying Potential Waste Resources

The first step in building a neighborhood-based approach to utilizing waste resources lies in identifying the potential assets available to a neighborhood. What are some of the waste products that can be turned into valuable resources while reducing the solid waste stream?

Food Waste—from individual kitchens or school, church, business and industry cafeterias or supermarkets, can be composted. The resulting compost can be utilized in community garden projects. Industrial food waste can also be utilized in more extensive agricultural fertilization projects.

Recyclable Goods—such as cans, bottles, paper, plastics, scrap metals, can be collected and sold to industries that remanufacture recycled goods. If collected goods can be sold to local industries, in effect closing the loop, benefits in the form of new jobs and local spending accrue to local neighborhoods.

Reusable Goods—such as furniture, clothing and appliances can be collected and resold. It is the most environmentally friendly method of dealing with waste resources. And the opportunity for value-added labor is substantial when dealing with reusable goods.

Toxic Wastes—like paint, turpentine, and other household products can be collected and redistributed at community exchanges instead of being dumped.

Landscaping Waste—such as tree trimmings can be used in a variety of capacities to create job opportunities and beautify local neighborhoods.

Gaining Access to Waste Resources

Local initiatives such as those of the Boy Scouts, school PTAs, hospital resale shops, etc., have provided the framework for the productive reuse of recyclable materials long before major waste disposal industries took an interest in recycling as a possible money-making venture. Since then, however, many of the smaller nonprofit organizations have been squeezed out of the recycling market as cities have begun to award curbside pickup contracts to larger businesses boasting greater capacity.

Nonetheless, smaller, community-based initiatives continue to be able to collect proportionally greater amounts, encourage efficient source separation and provide valuable education on recycling and the environment. A waste disposal industry sees recycling as only one small piece of its operation. Furthermore, community residents give up any control over local resources when they are turned over to a major waste disposal industry. As renewable resources are handed over, any potential for economic gain to local communities from the waste resources is lost.

But communities can regain control of their waste resources, and in dozens of cases they have. Many of the stories at the end of this section illustrate the ways in which local residents have identified and used the waste produced in their own communities for new community-building purposes.

More and more communities are discovering that once local waste resources have been identified and accessed, community-based projects can be put in place to utilize these resources. In many instances, community projects bring a clear economic benefit to the local economy: labor-intensive jobs are created for the poor and homeless; local buy-back centers pay cash to neighborhood residents or groups that have collected waste resources; locally collected resources are utilized in the manufacturing of locally produced materials; local waste resources can be refinished or recreated and resold. A valuable reference for community recyclers is "No Time to Waste: How Communities Reap Economic Benefits from the Shift to Recycling," Patrick Berry, Center for Neighborhood Technology, 2125 W. North Avenue, Chicago, IL 60647, $5.

But just as important as these economic benefits, the process of collecting waste resources, diverting them from the solid waste stream, reusing those materials and even selling them, creates an opportunity for building community.

Much of the success of neighborhood operations is attributable to educational efforts. Many neighborhood-based programs educate local residents on the benefits of recycling—both to the environment and to the local economy. Larger waste disposal companies simply cannot educate neighborhood residents in quite the same way that neighborhood groups can.

Community-based recycling projects also bring neighbors closer together. A neighborhood food waste collection site is the beginning of a wonderful community garden. A neighborhood buy-back center is the site of activity and conversation. The educational program of a neighborhood association reaches out to local schools, churches and other associations. Best of all, people simply feel good about preserving the environment while building community.

Making Energy Resources Work for the Neighborhood

Finally, while many community-based organizations and associations are actively turning waste resources from liabilities into assets, a number of organizations are also rethinking the opportunities for community-building presented by energy resources. For many, turning off a light switch when the light is not in use or deciding to use public transportation whenever possible are good individual ways to save on energy costs. But individuals working collectively within neighborhoods can have a much greater impact. What are some of the ways in which community groups have combined their efforts to save on energy costs, use energy resources more efficiently and even capture energy resources for their own use?

❦ A community organization has developed a series of projects aimed at making neighborhoods more energy independent. A home heating oil buyer's cooperative enables community residents to purchase fuel oil at bulk costs. An energy-use auditing project enables churches, nonprofits and multifamily rental units to maximize their savings on energy expenses. A reverse commuter project developed in cooperation with the public commuter rail line enables neighborhood residents to access manufacturing jobs in growing suburbs. (CFLS)

❦ A CDC in Baltimore conducts energy-use audits of low-income homeowners in the neighborhood. Homes are then targeted for weatherization, which increases the energy efficiency and energy cost savings of local residents. (BJEP)

❦ A coalition of community energy organizations formed an energy federation to coordinate the bulk purchase and sale of energy conservation materials. The federation supplies quality conservation materials to low-income weatherization programs, to nonprofit resource conservation groups, buying co-op members, and to other groups interested in conservation. The federation also coordinates technical services to its customers. (EFI)

Most of us are interested in conserving energy resources. Individuals are, however, often limited in their capacity to achieve maximum conservation potential because of lack of resources or information. Community organizations that conduct energy audits of institutions, nonprofit organizations, or multi- and single-family residences are one way to fill this gap. And local consumers are often prevented from purchasing energy-efficient products because of the immediate costs, even when long-term savings are guaranteed. Bulk purchasing member co-ops are often a solution to this problem.

Energy resources need to be used wisely, and they can be used most wisely when shared within the community. One community-based organization is thinking about that concept as it relates to local transportation. The group hopes to build a car share program in densely populated neighborhoods where parking is scarce and insurance rates are high. Families with only limited need for a second car or individuals with minimal need for a single car would be able to get rid of them and patronize a low-cost car-sharing operation on those occasions when the use of a car is essential. Individuals and families would save on fuel and insurance costs, be able to use public transportation networks more often, build a cleaner environment and help to create more local jobs. (CNT)

Energy and Waste Stories

Reuse

❧ A small recycling company collects, washes and redistributes wine bottles to wineries. Reselling bottles increases the profit margin of a group by 700% as opposed to selling glass that will be reprocessed. (Encore)

❧ A nonprofit organization benefits the local community by providing a buy-back materials center for salvaged waste, providing an opportunity for local entrepreneurs and craftsmen to refurbish salvaged materials and earn money through the "value-added" process, and creating local employment opportunities. The organization focuses on "total recycling." (Urban Ore)

❧ A foundation works with a community center that operates a tool bank. The foundation advises by sponsoring a fix-it workshop and providing hints on shopping for used appliances so that the low-income families can make their appliances last longer and so they don't always have to buy new products. (WCRF)

❧ A cooperative effort with a training and education program of a community college encourages parents in workshops to pack their daily lunches in such a way as to generate the least material for disposal or recycling. The workshop covers reduce, reuse and recycle issues and demonstrates how waste reduction is tied to saving money. (WCRF)

❧ Fed up with the crushing of glass at a local recycling center, a retired woman establishes a jar distribution business. Neighbors in the community and recycling centers from surrounding communities begin to bring jars to the new center. Jars are washed and distributed to neighborhood grocers as well as businesses and individuals from across the state. Neighbors also participate by helping to wash and sort. (The Glass Station)

❧ A recycling foundation consults with small groups throughout the state on recycling ideas. Instead of bringing brand-new ideas to groups, they try to build upon what is already happening with community-based groups. For instance, a community center in Seattle is hosting a summer barbecue series for kids. The Coalition works with the community centers to develop waste-free barbecues. (WCRF)

Recycling

❧ An alliance of 15 community-based recycling organizations supports existing community-based, source separation enterprises; assists the creation of new operations, supports a community-based marketing network that emphasizes job development among the poor, expands the source-separated network, educates the public, advocates source-separation recycling, waste reduction and job development, and encourages local secondary materials manufacturing. (CRA)

❧ A neighborhood source-separated collection site collects and processes about 10 tons of recyclable goods each month. The organization collects glass, metal, aluminum and tin, plastics. The collection site used to earn income by selling its recyclables to a Bronx buy-back center. When the buy-back center lost its funding from the city, a major portion of its funding went belly up. Now it is a volunteer neighborhood-based organization that draws its funding from membership drives and small grants. (ORE)

❧ A neighborhood recycling center provides educational outreach services to schools and neighborhood associations. Two or three volunteers from the association meet regularly with groups to discuss recycling concepts and provide tips. (ORE)

❧ One of the main thrusts of a CDC is to pave the way for already-existing companies to come into the community and reutilize abandoned industrial facilities. These companies are all engaged in remanufacturing recyclables. The CDC works with the companies on zoning, city regulations, favorable purchasing agreements through the city, etc., and fights for local hiring. The CDC then acts as a subcontractor. The CDC, as a subcontractor, picks up recyclables from the neighborhood and delivers them to the company for re-manufacture. (BJEP)

❧ A neighborhood group built a cottage industry around New York City's bottle bill law. The group opened a collection site for bottle bill materials and bartered the collected goods in exchange for labor from homeless and disadvantaged individuals. The individuals work at the collection site sorting and receiving materials in exchange for a portion of bottle bill materials. They then take the materials to local supermarkets to redeem the collected goods. An individual can make anywhere from $12 to $40 a day doing such work. (VGRT)

❦ Two redemption centers were opened on a nonprofit basis in response to the city's new bottle bill law and because many homeless individuals (and others) were not getting their five cents back on used containers. Homeless and poor persons are able to earn money from the centers in one of two ways: by bringing in bottle bill materials they have collected for redemption or by working at the center receiving, sorting and packing. The center employs between 23 and 35 (depending on the season) individuals and pays out $12,000 on a daily basis. (WECAN)

❦ A collection center operates several collection routes which employ seven drivers. The drivers collect redeemable bottles and cans from 2,500 office buildings in New York City that have agreed to "save cans for the homeless." (WECAN)

❦ A collaborative effort of an arts and recycling demonstration group uses business discards for participatory creativity workshops. Parents are given many ideas for low-cost toys that keep waste out of the landfill. (WCRF)

❦ A cooperative marketing association works with recycling drop-off centers by pooling materials and identifying markets for sale of collected materials. By establishing a cooperative approach to the sale of waste resources, individual collection centers gain easy access to major buyers in the state. (NHRRA)

❦ A marketing association provides educational and technical assistance for groups in preparing and marketing their materials for resale. The membership organization also explores the opportunities for developing new markets for recyclables. (NHRRA)

❦ A paint and solvent exchange has been implemented in some New Hampshire locales where folks simply exchange unused paints at a community event. Each of these events is part of an educational effort. (NHRRA)

❦ A recycling center operates a full-time buy-back center for recyclables and provides curbside pickup for the city. They try to hire ex-offenders and hard-to-employ youth whenever possible. They also focus on providing employment opportunities to low-income neighborhoods. To achieve this goal, the center has established relationships with numerous CBOs that have employment programs or referral services. Many ethnic service associations have employment referral services which the center utilizes when hiring. (TRICED)

❧ A buy-back center has a profit-sharing program with local groups: one-third of profits are shared among company employees, one-third of the profits are reinvested in the company and one-third of the profits are given back to the communities as grants. In the past, grants have included a youth program of the police department, a little league baseball team, beds for a homeless shelter and funding for a shelter for abused women. Income of the center is generated through a city contract, service fees from curbside pickup and sales of recyclables. The center pays premium prices on materials collected from community groups and does not assess a pickup fee. (TRICED)

❧ A recycling center operates a curbside recycling program based on a block leader approach. For each neighborhood to be introduced to the recycling program the center organizes 1500 households into regions and blocks. The general public is invited to a community recycling meeting at which time it is educated about the curbside program. Residents are recruited as block leaders to visit 15-25 households on an assigned block to further educate and prepare residents for recycling. Currently over 1200 volunteers in neighborhoods act as liaisons to the center. (Sun Shares)

❧ A recycling center receives and sorts materials, then bails and prepares them for markets. The center contributes to the local economy by providing stable work opportunities for eight employees, diverting 2,500 tons of materials per year from the county waste stream, saving suitable jars and bottles for local users, and providing community education on recycling. Part of the community education focuses on "precycling"— educating residents to think about purchasing products that come in "recyclable" packaging. The center is also a work site for individuals on community service sentencing programs. They also provide numerous volunteer opportunities and employ the developmentally disabled in this labor-intensive industry. (BRING)

❧ A coalition of 14 civic organizations provides volunteers
while the city provides the equipment and the pickup.
The city takes separated waste resources to a processing
center owned and operated by a mental health center.
Mentally handicapped workers are trained and
employed to process the materials. (Florence)

❧ Municipal crews pick up recyclables twice a month from
15 block corners where pick ups are made on Saturdays.
Some 45 to 50 blocks feed into the 15 collection sites. In
the past, grants were administered from a central source
for community groups hoping to improve their
neighborhoods. Improvements included planting trees,
flowers or creating gardens. Some community groups
have used the funds to help finance a local nursery
school program which allowed teen mothers to attend
school. (Block Corner)

❧ A CDC organized the local community to build a self-
help park in cooperation with the local park district.
Recyclable plastics were gathered from the
neighborhood and reused in the park as plastic "lumber"
for benches and playground equipment. Shredded and
treated tires were used as footing for a wading pool.
(Bethel)

❧ A CDC operates a materials recycling facility (MRF)
which is designed to receive mixed recyclable materials
from residential and commercial collection routes.
Materials received are sorted and processed (baled,
crushed, and ground) for shipment to end markets. The
MRF will employ 10 individuals initially and projects it
will employ 25 within three years. The CDC hopes to
attract small-scale manufacturing facilities to the
community that will use materials from the MRF as
feedstock for production. The initial source for materials
will come from a suburban curbside collection program.
(Bethel)

❧ A subsidiary of a CDC was one of the first multi-material
buy-back centers. The three main impacts on the local
economy have been in salaries and jobs to local
residents, money paid out in the buy-back operation
($1.4 million total) and in closing the loop on plastics in
the neighborhood. (R2B2)

❧ A coalition of recycling groups has a contract with the New York City Department of Sanitation. The coalition organizes tenants and owners for multimaterial collection. The coalition uses burlap bags, purchased from a local coffee distributor, to collect glass containers and collects plastic containers in local laundromats. (EAC)

❧ A recycling center collects 170 tons per month from curbside pickup. Through its buy-back operation, much of which is gathered by alley entrepreneurs, $600,000 to $700,000, is returned each year to the community. The center can, as a nonprofit organization, support a community buy-back program because it can afford to operate at a loss on some materials. The collection, sorting and processing site is staffed by 12-15 workers, most of whom would be otherwise "unemployable" by business standards. (Resource)

❧ A curbside recycling program serves 15,500 homes in a city whose population is 37,500. The program is operated by the city but uses neighborhood volunteers to help with the educational outreach program. Collected materials are sent to a center where developmentally disabled individuals are employed in the sorting, processing and baling process. The workers participate simultaneously in a life skills program. Ten of the graduates now have jobs with local businesses. (Florence)

❧ A joint venture with the assistance of a capitalization grant from the Clean Michigan Fund built a glass processing and corrugated cardboard processing plant. Sixteen jobs were created and 400 tons of materials were processed and sold each week. (ILSR)

❧ A recycling center buys back recyclable materials from "alley collectors" and provides curbside pickup and office paper collection. Since 1986, the Center has paid back over $1 million into the community through the buy-back system. (Uptown)

❧ A neighborhood association is conducting an intensive, door-to-door educational campaign to get local residents to handle household toxic substances in an environmentally responsible fashion. The association educates residents to look for alternatives to toxic substances, to recycle those substances that have already been purchased and finally to seek better disposal methods. The goal of the campaign is to create a chemical free neighborhood. (Good Works/FNC)

Composting

* A recycling center collects horse manure from the downtown horse stables. The manure is then sold to the Chicago Botanical Gardens which in turn makes it available to community garden practitioners. The composted manure is also sold to individual gardeners by the truckload or by the bag. (Resource)

* A curbside recycling program delivers landscaping waste and Christmas trees to a compost plant. The finished compost is sold back to the public and used by the city park service. Christmas trees are broken down into chips and used as mulching. (Florence)

* Fertilizer for a community gardening project is collected at the recycling center compost heap. Composting materials are gathered from neighborhood kitchens, local supermarkets and from the horse manure stockpiles of the local police precinct. Excess compost is made available to other community groups with garden projects and for neighborhood associations to mulch the base of trees. The group also provides technical assistance to community groups interested in developing gardening projects. (ORE)

* A community center built a vermicomposting bin. Children weigh their lunch waste and vermicompost it so that they can see and understand how much waste they are keeping out of landfills. The project is just getting started but the center hopes to use the compost for indoor plants in conjunction with the summer children's program. (WCRF)

* A composting operation hired handicapped residents to sort and transfer collected landscaping waste. Incoming landscaping waste is always contaminated and needs to be sorted before it can be composted properly. (McNally)

Landscaping Waste

❧ A recycling center provides tipping services to a city park district for tree trimmings. The wood resources are then processed into high- and low-grade chips for play lots or mulch, which is then resold in the community. (Resource)

❧ A local youth business initiative began six years ago when an illegal dumper of landscaping waste offered to bring only solid wood waste and wood chips to the field. Youth from a neighborhood center got organized: they printed fliers, made contacts with other landscaping companies, collected wood waste on their own and began to pass the word about a new firewood company. It is possible for kids to earn $100-300 a week selling firewood. (Seneca)

Energy Resources

❧ A cooperative venture between two community groups and the city (funded by a Federal community development block grant) identified participants in an OJT program of the Urban League for work on a project which delivers needed home repair services to residents of neighborhoods and around the city. Of those receiving services, 80% do not have to pay or receive subsidized rates for the services. (Mt. Vernon)

❧ A neighborhood center conducts energy audits for churches, nonprofit organizations, and multifamily rental buildings to determine where and how energy can be conserved. The audits usually result in significant long-term savings. (CNT)

❧ A community group transports public housing residents to jobs in suburban Chicago. Twelve employers in the suburb split costs with a CDC to transport 100 persons to jobs each week. (Accel)

❧ A community-based organization convinced a commuter train line to add two morning routes from the city to suburban job sites. The organization also worked in cooperation with other community groups to link city residents to manufacturing jobs in the suburbs. (CNT)

Energy and Waste Resources Contacts

Accel

Clarence Darrow Center for Community
Economic Development
Theresa Prim
4839 W. 47th Street, 2nd Floor
Chicago, IL 60638
(312) 735-9245

BJEP

Baltimore Jobs in Energy Project
Dennis Livingston
28 E. Ostend Street, Suite 200
Baltimore, MD 21230
(301) 727-7837

Bethel

Bethel New Life, Inc.
Mary Nelson
367 N. Karlov
Chicago, IL 60624
(312) 826-5540

Block Corner

Block Corner Recycling
Robert W. Pierson
1216 Arch Street
Philadelphia, PA 19107
(215) 563-4220

BRING

BRING
Alex Cuyler
P.O. Box 885
Eugene, OR 97440-0885
(503) 683-3637

CFLS

Community Family Life Services
Tom Knoll
305 E Street, NW
Washington, DC 20001
(202) 347-0511

CNT

Center for Neighborhood Technology
2125 W. North Avenue
Chicago, IL 60647
(312) 278-4800

CRA

Community Recycling Alliance of New York
Cindy Sweatt
101 Grand Street
Brooklyn, NY 11211
(212) 677-1601

EAC	Environmental Action Coalition Cindy Sweatt 625 Broadway New York, NY 10012-2611 (212) 677-1601
EFI	Energy Federation, Inc. Bradley Steele 14 Tech Circle Natick, MA 01760-1086 (508) 653-4299
Florence	Florence Municipal Curbside Recycling Hester Cope 1750 Eunice Avenue Florence, AL 35630 (205) 766-1531
FNC	Fremont Neighborhood Council Michael Gilbert Seattle, WA (206) 545-0063
Garbage	Garbage Reincarnation Mike Anderson Eureka, CA (707) 584-8666
The Glass Station	The Glass Station Alice Soderwall 2441 Hilyard Eugene, OR (503) 687-2069
Good Works	Good Works Karen Rudd 4223 Fremont Avenue, North Seattle, WA 98103 (206) 545-0630
Mt. Vernon	Geri Post Dept. of Planning and Urban Policy 9 S. 1st Avenue, 9th floor Mount Vernon, NY 10550
NHRRA	New Hampshire Resource Recovery Association (NHRRA) Peg Boyle P.O. Box 721 Concord, NH 03302-0721 (603) 224-6996

ORE   Outstanding Renewal Enterprises
                    Christina Datz
                    P.O. Box 20488
                    New York, NY 10009
                    (212) 420-0621

R2B2   R2B2
                    Mike Schedler
                    1809 Carter Avenue
                    Bronx, NY 10457
                    (212) 731-3931

Resource   The Resource Center
                    Ken Dunn
                    222 E. 135th Place
                    Chicago, IL
                    (312) 821-1351

Seneca   Seneca Neighborhood Center
                    Paul Lipson
                    1241 Lafayette Avenue
                    Bronx, NY 10474
                    (212) 378-1300

St. Nick's   St. Nicholas Neighborhood Preservation
                       Corporation
                    Michael Rashferd
                    Brooklyn, NY
                    (718) 388-5454

Sunshares   Sunshares
                    Peter Somers
                    1215 S. Briggs Avenue, Suite 100
                    Durham, NC 27703
                    (919) 596-1870

TriCED   TriCED
                    Richard Valle
                    33300 Central Avenue
                    Union City, CA 94587
                    (510) 471-3850

Uptown   Uptown Recycling Center
                    Dale Alekel-Carlson
                    4716 N. Sheridan
                    Chicago, IL 60640
                    (312) 769-4488

Urban Ore

Urban Ore
David Stern
1333 Sixth Street
Berkeley, CA 94710
(510) 559-4460, ext. 4454

Village Green

Village Green Recycling Team
Carl Hultburg
235 Second Avenue #4C
New York, NY 10003
(212) 995-3357

WCR

Washington Citizens for Recycling
David Stitzel
157 Yesler, #309
Seattle, WA 98104
(206) 343-5171

WECAN

WECAN Redemption Center
Guy Polhemus
630 Ninth Avenue, Suite 900
New York, NY 10036
(212) 262-2222

Other Important Contacts:

Institute for Local Self Reliance
Neil Seldman
2425 18th Street, NW
Washington, DC 20009
(202) 232-4108

American Council for Energy Efficient Economy
1001 Connecticut Avenue, NW
Washington, DC 20036
(202) 429-8873

ASSET-BASED COMMUNITY DEVELOPMENT: MOBILIZING AN ENTIRE COMMUNITY

Across the country, community builders are refocusing attention on capacities and assets, and are inventing new methods for mobilizing neighborhood residents. Most often, however, these efforts concentrate on one or two local assets, generating new relationships and influence for a particular school, or church, or park, or community organization. Before us lies the challenge of a more comprehensive asset-based strategy, one which might involve virtually the entire community in the complex process of regeneration.

What might such a process look like? What are the basic building blocks which, when fully mapped, would constitute a more or less complete inventory of a community's assets? How might these building blocks be combined into a strong and dynamic community building strategy? How do the disciplines of community organizing, community economic development and community-based planning inform this whole community strategy? Who might be appropriate conveners for this process, providing it with the leadership which invites investment and vision?

INTRODUCTION

Five Steps Toward Whole Community Mobilization

The following five steps do not presume to add up to a complete blueprint for asset-based community development. Rather, they are intended to identify some of the major challenges facing community builders, and to point at least toward the beginning of a walk down the path that would mobilize an entire community's assets around a vision and a plan. Such a path would cover at least these five basic steps:

- ❧ Mapping completely the capacities and assets of individuals, citizens' associations and local institutions.

- ❧ Building relationships among local assets for mutually beneficial problem-solving within the community.

- ❧ Mobilizing the community's assets fully for economic development and information sharing purposes.

- ❧ Convening as broadly representative a group as possible for the purposes of building a community vision and plan.

- ❧ Leveraging activities, investments and resources from outside the community to support asset-based, locally-defined development.

Taken together, these five steps begin to point the way down a community building path which is, in fact, asset-based, internally focussed and relationship driven. Let us examine each of these steps in a little more detail.

Step 1—Mapping Assets

The commitment to mapping an entire community's assets is the place where this path begins. Once begun, however, the process of locating and making inventories of the gifts and capacities of individuals, of citizens' associations and of local institutions must be ongoing. Because the fully mobilized community is one which always begins to address its agendas and challenges with the question, "What resources do we have to solve this problem ourselves?" community builders need a continually updated "map" of those resources.

Step 2—Building Relationships

Building strong relationships among the community's assets constitutes the second step down the community building path. The community becomes stronger and more self-reliant every time local residents, and particularly the "strangers" within, are linked with others for problem solving purposes; every time an association of citizens connects with a local school or park to take on tasks together; every time a local business builds ties with the youth of the community. Communities discover that a new set of expectations begins to take root in the neighborhood, that people come to believe that they are capable of acting as effective problem solvers, and that their community is filled with much greater capacity for self-direction than they had ever suspected. And gradually, as the web of ties among assets inside the community is rebuilt, and as the demonstrations of local competence multiply, residents cease to look first toward the outside for help in addressing the most important local concerns.

Each of these first two steps—mapping local assets and building strong ties for problem solving purposes—has been emphasized throughout the guide. It may be helpful here to bring together some of the approaches covered in earlier chapters, and to combine them in summary fashion. The following six-point "Community Asset Check List" will help both to provide a guide for the construction of inventories, or maps, and to summarize some of the major challenges involved in beginning to build relationships among a community's assets. Community builders can use this check list as a guide to building their own unique path toward regenerating an entire community.

Community Asset Check List

Have We Found and Mobilized:

    ✔   The Capacities of Individuals

    ✔   The Gifts of "Strangers"

    ✔   The Associations of Citizens

    ✔   Local Private, Public and Non-Profit Institutions

    ✔   The Community's Physical Assets

    ✔   The Capacity Finders and Developers

Capacities of Individuals

How might the gifts and talents of every individual in the community be discovered? Community builders may want to adapt or modify the "capacity inventory" in Chapter One of this guide, or to construct one of their own.

Once collected, how might the gifts of individuals be activated in community building work? In particular, how might these capacities be connected with each other to enhance the work of local associations and institutions, and of the whole community development process?

Gifts of Strangers

Who are the "strangers" in this community? A community which pays particular attention to locating and mobilizing the gifts of the strangers in its midst is one which clearly welcomes the contributions of all its members to the community building process. Whether these marginalized citizens are young people or older residents, or various kinds of labelled people, the fact that they too are involved not as clients or recipients but as citizens and contributors can help to define this path as one which everyone can travel.

Once the strangers have been identified, the community builders will want to begin to connect them with other individuals, associations and institutions in the community. Where are those points of connection? Who might begin to do this important work?

Again, the challenge of finding the gifts of strangers, and of reconnecting them as contributors to the community mainstream, is anything but a one-time challenge. This work is ongoing, and becomes fully a part of the community building process only when it becomes virtually habitual.

Associations of Citizens

What associations are present in the community? Some, such as churches or ethnic associations, will be easy to locate. But others, often informal and less public, will be more difficult to map. Since citizens' associations represent such a wealth of untapped resources for community building, constructing this inventory will be well worth the effort. Methods for uncovering the associational life of the community are outlined in Chapter Two.

Once the local associations have been located and mapped, the process of mobilizing them for the additional purposes of community building can begin. How might they be connected with each other, or with the institutions in the community, or with the community's strangers? What other roles might they consider taking on in the community? Can some associations begin to contribute to the economic development agenda? Might some be useful as part of a revitalized local communications and information-sharing system? Since the very essence of an association of citizens is its voluntary nature, these groups will want to play a major role in defining their own revised and expanded agendas. They also represent a constantly renewable source for finding new leaders who are willing to step into the larger community building arena.

Local Institutions

Once again, the first step involves mapping. What public institutions, not for profits, and businesses are located in the community? In some areas, listings will be readily available, and many local institutions will be highly visible. In many instances, however, no reliable inventory of local businesses or other institutions exists. The methods used for locating these institutions will be similar to those used in mapping local associations.

As noted in Chapter Three, the physical presence of an institution within the community does not necessarily indicate its responsiveness to community agendas. So the process of involving institutional leadership in community building efforts must begin with the challenge of resident control, or at least of serious resident input into the institutional agenda.

Once the local institutions have committed themselves to the tasks of community building, the steps toward involving them further are familiar. How might these institutions reach out to a variety of individuals in the community, especially the strangers? How can these organizations be connected to each other, and to local citizens associations, for mutually beneficial problem solving?

Perhaps most importantly, how might these local institutions expand their roles in rebuilding the neighborhood economy? Can they begin to purchase more goods and services locally, hire more local residents, invest in the community, contribute to training and education agendas? Can they provide resources which enhance the community's capacity for discussion and planning? And can they begin to use their relationships with resources outside the community for community building purposes? Clearly a community whose local private, public and nonprofit institutions are mobilized and committed to cooperative efforts is well positioned for community building success.

Physical Assets of the Community

Mapping the physical assets of the community presents another obvious starting point for the community building process. What are those assets? What does the community have in terms of land, buildings, streets and transportation systems, infrastructure, etc.?

There are at least two purposes for mapping a community's physical assets. First, residents can begin to appreciate, value, enhance and mobilize what is already there. And second, if the inventories of physical assets pay special attention to those parts of the community which are underused, such as vacant land or abandoned residential or industrial buildings, new agendas for putting these assets to productive use will begin to emerge.

Thus, after mapping the physical assets, community builders will want to raise some familiar challenges: How might these assets be connected to individuals, associations and institutions in the community? How might the community begin to imagine and institute new uses for underused assets? Who might best be able to use the land, or the buildings, and who can begin to put the redevelopment process in motion? Again, as many neighborhood groups have discovered, a successful effort to reclaim what was once an eyesore or even a danger can provide inspiration for an entire community building effort, and can be a powerful signal of a community which is seriously on the move to rebuild itself.

Capacity Finders and Developers

Perhaps the most important challenge facing community builders involves leadership. Building a team of community leaders who are clearly oriented toward finding and mobilizing the already existing gifts and capacities of residents and their associations is crucial to the success of the community building enterprise. Since many current leaders are much more accustomed to "playing the deficit game," to gathering resources from the outside based on the community's needs and problems, new leadership will inevitably be needed. Fortunately, every community is blessed with residents who are fundamentally committed to what might be called a capacity-oriented view of the world. These are the folks who understand well the fact that the proverbial glass is both half empty and half full, but who insist always on focussing first on the fullness, on the gifts and capacities of their families, friends and neighbors. These are the folks who must now be brought into the community building process. These are the local leaders who can commit themselves to constantly expanding the numbers and kinds of people involved in various forms of leadership, and who can explore all of the ways in which the community's power to find, enhance and build upon capacities can be strengthened. Finding the capacity finders—that is a crucial step along the path to rebuilding community.

Step 3—Mobilizing for Economic Development and Information Sharing

Beyond locating and beginning to build relationships among the six basic categories of community assets, the path toward rebuilding the entire community involves mobilizing all of the community's assets for two important purposes, developing the local economy and strengthening the neighborhood's capacity to shape and exchange information.

Developing the Local Economy

A community which has fully mobilized the economic power which it already possesses is in a good position to grow its local economy even more vigorously. As this guide has emphasized before, this challenge involves first, locating and mobilizing all of the skills of individual residents which can be used for economic development purposes. Then each local citizens' association and institution must be urged to begin making its own set of contributions to the neighborhood economy.

Finally, the asset-based community developer will begin to take a new look at the possibilities of the local market. What markets can be developed by simply connecting existing institutions and activities? And, to revisit economist Jane Jacobs' sage advice about rebuilding urban communities, the community builder will want to ask, what goods and services might this community export? How can this neighborhood provide more for itself and decrease its imports?

Clearly these challenges are offered not as a full and exhaustive treatment of community economic development, but as an asset-centered addition to the excellent work already being done by community development groups across the country.

Controlling Community Information

Any community which is seriously engaged in the work of regeneration simply must assume more control over the images which help to define it, and over the flows of information upon which the success of local plans and strategies depend.

As this guide has noted, ancient villages often centered their lives around the "village well." The well was much more than a place which offered water; it was a nerve center for the entire community, a place where gossip, stories, and information of all kinds were exchanged.

Obviously, the capacity to exchange information is central to the success of the community building project. So it is very important that community builders first locate all of those places and circumstances within the community where communication of at least a semi-public nature already takes place. Who are the local communications leaders? How might the current places of information exchange—beauty parlors and barber shops, churches and clubs, even taverns and street corners—be validated, strengthened and expanded?

Then, as an integral part of the community building agenda, plans for increasing the capacity of the community to exchange its own definitions and plans and vital stories must be set into motion. Already thousands of local communities continue the tradition of producing their own newspapers. More and more localities have access to lower watt radio stations, while others explore cable and video potentials. Strengthening the village well rebuilds the central nervous system of a community, without which the process of restoring health and wholeness becomes unimaginable.

Step 4—Convening the Community to Develop a Vision and a Plan

Who are we in this community? What do we value most? Where would we like our community to go in the next five, ten, twenty years? These simple but compelling questions lie at the heart of the community building challenge. For without a commonly held identity and a broadly shared vision the hard work of regenerating community is very difficult to sustain.

In many communities, a process of community based planning provides the vehicle for defining and developing a local vision, and for attaching that vision to strategies which begin to move toward making the vision a reality. Community planning models and approaches abound and even more are being developed as localities recognize the usefulness and power of a consensus building process which leads to a plan.

Clearly, some version of a community planning effort is an integral part of the process of asset-based community development. It is well beyond the scope of this guide to outline a particular community planning model, and since a number of technical assistance providers have already produced very helpful guides, it is unnecessary as well. (One recent and very useful example, *From the Bottom Up: Building Communities From Within*, is available from the Community Workshop on Economic Development, 100 S. Morgan, Chicago, IL 60607)

For the asset-based community builder, the community planning process presents a marvelous opportunity to set the tone for the entire regeneration effort. From the very beginning, an orientation toward finding and mobilizing local capacities should form the core of the process. In fact, three simple commitments, agreed to at the inception of the planning process, will help to ensure that the community planning effort becomes a magnet which attracts and coordinates the full array of local capacities.

Commitment 1—Begin with assets. Start the process with a thorough inventory of the individual, associational and institutional capacities of the community. From the beginning, attempt to set a tone which is filled with promise and potential. "We really do have a surprising array of assets here in this community. This place is well worth preserving and improving." Avoid the temptation to begin with a traditional "needs survey," since this will lead inevitably to a strategy largely dependent upon outside help. (Even the more neutral sounding "barriers and opportunities" exercises can result in an unproductive emphasis on roadblocks, especially when introduced before a full sense of local capacity has taken root.)

Commitment 2—Expand the table. Many community planning efforts achieve limited results because only the recognized, visible leaders of the community are invited to participate. One result is that since the full range of local problem-solving potential is not at the table, the planning leaders are constantly pulled toward a dependence upon only external resources.

An alternative approach attempts not only to make the planning process as open and participatory as possible, but also to pay particular attention to including people as *representatives of community assets.* Thus an expanded community planning table would include many participants not normally thought of as community leaders. These participants would each, in a sense, be bringing the assets of his/her own group to the table as part of the larger community problem-solving capacity. A table which included business owners and local association representatives, along with people representing the school, library, police, community college, park and church—such a table would represent a great wealth of local resources which could be used to move agendas and solve problems without first turning to the outside for help. And clearly, if a broadly representative table such as this can reach consensus around a vision for the community's future, that vision will assume a powerful role in the life of the community.

Commitment 3—Combine planning with problem-solving. Sometimes a planning process can float away from the reality of everyday life, becoming a totally future-oriented, abstract exercise. But if community planning contains at its core a commitment to finding and mobilizing local capacities for problem-solving purposes in the here and now, the longer range strategizing will remain connected to the present, and citizens will experience concrete results from their participation.

In one of the most powerful and creative community planning efforts, the Dudley Street Neighborhood Initiative in Boston, the leaders recognized from the beginning the necessity to combine planning with what they referred to as "organizing." As a result, neighborhood residents experienced small but significant concrete victories based on their ever increasing confidence and capacity—illegal trash dumping halted, streets and lots cleaned up, new efforts to involve young people in community building. These smaller but very tangible products lent a sense of concrete reality to the larger community planning process, and gave DSNI the credibility to win from the City of Boston the power of eminent domain. This story is reported in *Streets of Hope: The Fall & Rise of an Urban Neighborhood,* Peter Medoff & Holly Sklar, South End Press, Boston, MA (1994).

A planning process which solves problems as it evolves can mobilize an entire community around its own capacity and vision. Such a process, built solidly on a community's strengths and involving the broadest possible array of participants, can successfully propel a community down the path of regeneration.

Step 5—Leveraging Outside Resources to Support Locally Driven Development.

What is most important about this step is that it comes last in the asset-based community development process. Only when all of the capacities of local individuals, associations and institutions have been inventoried thoroughly; only when these local assets have begun to look first to their relationships with each other for solving problems; only when the local economic development potentials have been released and information is flowing freely; only when a broadly representative group of citizens have begun to solve problems together, and to hammer out a shared vision and set of strategies—*only then* should the community begin to consider leveraging resources from the outside.

Clearly a community which has mobilized its internal assets is no longer content to be a recipient of charity. Rather, this mobilized community offers opportunities for real partnerships, for investors who are interested in effective action and in a return on their investment. Let it be said once again that the task of attracting outside resources continues to be very important, particularly for lower income communities. Relegating this task to the last of our five steps is not, therefore, a judgment about its relative importance, but a statement about the necessary relationships between outside help and inside capacity.

Traditionally, any number of neighborhood-based groups and institutions have been focussed on the challenge of attracting outside resources. Both multi-issue community organizations and local community economic development groups in particular have scored valuable successes. If these groups can add to their own well developed perspectives and strategies a renewed commitment to finding and mobilizing the full range of local community capacities, their continuing leadership in community building can only be strengthened. The bridges and relationships which they have already built with outside public, private and non-profit resource providers, when combined with the relationship to the outside which local institutions such as churches, schools, parks and libraries have as part of their larger identity—these bridges can contribute invaluable support to the community building process.

The next section explores further some of the ways in which "outsiders," particularly in philanthropy and government, can provide assistance to the asset-based community development process.

PROVIDING SUPPORT FOR ASSET-BASED DEVELOPMENT : POLICIES AND GUIDELINES

Most of the material in this guide is designed to help local community leaders locate, assess and mobilize all of the assets in their neighborhood. Clearly, however, the development approaches outlined here deserve help and support from interested individuals and organizations outside the community. This final section offers some initial advice to a variety of potential helpers, including funders and government agencies.

INTRODUCTION

Support From Funders

Most funders of community activity have traditionally asked that proposals begin with a "needs" or "problem" statement, often reinforced with a "needs survey." But providing support for asset-based development calls for a different strategy. Funders will want, first of all, to send a clear message to the community—one that encourages local residents to maximize the use of their own skills and resources to solve problems. Therefore, this section includes five guides to establishing a capacity-oriented approach to philanthropy.

First is a sample set of guidelines that can be adopted and developed by philanthropic groups such as foundations, United Ways and church groups. It is the Guide to Capacity Oriented Funding on the next page.

Following this Guide are copies of the capacity-oriented guidelines of three foundations—The Tucson Community Foundation, the Community Foundation of Greater Memphis, and the Community Foundation for Southwest Washington.

This section concludes with a description of a new form of philanthropy—a neighborhood-based asset development foundation called The Neighborhood Development Trust. This kind of foundation could be sponsored, supported or funded by a philanthropic group that does not want to use intermediaries. It is a way to provide funds to trigger local groups to create, support and develop their own asset development fund.

A Guide to Capacity-Oriented Funding

We support proposals from community-based groups that:

Clearly identify the skills, abilities, capacities and assets which local residents will contribute to the proposal. How will local residents' capacities be used to address the issues identified? Have you developed an inventory of the capacities and skills of local residents to help guide this process? We are particularly interested in how you will discover and use the gifts and abilities of the "strangers" in your community—those people who have been marginalized and overlooked because of labels such as disadvantaged, underclass, elderly, developmentally disabled, ex-offender, physically disabled, mentally disabled, mentally ill, etc.

❧

Clearly identify the capacities of your community's citizens associations, and indicate how they will be involved in both governance and problem-solving in your proposal. We are interested in the involvement of groups such as arts organizations, business associations, church groups, organizations of the elderly, organizations of men or women, ethnic associations, health groups, self-help groups, outdoor organizations, block clubs, school groups, political organizations, unions, service clubs, youth groups, veteran's organizations, etc.

❧

Indicate how this proposal will mobilize, utilize, enhance and expand these local capacities. How will local citizens and groups be stronger at the end of this proposal? How will they be better able to develop local assets?

❧

Contribute to building the local economy by, for example, employing community residents, enhancing local purchasing, capturing public budgets for local use, etc.

❧

Show evidence of significant investments of resources and time by local residents and organizations before our funding is initiated. We are particularly interested in projects which local residents design, carry out and control themselves.

Tucson Community Foundation: Investing in the Strengths of People and Communities—Request for Proposals

The Tucson Community Foundation believes communities are strengthened when people begin to see themselves as resources, and find successful ways of marshalling their talents, and the talents of local people and organizations to solve problems. TCF, therefore, has placed a high priority on investing in projects that 1) involve people expected to benefit from the projects in the development of those projects, 2) recognize and build on the existing capabilities of the people and communities served by those projects, and 3) build on the strengths of people who are often excluded—in other words, people traditionally labeled "disadvantaged" and "underserved."

Your application should include the following:

- A proposal cover sheet that includes the following in this order:
  - contact name
  - contact phone number
  - organization name and address
  - amount requested
  - purpose of your organization (50 words or less)
  - concise description of your project (50 words or less)

- One copy of your proposal, no more than three typewritten pages in length. Please address the following questions in that space:

  - Describe the project you would like funded. What are your goals? How will you implement the project? What results do you wish to achieve? How will you measure your progress and success?
  - How will you involve the people expected to benefit from your project in the development of the project?
  - How will those people's skills be utilized in the implementation of the project?
  - How will those people's skills be enhanced through their involvement in this project?
  - Who are the stakeholders (groups and people) and how are they collaborating with you on this project?

- Your organization's operating budget (statement of revenues and expenses) for the last completed and current fiscal year. Also include a budget for the project you wish to have funded. Indicate other sources of revenue, i.e. government, foundations, corporate, and individuals.

❧ If your organization is tax exempt, please include your IRS ruling letter. If not, please include a description of how your group is structured. We will consider funding grassroots groups that have come together for a charitable purpose if they consist of five or more people and have some type of governing body.

❧ A list of the board of directors or those responsible for your organization.

❧ A letter from the board chairman or volunteer leader of your group that approves your application for funding.

❧ Letters from groups that are working together with you on this project, specifically outlining how you will work together.

Community Foundation of Greater Memphis: The Greater Memphis Fund (Excerpts)

Mission

The Greater Memphis Fund was established by the Community Foundation of Greater Memphis as a way for the Community Foundation to enter into partnerships with nonprofit organizations that are committed to and actively involved in building their community. Grant-making through the Greater Memphis Fund is based on the belief that all communities have strengths as well as weaknesses, and that positive, long-term change occurs when a community's strengths serve as the basis for action. The Greater Memphis Fund will support organizations that help people rebuild their communities from the inside out by focussing on assets and mobilizing relationships between local institutions, businesses and residents.

Criteria

Applications for The Greater Memphis Fund will be reviewed according to the following criteria:

- ❦ Applicants must be nonprofit, tax-exempt organizations that are involved in enhancing the quality of life for citizens in metropolitan Memphis. west Tennessee and northern Mississippi. Organizations that have not been recognized as tax-exempt by the IRS may apply if they have a fiscal agent relationship with a 501(c)(3) nonprofit organization.

- ❦ Applicant organizations should be able to describe their "local community" and have a vision that will shape their future relationship with that community.

- ❦ Applicant organizations should demonstrate a commitment to incorporating widespread participation by local residents, organizations and institutions in their on-going programs. Furthermore, they should actively seek to involve local residents in the governance and decisionmaking aspects of their organization.

- ❦ Applications should identify the strengths and capacities which local residents, organizations and institutions will contribute to the proposal, and should indicate how the proposed project will mobilize, utilize, enhance and expand these local capacities.

❦ Applications should show evidence of significant investments of resources and time by local residents and organizations.

❦ Applications should indicate how the proposed project will contribute to building their local economy by, for example, employing community residents or enhancing local purchasing.

Community Foundation for Southwest Washington: Building Better Communities (Excerpts)

The Community Foundation believes in supporting community-based efforts to address local issues. This grant application and the questions asked reflect our interest in understanding how your proposal builds on the community's strengths, and on the potential of its citizens.

To clarify our "asset-oriented" focus, the following guidelines may be helpful.

❦ What are the skills, capacities, assets of the local residents you propose to involve in this proposal?

❦ Having identified the capacities and assets of the local residents, how does your proposal enhance, mobilize, expand these capacities? (We are especially interested in how your organization would incorporate the skills of people who are traditionally overlooked in community-building efforts.)

❦ Will this proposal contribute directly to the power and economic base of the local community? Do local people hold a majority of positions on the governing board of your organization, will local businesses and enterprises be the providers of services or goods funded? (This question attempts to see how the grant funding will be used to strengthen local governance, associations, businesses, and enterprises.)

❦ How will local associations be involved in this proposal? (We believe a critical asset of every community is its associations of citizens. These would include arts organizations, organizations for men or women, political organizations, unions, service clubs, youth groups, etc.)

The Neighborhood Development Trust

The primary resource for revitalization of older urban neighborhoods is neighborhood people and their associations and enterprises. However, most policies and programs focused upon the residents of these neighborhoods identify the primary resource as professional and technical expertise drawn from outside the neighborhood.

This proposal outlines a method to mobilize resources inside the neighborhood to enhance local development and enterprise. It assumes that, in the long run, the primary neighborhood development resource must be the investment of time, money and problem-solving capacity by the people in the neighborhood. Therefore, the proposal creates a local structure called the Neighborhood Development Trust that will stimulate and multiply these investments over the long term.

Why a Neighborhood Trust?

Often, the most significant seeds for revitalizing new neighborhoods involve nearly invisible small scale entrepreneurial or developmental efforts. Therefore, only a *local* structure can find and enhance these projects, and connect them with larger development strategies. Large foundations are generally not designed to make these micro-investments. The Neighborhood Trust is a local structure specifically designed to identify, support and invest in small local community enterprises.

The Goals of the Trust

In order to develop older neighborhoods, there must be a local emphasis upon:

- ❧ community
- ❧ constituencies
- ❧ capital
- ❧ continuity

Community commitment is the first essential. In places of high mobility and individual isolation the call to the common good of a place and its people has often been unheard. This call needs to be greatly amplified. The Neighborhood Development Trust is a powerful amplifier.

Many local *constituencies* must be reached to mobilize effective community investment. Instead of programs and policies that are primarily focused upon helping one needy person, the Trust will focus on mobilizing local groups with broad membership representing people of diverse backgrounds.

The *capital* of local residents must be invested in local enterprise. This capital is held by local individuals, associations, enterprises and public bodies. It is commonly expended or invested outside the neighborhood or spent locally with institutions and enterprises that invest the capital elsewhere. The Trust is a community magnet to draw the local investment potential into the neighborhood economy.

Older, inner city neighborhoods are usually described as "changing neighborhoods." This idea about the neighborhood creates a sense of uncertainty, impermanence and decline that leads many residents to feel that the risk of investment is too great. The Neighborhood Development Trust is a local investor with a long term commitment that provides the *continuity* that is essential to the development process.

In sum, the Trust is a vehicle that will establish a local institution that convenes many community interests to enhance long-term investment in the neighborhood's future.

The Structure of the Trust

The Trust would be initiated by creating a local neighborhood endowment. The endowment would be a grant designated for purposes of development in the local neighborhood. The grant would have four special features:

- To stimulate continuity and community commitment, only the proceeds of the endowment could be used annually. The corpus would remain intact although it could be prudently invested in local enterprises.

- To stimulate community capital investment, the grant would provide for dollar matching each year for several years up to a maximum amount. For example, the grant would match every community dollar invested in the Trust up to $50,000 a year for 5 years. The investors could be individuals, churches, businesses or local associations. The Trust could receive and encourage gifts and bequests. Property of residents who die without a will could be assigned to the Trust. Tax delinquent properties or government-owned properties could be given to the Trust. These bequests or proceeds of properties would become a part of the corpus.

- To insure broad constituencies for the Trust, in both securing contributions and making effective investments, the directors of the Trust would be neighborhood people with diverse constituencies.

❧ To provide for effective initial management of the Trust, the grant could provide funding for a manager for several years at a descending rate of support to provide an incentive for local self-sufficiency. The manager would be selected by the local directors and be accountable to them.

Thus, the Trust would be initiated by a grant that would be 1) sufficient to provide an initial endowment, 2) provide matching funds of a limited amount for a specified number of years and 3) provide initial funding of a manager whose salary would be supported in descending amounts for a specified number of years.

In practice, the grant could be for any amount. One example might be:

Endowment	$500,000
Matching endowment	$250,000
($50,000/year for 5 years)	
Manager support	$180,000
($40,000 first year decreasing	
$5,000/year over 8 years)	
Total	$930,000

A neighborhood endowment of $930,000 might be compared with the amount of public welfare money spent for support of low-income people in Cook County in 1984—$4,851,000,000. The cost of such a neighborhood endowment for all 75 Chicago neighborhoods would be $70 million or 1.5% of the annual investment in poverty.

If a Trust were established in each of Chicago's poorest 25 neighborhoods at the above rate, the grant cost would be $23 million dollars. If each neighborhood match of $250,000 was met, the Trust would leverage $6,250,000 in local capital.

If a plan to create Funds in the poorest 25 neighborhoods was implemented in 1/5 of the neighborhoods over each of 5 years, the annual grant would be $4,650,000.

Directors of the Fund

Those appointed to be Directors of the fund would be individuals, most of whom own, lead or represent local enterprises or institutions with investment potential. There are many variations that are possible. These include but are not limited to a Board of Directors composed of:

❧ Any neighborhood person contributing $1,000 or more to the Fund as an individual or in behalf of a local enterprise or association.

    ❦ All neighborhood churches that make a significant contribution to the Fund with a minimum contribution scaled to the size of the congregation. This could stimulate church-based community development corporations in these neighborhoods and provide models for similar corporations in other neighborhoods.

    ❦ All local businesses that contribute $1,000 to the Fund. This could stimulate coalitions of local businesses focused on community enterprise development—a function not usually performed by local Chambers of Commerce.

    ❦ The leaders of all local associations, clubs and organizations that contribute $500 to the Fund. This could create a Congress of Community Organizations focused on community enterprise development.

The possibilities for governance are limitless. A mix of any of the foregoing interests is possible. The point is that the Trust is a magnet to:

    ❦ convene groups and interests around development issues;

    ❦ stimulate investment in small local community enterprise;

    ❦ create a focus for a long-term vision for the neighborhood.

Uses of the Fund

The primary purpose of the Trust would be to develop the local economy and stimulate local citizen problem-solving. The Trust would utilize both grants and Program Related Investments in its development strategy.

The economic purposes would be achieved by investing in existing or new enterprises, job creation activities and methods to capture for local purposes the spending and savings of local residents. Special emphasis would be placed upon micro-enterprises and local development initiatives that are uneconomic for larger philanthropies or investors to find and capitalize.

Examples of local initiatives that could be supported by a Neighborhood Development Trust include:

❦ Micro enterprises for which small loans or grants of $200 to $2,000 are crucial. For example, materials costs for a group of Guatemalan immigrant families seeking to initiate a business selling their own traditional hand crafts; an equipment loan for a home beauty parlor business; a start-up grant for a small family run restaurant, etc.

❦ A grant or loan to launch a neighborhood newspaper and/or radio station designed to provide inexpensive advertising for local enterprises and report on successful community and personal initiatives—proclaiming the *good* local news.

❦ Funding to initiate a local facility or market for artisans, craftspeople and entrepreneurs without resources to reach the public with their wares.

❦ Financing local research on consumer spending patterns and market potential, studies to guide entrepreneurs and enterprise development strategies.

❦ Incentive grants for local businesses to create intern and apprentice-like opportunities for local high school students.

❦ Matching funds for local residents to travel to other cities or neighborhoods to observe creative new enterprises that could be initiated in the local neighborhood.

❦ Grants or matching gifts for local high school students to visit selected colleges and junior colleges. This experience (already proven in one city) often greatly expands the aspirations of local youth and provides a long range investment in local people who can return as managers, entrepreneurs and investors.

❦ Grants to support local experiments in energy conservation to increase local purchasing power.

❦ Loans to provide start-up for local waste recycling enterprises.

❦ Grants to initiate conversion of vacant land to gardens or parks.

❦ Loans to redesign local vacant facilities for new productive uses.

❧ Small grants or awards to local block clubs that create new initiatives for child care, gardening, energy conservation, youth employment, etc.

Finally, the citizen problem-solving purposes of the Fund can be achieved by limited investments in local planning processes that convene a broad range of community investors to create a vision for the neighborhood's future and plans for mobilizing a wide range of constituencies in implementation. The economic investment elements of such a plan would be eligible for Neighborhood Development Trust funding.

Governments at all levels aspire to assist in the community development process. They are clearly the trustees of many resources that can be vital to neighborhoods involved in regenerating themselves from the inside out. However, these resources are often provided in ways that dominate, stifle and often misdirect local efforts to revive community life. This is because governments (and other funders) often see themselves as the central actor in the process of local community building.

Effective support of asset-based development requires governments to shift their role from defining problems and creating solutions to following community definitions and investing in community solutions. This shift will result in government leaders fulfilling their legitimate roles as public *servants*. And as the effective role of a public servant is discovered, we will be reinventing government.

Local Government Invests in the Community

Local governments can helpfully invest their resources in three important neighborhood assets and processes: citizen problem-solving, community plans and local economies.

Local Government and Citizen Problem-solving

As this guide has reported, across America successful problem-solving involving the identification and mobilization of the skills and capacities of local citizens has led to the beginning of processes which reinvigorate the economic and physical assets that surround them. A first step in investing in this process is to reinvent government programs and personnel so that they are able to support local people in identifying and mobilizing their local assets. This means that rather than asking local citizens for "needs surveys" and "problem inventories," local government can identify local problem solvers and the types of local assets described in this guide. Then, the appropriate development question can be asked: how can these problem solvers be supported and the assets strengthened and connected? Cited throughout this guide are many examples where local governments have been useful supporters of local citizen problem-solving.

The essential focus of this support has been representatives of local government who have asked **how they can assist local citizens** in their development efforts rather than how local citizens can participate in the government's efforts. When local civil servants are supporting citizen efforts, they will then be able to interpret to their supervisors and elected officials how resources can serve rather than stifle.

SUPPORT FROM GOVERNMENTS

A useful first step in reinventing local government involves frontline personnel in creating an asset map of a local neighborhood. Shared with local associational leaders, this map can be the beginning of a local discussion about the appropriate supportive role of government resources.

In one city, Savannah, Georgia, local officials created an especially innovative method of identifying local assets and problem-solving leaders. They established a fund and announced throughout the neighborhoods that any block organization or local association with a community building idea for their area could apply for a grant of up to $500. The grant program stimulated many local groups to consider what more they could do with their members to develop their area. The city had high leverage with limited dollars and a map of local assets and problem-solving leaders emerged from the applications.

Local Government and Community Planning

Increasingly, neighborhood leaders are forming local coalitions and collective associations to multiply their capacity to regenerate their communities from the inside out. The focus of these groups varies. Some are general neighborhood advocacy organizations. Others focus on development activities related to housing, education, health, economic development, etc. Some have created broad based community development groups that attempt to mobilize the assets of the entire community, as described in the previous chapter.

These new forms of neighborhood capacity building establish "tables" where people representing local assets sit, create a local vision, and work out the interrelationships necessary to implement their plans.

Local governments need to identify these tables and seek permission to sit as a participant. In this way, the concept of citizen participation in government can be transformed to *government participation* in citizen initiatives.

Once seated at these tables, public servants will understand how government resources can invest in the asset development strategies of local communities. This investing generally takes four forms: money, information, technical assistance, and public authority.

While local governments are accustomed to understanding funding, information and technical assistance as resources directed toward local use, public authority is usually understood as the exclusive domain of government. However, as neighborhoods create new structures for rebuilding community, they are now finding that they need to command some of the powers and authority held by municipal governments.

Two examples of shared government authority that have been critical in rebuilding local neighborhoods involve Chicago and Boston. In Chicago, the Board of Education, as a result of state legislation, transferred much of its power to the local schools. Each local school now has a legally constituted school board elected by local residents. This board has significant power over the local budget, curriculum and selection of administration. As a result, community residents have control over and responsibility for the preparation of their young people for adult life.

In Boston, a coalition of associations of local residents developed a new vision for their neighborhood. Because such a large portion of all the local land was vacant or abandoned, their plan to develop their primary asset called for increased authority. Therefore, the Dudley Street Neighborhood Initiative persuaded the city government to transfer its power of eminent domain, thus allowing the neighborhood to gain control over all property necessary to implement its community plan.

In both the Chicago and Boston cases, the power to develop local capacities and assets depended on the investment of government authority in local groups. Often, it is the authority being localized that allows government money, information and technical assistance to be most effectively utilized.

Local Government Building Local Economies

It is very clear that investments by government are an important part of many local economies. These investments take many forms. They may be federal defense contractors hiring local people, state highway programs which hire local contractors or city schools contracting for food services from local caterers hiring neighborhood residents. Wherever government spends the taxpayer's money, it is investing in an economy. The critical question for local neighborhoods is whether the government is investing in its local economy.

Unfortunately, in lower income communities, what often appears to be substantial local government expenditures are actually not investments in the local economy. This is because the expenditures largely go to individuals or businesses that are not from the neighborhood. This is especially true of the expenditures for health and human services. The government expenditures for medical services are received by professionals who usually reside outside the neighborhood, and companies servicing the medical personnel that are also non-local. The same is generally true of other educational and social services. The service providers and the companies that support them are usually outside the neighborhood. This is the reason the local government ledgers that appear to show considerable investment in lower income neighborhoods are misleading. The government is investing in services **for** the neighborhood but not **in** the neighborhood economy.

Therefore, the reorientation necessary by local governments requires a new ledger. This ledger is a balance sheet that shows *who received the local public expenditures* as well as who received the services. It will show what percentage of local government dollars spent in behalf of neighborhoods resulted in the employment of local residents, purchases from local enterprises and contracts with local businesses.

When the balance sheet shows that most public expenditures are invested in the local economy, the need for social welfare expenditures will decrease as the economic well-being of local residents increases.

The earlier chapter on Rebuilding the Local Economy provides a specific guide for local governments seeking to convert their expenditures into local investments in support of rebuilding local economies.

State and Federal Government Investments in the Local Community

It is much more difficult for State and Federal governments to become supportive investors in local neighborhood asset building activities. Both the distance and the large size of these governments make it less likely that they can join at the community table. Nonetheless, these governments can support asset-based local development by adopting three important policies:

Gathering Data on Local Assets. State and federal governments usually require localities to count up their deficiencies, problems and needs in order to access public investments. As a result, the investments usually go to needs-meeting providers who expend most of their money on personnel and companies outside the neighborhoods. An alternative policy would seek data regarding local assets and their development with indications of how government money would support the local initiative. The guidelines for funders outlined earlier in this chapter—A Guide for Capacity Oriented Funders—can be used as a model for asset-based funding by government as well as philanthropies.

Investing in the Local Economy. In lower income neighborhoods, two-thirds of all government expenditures generally go to health and human service providers and businesses providing commodities and housing. (See the study, "Government Spending for the Poor in Cook County, Illinois: Can We Do Better," by Diane Kallenback and Arthur

Lyons, Center for Urban Affairs and Policy Research, Northwestern University, Evanston, Illinois 60208, $7.) Because the economic benefi- ciaries of these expenditures are not usually local residents or their enterprises and businesses, an asset-based investment strategy would shift policies toward insuring that a substantial percentage of govern- ment expenditures provide direct economic benefit in the form of local jobs, contracts and purchases. The earlier chapter on Rebuilding the Local Economy provides specific guidelines for implementing these policies.

Removing Barriers to Local Innovation. State and federal govern- ments are comprised of hundred of departments, divisions and bu- reaus. Each administers distinctive programs. At the neighborhood level, groups seeking to develop a comprehensive and integrated asset development strategy are faced with hundreds of categories of outside public resources, each wrapped in red tape of its own. As a result, government programs demand that these local coordinating groups develop *categorical, divided, specialized, limited, technical, defi- ciency-focused* proposals.

Practically speaking, it is impossible for local associations and coali- tions to expend their time, money and energy to weave back together the hundreds of separate strands the larger governments have dangled before them.

The alternative policy is for these governments to create mechanisms that set aside the categories and red tape when local asset develop- ment groups seek support for a holistic local initiative. The name for such a set-aside at the Federal level is a waiver. A programmatic method for creating uncategorical and de-red-taped grants is to estab- lish an inter-agency waiver council. Such a body, under the direct auspices of the elected executive, would have the responsibility to convene the multiple agencies for joint review of comprehensive local proposals. The agencies would also provide waivered grants within a specific brief time period, or provide an explanation to the executive as to why the waiver is not recommended.

A waiver council of this nature operated successful for several years in the Domestic Affairs Office of the Reagan White House.

Precautions for all Governments

Because governments are usually large, complex and formal, it is often difficult for them to deal effectively with small, simple and informal local asset development groups. Often government efforts to support are dominating, distorting or demeaning. There are a few principles that can help government officials avoid this overbearing propensity.

* "Public servant" is the best definition of a government worker or program. A servant supports and does not control. A servant never suggests that the employer could "participate" in the servant's work. The servant "supports" the employer's work.

* Be clear about the limits of government. If government replaces the work of citizens and their associations, it will not have created a good society. Instead, the evidence is clear that it will have created a dependent society. And because it will not be able to fulfill all its claims, local problems will grow worse. There can never be enough schools to create effective young people. There can never be enough clinics to create health. Secure, wise, just and healthy communities are created by citizens and associations and their enterprises, **supported** by governments making useful investments in local assets.

* Leave the credit to local citizens and their associations and enterprises. Too often, governments that have been a part of a local development effort take most of the public credit for the activity, overshadowing the efforts of local citizens and their community. The Mayor cuts the ribbon. The Governor announces the grant. Those who do the work go unrecognized.

* Don't replace local associations and institutions with new systems, institutions, centers or agencies. One of the most significant causes of weakened local citizen initiatives, associational work and institutional capacity has been the introduction of new government sponsored structures and organizations. As new organizations appear in the neighborhood with impressive buildings or offices, lots of money, and well paid outside professionals, they unintentionally but necessarily replace some of the power, authority and legitimacy of local groups. Although they assert that they are there to strengthen community, they are as likely to replace community initiatives. Therefore, government representatives can ask, "What do you community folks

think we should do to support you?," rather than, "We have this new program that we're bringing into your community."

- ❦ "One size doesn't fit all" at the neighborhood level. The essential characteristics of local associational life are diversity, proliferation and informality. Higher levels of government, on the other hand, are characterized by uniformity, standardization and formality, seeking to establish general guidelines and regulations that will "fit all." It is this generalizing imperative of central governments that is structurally at odds with creative local initiatives. And yet, it is creative local initiatives that are the essential power for regenerating community. Therefore, great flexibility is necessary if large governments are to support community building. And if this flexibility is not possible, it may be best for large governments to learn how to get out of the way of local efforts.

Final Thoughts on the Limits and Potential of Building Communities From the Inside Out

As we have researched the local initiatives and followed the development paths that have led to writing this guide, we have been inspired by the creative local energies that are busily at work against great odds. But we have also been impressed by the odds. Because those odds seem so great to many observers, we have repeatedly been asked some hard questions about the strategies outlined in this guide. There are no easy answers. Nonetheless, the following answers seem most realistic to us.

Do you really think these internally focused strategies will work?

It seems to us that these strategies are more likely to work than many others being proposed because the others have so little prospect of being implemented.

What are the external resources and strategies that are more likely to regenerate neighborhood in the 1990s? Are we to expect the deficit focused Federal, State and local governments to provide a new wave of resources? Are we to rely on new corporate plants, facilities, and employment to provide important economic opportunity in neighborhoods and for neighborhood people? Can we expect the human service industries to finally develop comprehensive, coordinated, integrated local inter-agency, multi-source local delivery systems? Who would advise local citizens that they should depend upon these megasystems to deliver a hopeful future?

It seems to us that the obvious *necessity* in this decade is for citizens to use every resource at their local command to create the future. And indeed, it is clear in inner city neighborhoods across America that most residents have reached that conclusion themselves. It is from that conclusion that tens of thousands of local initiatives have grown. And it is a sample of those initiatives that are reported in this guide.

A second reason for believing that internally focused strategies can work is that the evidence is overwhelming in developing societies that if outside plans and resources dominate and overwhelm local initiatives and associations, massive social and economic disasters occur. The evidence is in from several continents and it clearly suggests that development must start from within. The process must respect local structures, support local visions and invest in local productive capacities.

The same lesson can be learned about local development efforts in the United States. We can see in many cities the hollow shells of the designs of outsiders imposed on local communities. Therefore, it needs to be realistically recognized that if all the outside resources did suddenly begin to be available in low income neighborhoods, without an effective and connected collaboration of local individuals, associations and institutions, the resources would only create more dependency and isolation before they were finally dissipated.

> *It is possible that internally focused strategies might work in some places, but how can they be replicated and reach a critical scale that makes a "real" difference?*

This question goes to the heart of a basic understanding of how things change in a society. Consider how the European settlers created their new communities in North America. In thousands of places in thousands of different ways they utilized their very limited capacities to create a new society. They did not have models for replication or plans to reach a significant scale. In some places they created Chicago and in others, ghost towns. In sum, they created a new society but it was achieved, local part by local part, sometimes creating centralized institutions from the bottom up.

The unique policy question we face today is whether existing centralized institutions can *support* local invention rather than act as the inventor. It is an exciting challenge for it calls for a new way to reinvent cities. If we succeed, the new way will result in structurally reformed enterprises, services and governments—redefined by their new capacity to *respond* to community rather than manage, replicate and proliferate local initiatives.

Isn't there a danger that local communities and groups won't be inclusive? Isn't parochialism and discrimination a problem with many local groups and associations?

Yes. One sociological definition of a community is that it is a group of people who perceive that they are all incorporated by the same boundary. Therefore, it is part of the definition of community that the collective commitment is somehow bounded. There are those included and, de facto, those who are not.

From this perspective, the critical question is whether the boundary has a welcome. Does it have a door or is it an impenetrable wall? There is no avoiding the fact that some groups create walls. The response to these walls may be to use law to breach them, education to influence their members or traditions that emphasize hospitality rather than exclusion.

The effort to create open communities has been, and will be, a never-ending struggle.

Aren't there some communities where there is not much associational life among local citizens? What do you do then?

Communities vary greatly regarding the number and formality of local associations. In some newly formed communities such as suburban developments, associations may be sparse because local citizens haven't had time to create them. And in some lower income communities and housing developments, there are so many institutions to manage and serve the local residents that associational life may have atrophied for lack of functions.

Nonetheless, it is clear that even in suburbs and inner cities, there are many informal associations doing critical community work. Just because they do not have a name or officers does not mean they are not there. It does mean that effective development work and community organizers must find, honor, and enhance the associational relationships already at work.

Does the "inside out" emphasis of this guide mean that outside resources don't really count?

No. Especially in lower income inner-city neighborhoods, outside resources are essential to the renewal process. There are, nonetheless, two critical qualifications to this answer.

First, outside resources will largely be wasted if the internal capacity of the community is not developed. Here, the question is the order. The inside capacity must be there **before** the outside resource can be effectively leveraged. That is why this guide is described as focusing on development "from the inside out." It is a process from the inside *to* the outside.

Second, outside resources that overwhelm, dominate or replace the work and potential of local citizens, their associations and the institutions they control will weaken rather than enhance the development process. We can see this most clearly in a few neighborhoods and housing developments that are virtual colonies dominated by local outposts of outside systems. These places have become very powerless in citizen and associational capacity. We can easily recognize this kind of powerlessness. The name for it is dependency.

In summary, this guide basically describes a path. It is a path where local people must take the first steps. Those steps are toward the interdependence of citizens and their local associations and institutions. The capacity to take those steps is the necessary prelude to an effective relationship with outside resources.

The Mondragon Cooperatives in Spain have a motto that best sums up the message of this guide:

"We make the path by walking it."

The Asset-Based Community Development Institute
is funded by
The Chicago Community Trust
and
The Kellogg Foundation

Design by Valerie Lorimer